UNITED STATES
Supreme Court Education Cases

Seventh Edition

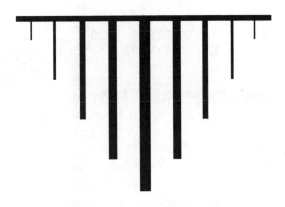

Oakstone

Oakstone Legal & Business Publishing, Inc.
11975 Portland Avenue South, Suite 110
Burnsville, Minnesota 55337

> "This publication is designed to provide accurate and authoritative information in regard to the subject matter covered. It is sold with the understanding that the publisher is not engaged in rendering legal, accounting or other professional service. If legal advice or other expert assistance is required, the service of a competent professional person should be sought." *-from a Declaration of Principles jointly adopted by a Committee of the American Bar Association and a Committee of Publishers and associations.*

Library of Congress Cataloging-in-Publication Data

U.S. Supreme Court education cases.—7th ed.
    p.cm.
  Includes index.
  ISBN 0-939675-87-0
  1. Educational law and legislation—United States—Cases.
2. Discrimination in education—Law and legislation—United States—Cases. 3. United States—Constitutional law—Cases.
I. Data Research, Inc. (Rosemount, Minn.) II. Title: US Supreme Court education cases.
KF4110.U15   1999
                344.73'07'02643—dc20
                [347.304702643]
                                  93-072358
                                    CIP

Library of Congress Catalog Number 93-072358

TABLE OF CONTENTS

CHAPTER ONE
  Desegregation

TABLE OF CONTENTS

TABLE OF CONTENTS

CHAPTER TWO
Private Schools

TABLE OF CONTENTS

TABLE OF CONTENTS

CHAPTER THREE
Student Rights

TABLE OF CONTENTS

TABLE OF CONTENTS

TABLE OF CONTENTS

TABLE OF CONTENTS

TABLE OF CONTENTS

TABLE OF CONTENTS

CHAPTER SIX
Students with Disabilities

TABLE OF CONTENTS

INTRODUCTION

When legal issues are discussed, people invariably want to know how the United States Supreme Court has ruled on the particular legal issue. The inquiry can often be a frustrating one, because the Court has not and will never rule on every legal topic which comes up in daily life. Fortunately, when the Court does rule on specific legal issues, the precedent it sets is useful in establishing law in other areas. A ruling on a particular point may be used by analogy to establish the law in a similar area.

One reason the U.S. Supreme Court will not consider each topic in education law is that it often is without jurisdiction to accept education law cases. According to the U.S. Constitution, the Court's role is generally limited to appeals involving cases and controversies arising under federal law, or the federal constitution, and to cases for which the litigants have already obtained federal court jurisdiction. See Article III of the federal Constitution, which is reproduced in its relevant parts in Appendix A of this volume. Unless the case involves federal laws or funding, education cases are generally filed in state courts, in which case the state's supreme court will make the final determination. Nonetheless, state education and antidiscrimination laws are often based upon similar federal statutes and regulations, and U.S. Supreme Court decisions are frequently cited by state courts as authority for their rulings in state law cases. The competent lawyer or education professional will be aware of both state and federal legal requirements. Although the Court has not ruled on as many cases in education law as it has in more highly regulated areas, educators will find this volume to be a comprehensive and complete guide to education law.

Steve McEllistrem, Esq.
Editorial Director
Oakstone Legal & Business Publishing

i

GUIDE TO THE USE OF
U.S. SUPREME COURT
EDUCATION CASES

The organization of this volume is chronological by subject matter. Each chapter constitutes a particular subject matter area, and subpoints under Roman numerals appear where warranted. Within each chapter and subpoint, the cases appear in chronological order. Find your topic in the table of contents or index and consider the cases in the particular subpoint or chapter for the Supreme Court's analysis of your education law issue. The cases in this volume contain important legal precedents. Even cases like *Plessey v. Ferguson*, found in Chapter One of this volume, which established the now invalid "separate but equal" doctrine, have never been completely overruled. Supreme Court cases which are no longer recent are still extremely important and need to be considered in confronting any legal topic.

Depending upon the interest of the reader, this volume can be the starting point for researching education law topics. For each case, a full legal citation has been given. With this citation, the reader can obtain the actual case opinion from any law library for scholarly research. Lawyers are familiar with this procedure, but educators should not be intimidated by the prospect of visiting a law school or public library law collection to do further research. An easy way to keep abreast of changes in education law is to maintain your subscription to Data Research education law periodicals. The editors recommend use of this volume in conjunction with other Data Research publications to compare recent state and federal court decisions with the Supreme Court precedents contained here for a broad view of the entire education law field.

ABOUT THE EDITORS

Steve McEllistrem is the editorial director of Oakstone Legal & Business Publishing, Inc. He co-authored the deskbook *Statutes, Regulations and Case Law Protecting Individuals with Disabilities* and is a former editor of *Special Education Law Update*. He graduated *cum laude* from William Mitchell College of Law and received his undergraduate degree from the University of Minnesota. Mr. McEllistrem is admitted to the Minnesota Bar.

James A. Roth is the editor of *Special Education Law Update* and *Legal Notes for Education*. He is also a co-author of the deskbook *Students with Disabilities and Special Education*. He is a graduate of the University of Minnesota and William Mitchell College of Law. Mr. Roth is admitted to the Minnesota Bar.

Patricia Grzywacz is the Managing Editor of Oakstone's Education Newsletters. She is the co-author of the deskbook *Students with Disabilities and Special Education*. Ms. Grzywacz graduated from Widener University School of Law and received her undergraduate degree from Villanova University. Prior to joining Oakstone, she was the Managing Editor of the *Individuals with Disabilities Education Law Report*® and authored the *1999 Special Educator Deskbook*, both published by LRP Publications. She is admitted to the Pennsylvania and New Jersey bars.

TABLE OF CASES

TABLE OF CASES

TABLE OF CASES

TABLE OF CASES

DEFENDANT - PLAINTIFF
TABLE OF CASES

DEFENDANT - PLAINTIFF TABLE OF CASES

DEFENDANT - PLAINTIFF TABLE OF CASES

CHAPTER ONE

Desegregation

I. "SEPARATE BUT EQUAL" FACILITIES

Early attempts to desegregate public facilities were rejected by the U.S. Supreme Court. Although it validated segregation, it required that separate facilities be equal in quality.

A man who was one-eighth black and seven-eighths white attempted to sit in the "white" section of a passenger train. When the conductor told him to sit in the "black" section, he refused to do so. He was charged with violating a Louisiana law which required separate railway carriages for whites and blacks. The U.S. Supreme Court refused to hold the statute unconstitutional as a violation of the Fourteenth Amendment's Equal Protection Clause. The Court rejected the notion that the conflicts between whites and blacks could be overcome by legislation. It held that as long as equal facilities are provided for each race, a state could require racial separation. *Plessey v. Ferguson*, 163 U.S. 537, 16 S.Ct. 1138, 41 L.Ed. 256 (1896).

II. RACIAL DESEGREGATION MANDATED—*BROWN I*

The landmark case of *Brown v. Board of Education* in 1954 rejected *Plessey*'s "separate but equal" doctrine. For the first time, the U.S. Supreme Court held that racial segregation violated the Fourteenth Amendment's Equal Protection Clause.

Brown v. Board of Education involved a challenge by black children in Kansas, South Carolina, Virginia and Delaware to state statutes requiring racial segregation in public schools. Each group challenged the laws in federal district courts, alleging that the laws violated the Equal Protection Clause of the Fourteenth Amendment. Each court adhered to the "separate but equal" doctrine and held that as long as the school facilities for blacks were equal to those of whites, segregation could be upheld. The U.S. Supreme Court granted certiorari.

The black children argued that segregated public schools are not equal and cannot be made equal by virtue of the fact that they are separate from white facilities. The Court examined the effect of separate facilities on the public school system and concluded that separate but equal facilities are inherently unequal. Segregation has a psychological effect on black children, which gives them a sense of inferiority and affects their motivation to learn. The Court held that segregation in public schools violated the Equal Protection Clause of the Fourteenth Amendment. It held that further litigation was necessary to formulate decrees on how the districts should be desegregated. The case was restored to the Court's docket. *Brown v. Board of Education*, 347 U.S. 483, 74 S.Ct. 686, 98 L.Ed. 873 (1954). *(Brown I.)*

The *Brown* mandate did not apply to school districts in the District of Columbia because the Fourteenth Amendment's Equal Protection Clause only directs "states." The District of Columbia is not considered a state, but rather part of the federal government. Thus, the Court had to find another constitutional provision which would prohibit racial segregation in D.C. schools.

A group of black children who were refused admission to a District of Columbia public school solely because of their race challenged segregation in the D.C. federal district court. The group alleged that segregation deprived them of due process of law under the Fifth Amendment. After the district court dismissed their complaint, the U.S. Supreme Court granted certiorari.

The Supreme Court first acknowledged that the Fourteenth Amendment's Equal Protection Clause prohibited segregation in state schools, as established in *Brown v. Board of Education*, decided the same day. It noted that the Fifth Amendment, applicable to the District of Columbia, did not contain an equal protection clause. The Court held that the concepts of equal protection, however, were not mutually exclusive and that racial segregation could be so unjustifiable as to be violative of due process. It concluded that since segregation could not be reasonably related to any governmental objective, the system imposed a burden on black children constituting a violation of due process. Since the Constitution prohibits states from segregating public schools, it would be unthinkable to impose a lesser duty on the federal government. The Court held that racial segregation in D.C. schools violated the Fifth Amendment's Due Process Clause. *Bolling v. Sharpe*, 347 U.S. 497, 74 S.Ct. 693, 98 L.Ed. 884 (1954).

III. IMPLEMENTATION—*BROWN II*

After the Supreme Court's landmark decision in *Brown I*, which held that racial discrimination in public education is unconstitutional, the Court faced the monumental task of sorting out the complexities of turning dual, segregated school systems into unitary desegregated systems.

In *Brown II*, the Court heard the opinions of the parties involved and of the state and federal attorneys general. The Court concluded that the cases involved in *Brown I* should be remanded to the federal district courts, because of their close proximity to local conditions. It further held that school authorities have the primary responsibility of implementing the *Brown I* mandate. It ordered that implementation had to take place with "all deliberate speed." Federal courts reviewing school district efforts must determine whether there has been a good faith implementation of the *Brown I* mandate.

The Court stated that the district court could, in reviewing implementation plans, consider problems related to administration arising from physical condition of the school plant, the school transportation system, personnel, revision of school districts and attendance areas, and revision of local laws and regulations. District courts were also to retain jurisdiction of the case during the implementation process. Armed with these mandates, the federal district courts set out to supervise the transition from dual, segregated school systems to unitary, desegregated school systems. *Brown v. Board of Education*, 349 U.S. 294, 75 S.Ct. 753, 99 L.Ed. 1083 (1955). (*Brown II.*)

A. Desegregation Plans and Efforts

1. Challenges to Segregation

After segregation was no longer constitutional, school boards were forced to implement plans to establish unitary school systems. The result was often decades of litigation.

Under an approved desegregation plan of public schools in Arkansas, black children were ordered to be admitted to a previously all-white school. While the school board made provisions for the plan's implementation, other state officials actively opposed the plan and passed laws to perpetuate segregation. On the day the blacks were to start school, the state sent its National Guard to prevent them from entering the schools. The black students were finally able to attend previously all-white schools, accompanied by federal troops. However, their attendance resulted in turmoil in the school, interrupting the educational process. A federal district court granted the school district's request to suspend the desegregation plan for two and one-half years and ordered the students back to segregated schools. The U.S. Court of Appeals, Eighth Circuit, reversed and ordered the plan reinstated. The U.S. Supreme Court granted certiorari.

Before the Court, the board contended that it had made a good faith effort to implement the plan, but that educational quality had been adversely affected. Although the court sympathized with the board, it affirmed the court of appeals' decision ordering the plan reinstated. It rejected the board's suggestion to do away with the plan until *Brown*'s holding could be further tested in the courts. The Court condemned the state officials' conduct and declared that *Brown*'s effect could not be nullified. It reaffirmed the supremacy of federal law and ordered the plan's continued implementation. *Cooper v. Aaron*, 358 U.S. 1, 78 S.Ct. 1401, 3 L.Ed.2d 5 (1958).

After *Cooper v. Aaron*, the Court encountered efforts by the state of Louisiana to avoid integration. The Court rejected the state's argument that it had "exclusive control" over the field of education. An injunction which had stopped the state from continuing to segregate was held valid.

The state of Louisiana enacted various measures with respect to school integration which were challenged in a federal district court. The court granted an injunction which nullified the state legislature's enactments. On appeal to the U.S. Supreme Court, it was held that the state did not have exclusive control over the field of public education. Accordingly, the injunction was valid and could not be stayed. *United States v. State of Louisiana*, 364 U.S. 500, 81 S.Ct. 260, 5 L.Ed.2d 245 (1960).

In a Virginia case, the U.S. Supreme Court ordered that district courts rule whatever is "necessary and proper to admit [complainants] to public schools on a racially nondiscriminatory basis with all deliberate speed . . . ."

Efforts to desegregate Prince Edward County's schools in Virginia met with resistance. The state passed laws to close and cut off the funds of public schools that were not desegregated. After the legislation was struck down by Virginia courts, the state adopted a "freedom of choice" program and left school attendance to localities. The U.S. Court of Appeals, Fourth Circuit, ordered the end of discriminatory practices in the district. The county then refused to levy taxes for the next school year. As a result, schools were closed for a few years, during which time private schools for white children were operated. The private schools received tuition grants and tax credits from the state. A federal district court ruled that these actions were attempts to prevent desegregation and ordered that the schools be reopened. The county and school board requested that the district court stay proceedings pending a state court suit which would determine the validity of the tax breaks and grants and whether public schools could be closed under the Virginia Constitution. The district court refused, but the court of appeals reversed. The U.S. Supreme Court granted certiorari.

The Court reversed the appellate court's decision and reinstated the district court's ruling. It held that black children in Prince Edward County had been denied equal protection of the laws because white children could attend private schools, whereas black children did not have access to such schools. It concluded that public schools had been closed for the sole reason of preventing white and black children from attending the same schools. This was especially apparent given that private white schools were basically state supported. The Court remanded the case to the district court to enter a decree ensuring that black children would receive an equal education in public schools along with white children. *Griffin v. County School Board*, 377 U.S. 218, 84 S.Ct. 1226, 12 L.Ed.2d 256 (1964).

The meaning of "all deliberate speed" was held in *Alexander v. Holmes County Board of Education*, below, to mean immediate dissolution of dual school systems.

The segregated status of black school children in Mississippi was challenged in 1969. The U.S. Court of Appeals, Fifth Circuit, allowed the school districts more time to desegregate under the standard of allowing "all deliberate speed," as established in *Brown II*. The U.S. Supreme Court granted certiorari and struck down the court of appeals' decision. It ordered the immediate termination of the dual school system operation and declared that the districts could only operate desegregated unitary schools. *Alexander v. Holmes County Board of Education*, 396 U.S. 19, 90 S.Ct. 29, 24 L.Ed.2d 19 (1969).

**After the Court's decision in *Alexander v. Holmes County Board
of Education*, above, the Court took on cases to clarify the decision's
meaning.**

In one case, the U.S. Court of Appeals, Fifth Circuit, deferred
student desegregation in several school districts. The Supreme Court,
in a per curiam opinion, reversed the court of appeals' decision and
stated that its *Alexander* decision had been misconstrued by the lower
court. Justice Harlan, in a concurring opinion, offered his view of how
Alexander should be interpreted. He stated that the burden of proof
should be shifted to the defendant school districts. This meant that if
segregation challengers could show a chance of trial success, the school
district would have to provide immediate relief from the unconstitutional dual school system. He wrote that the time between a finding of
the school district's noncompliance and the institution of relief should
be no more than eight weeks. The case was remanded to the court of
appeals for expedient resolution. *Carter v. West Feliciana School
Board*, 396 U.S. 290, 90 S.Ct. 608, 24 L.Ed.2d 477 (1970).

*Editor's Note: A concurring opinion is not binding. It is an opinion
in which the justice agrees with the majority's result in the case,
although he or she separately states the reason for doing so.*

**In *Northcross*, below, the Court ruled that the court of appeals
should not have substituted its findings—that a school district was
operating a unitary system—for the district court's finding that a
dual system was still in operation.**

A federal district court approved the Memphis board of education's
desegregation plan. It later ordered the board to revise its plan to
eliminate unrestricted free transfers and provide for complete faculty
desegregation. It also ordered the board to file a map of proposed zone
boundaries and enrollment figures so that the court could adequately
evaluate the revised plan. Parents moved for an order that would force
the school district to establish a unitary system, relying on *Alexander*.
The U.S. Court of Appeals, Sixth Circuit, denied the request.

The U.S. Supreme Court reversed the court of appeals' decision. It
ruled that the appeals court had erroneously substituted its finding (that
the school district was operating under a unitary system) for the district
court's finding that it was still operating a dual system. The appeals
court had also prematurely ruled that the board had converted to a
unitary system when the revised plan was not before the court for

review. Finally, the Court held that the *Alexander* decision, above, applied to this case and it ordered the school district to promptly achieve a unitary system. *Northcross v. Board of Education*, 397 U.S. 232, 90 S.Ct. 891, 25 L.Ed.2d 246 (1970).

In 1971, Justice Marshall denied a stay which would have prevented the implementation of a desegregation plan because of the "irreparable damage" segregation caused.

In 1963, the Jefferson Parish, Louisiana, School Board submitted desegregation plans to a federal district court. Litigation over the plans became protracted. In 1971, the board sought a stay from the court to prevent the plans' implementation. It asserted that the parish would experience transition difficulties. The court refused to grant the stay. The board appealed to the U.S. Court of Appeals, Fifth Circuit. Supreme Court Justice Marshall wrote the circuit court's opinion as a circuit justice. Justice Marshall upheld the stay denial, noting that there were no mitigating factors other than those normally incident to the transition from dual to unitary school system status. Because of the irreparable damage to students who were still forced to attend segregated schools, Marshall wrote "the rights of children to equal educational opportunities are not to be denied, even for a brief time, simply because a school board situates itself so as to make desegregation difficult." *Dandridge v. Jefferson Parish School Board*, 404 U.S. 1219, 92 S.Ct. 18, 30 L.Ed.2d 23 (1971).

Purposeful maintenance of segregated schools in a substantial part of the school system is evidence of racial discrimination in violation of the U.S. Constitution.

Students in Columbus, Ohio, brought a class action suit against their school district. They alleged that school officials had continually pursued a system of perpetuating racial segregation. A federal district court found that the school district had intentionally operated a dual system at the time *Brown I* was decided. It also determined that since *Brown II*, the district had failed to implement a unitary system, but instead had engaged in intentional conduct to perpetuate and maintain the segregated system. The court then enjoined the school district from discriminating on the basis of race and ordered it to submit a system-wide desegregation plan. The U.S. Court of Appeals, Sixth Circuit, affirmed the decision. The U.S. Supreme Court granted certiorari.

The Court also affirmed the decision, ruling that a purposeful and effective maintenance of segregated schools in a substantial part of the system was evidence that a dual system existed. The school district had taken actions having a foreseeable and disparate impact and this was enough to prove the district's action was a constitutional violation. The Court upheld the district court's order. *Columbus Board of Education v. Penick*, 443 U.S. 449, 99 S.Ct. 2941, 61 L.Ed.2d 666 (1978).

While much of the South was forced to desegregate due to suits filed by black students, California was experiencing problems of a different kind. Attempts to create a unitary school system in San Francisco were resisted by students of Chinese ancestry. The Supreme Court handled this unique situation by applying the *Brown* decisions to all racial minorities and upholding the school district's plan. The Court expressly ruled that the Fourteenth Amendment protects not only blacks, but all racial minorities.

American children of Chinese ancestry sought a stay of a federal district court order reassigning students of Chinese ancestry to elementary schools in San Francisco. The students feared that Chinese language and cultural classes would be eliminated under the desegregation plan. The classes affected by this lawsuit were filled predominantly with children of Chinese ancestry. California had historically provided for the establishment of separate schools for the Chinese under state law. After the Supreme Court's decision in *Brown I*, state school districts had to eliminate the effects of *de jure* segregation.

The San Francisco school district redrew school attendance lines to promote racial desegregation. The plan was approved by the district court. The U.S. Court of Appeals, Ninth Circuit, also denied the children's request for a stay pending a hearing on the plan in the district court. Writing as a circuit justice, Justice Douglas held that the Equal Protection Clause of the Fourteenth Amendment was not written for blacks only. Racial desegregation applied to all racial minorities. The board's plan seemed to be thoughtfully devised. The Court denied the stay. *Guey Heung Lee v. Johnson*, 404 U.S. 1215, 92 S.Ct. 14, 30 L.Ed.2d 19 (1971).

In *Gomperts v. Chase*, Justice Douglas, writing as a circuit justice, considered a California case involving the distinction between *de jure* and *de facto* segregation. The latter form has been identified as segregation resulting from housing patterns rather than by legislative mandate or school board action.

A California school approved desegregation plans less than fifteen months before the opening of the 1971 school year. The plans created a great deal of controversy, and a school board election resulted in a change in the board's composition. The new board submitted a revised plan which was based solely on voluntary student transfers. A group of parents and students contended that the absence of mandatory integration measures would restore the segregated school system. The group sued the board in a federal district court, seeking an order to compel an end to segregated schools within the district. The court refused to grant the order, and the group's appeal to the U.S. Court of Appeals, Ninth Circuit, was unsuccessful. The group's appeal for an order pending the filing of a petition for writ of certiorari to the U.S. Supreme Court was received by the Court only three days prior to the onset of the 1971 school year.

Justice Douglas wrote that had the case been a classical *de jure* segregation case, an order would be forthcoming. However, it was not clear that the district schools had become segregated by legislative mandate or school board action. The group had argued that the state had created segregated schools by constructing a freeway which isolated a black neighborhood so that the neighborhood high school became predominantly black. It also argued that state planners, local realtors and banks had played roles in creating residential segregation with the resulting school segregation. Under that theory, state action was present, and *de jure* segregation had taken place. Further, there was evidence that the predominantly black high school in the district was an inferior facility. Despite these arguments, Justice Douglas refused to grant the requested order. There was no ready alternative to the revised plan which could be effectively implemented in the three remaining days before school opened. *Gomperts v. Chase*, 404 U.S. 1217, 92 S.Ct. 16, 30 L.Ed.2d 30 (1971).

2. Free Transfers and "Freedom of Choice" Programs

A common scheme among school districts attempting to avoid the desegregation mandate was to adopt a "free transfer" policy for students. The use of free transfers invariably led to student reassignment to racially identifiable schools. One such transfer policy was struck down in Tennessee as violative of the *Brown* mandate.

A group of black children in Tennessee challenged their school board's desegregation plan in a federal district court. The plan provided for rezoning of school districts without reference to race. However, the plan also provided that a student could request to transfer from the school to which he or she was reassigned, back to his or her former segregated school where his or her race would be in the majority. The plan was approved by a federal district court and by the U.S. Court of Appeals, Sixth Circuit. The U.S. Supreme Court granted certiorari.

The black children contended that the district's transfer policy tended to perpetuate racial segregation. They pointed out that although transfers were available to those who chose to attend school where their race was in the majority, there was no provision whereby a student could transfer to a school in which his race was in the minority, unless he or she could show "good cause" for the transfer. The Court agreed and struck the plan down as constitutionally insufficient to fulfill the *Brown* requirements of desegregation. The Court ruled that if the plan had provided for transfer provisions regardless of the students' race or of the schools' racial composition, the plan would have been constitutional. Classifications on the basis of race for transfer purposes between schools violates the Fourteenth Amendment. The Court struck the plan down. *Goss v. Board of Education*, 373 U.S. 683, 83 S.Ct. 1405, 10 L.Ed.2d 632 (1963).

A Virginia county's freedom-of-choice program was struck down because it unconstitutionally placed the burden of desegregation on parents and students.

New Kent County in Virginia maintained two segregated schools in its district. One-half of the county's population was black. The county continued the dual schools even after the Court ruled in *Brown II* that Virginia's statutory and constitutional provisions requiring racial segregation were unconstitutional. After the federal government threatened to cut off its aid, the county adopted a "freedom of choice" program. The program, which allowed pupils to choose which school they wanted to attend, was approved by a federal district court. The U.S. Court of Appeals, Fourth Circuit, approved it also, although it required a more specific order regarding teachers. The plan's result was that 85 percent of the county's black students still attended an all-black school. The U.S. Supreme Court granted certiorari.

The Court held that the freedom-of-choice program was not constitutionally acceptable in light of *Brown II*, which required school districts to implement desegregation plans immediately. Although the freedom of choice plan was not itself unconstitutional, its effect was to place the burden of desegregation on parents and children. *Brown II* required the burden to be placed on the school board. It ruled that there is no one right plan to desegregate and that subsequent plans had to be approved by the district court. The case was remanded. *Green v. New Kent County School Board*, 391 U.S. 430, 88 S.Ct. 1689, 20 L.Ed.2d 716 (1968).

In a similar case to *Green*, the Court struck down a "free transfer" plan because it had been administered discriminatorily.

Tennessee passed a law giving local school boards exclusive authority of approving pupil reassignments. Subsequently, no white had requested enrollment in a black school and only seven blacks were allowed to attend white schools. The U.S. Court of Appeals, Sixth Circuit, invalidated the system. Black students sought an order from a federal district court directing the admission of black students to white schools and forcing the school district to implement a desegregation plan. The district court granted the orders. A plan was later approved which provided for pupil assignment with attendance zones. However, the plan also contained a "free transfer" provision which allowed a student to transfer to the school of his or her choice. After one year, the plan had not significantly promoted desegregation and the district court held that the plan had been administered discriminatorily.

The U.S. Supreme Court held that the "free transfer" provision of the plan had not furthered racial desegregation and did not meet the board's responsibility of implementing an effective plan. The Court relied on its previous decision in *Green*, above, to strike the provision down. The school district was ordered to formulate a new plan which would promptly create a unitary and nondiscriminatory school system. *Monroe v. Board of Commissioners*, 391 U.S. 450, 88 S.Ct. 1700, 20 L.Ed.2d 733 (1968).

Another "freedom-of-choice" plan was struck down in *Raney*, below, with an observation by the Court that federal courts should oversee desegregation cases to ensure that desegregation goals are met.

An Arkansas school district had a racially segregated school system in which black and white students were almost totally separated. The district continued the system even after the *Brown* decision and took its first steps toward desegregation in order to remain eligible for federal financial aid. It adopted a "freedom-of-choice" program which required students to choose the school they wanted to attend. The result was that no white children attended the black school and almost 85 percent of the black children still attended the same school.

A group of black students who had applied to attend the white school were refused admittance because available spaces had allegedly run out at that school. They sued for injunctive relief in a federal district court. Meanwhile, the school district made plans to build a new black high school on the same site as the old black high school. The students sought further to enjoin the high school's construction, arguing that building a new school at the same site would perpetuate the segregated system. The district court denied all relief, concluding that because the school district had adopted a plan without a court order and some blacks were attending the white school, the plan was not just a sham or pretense of carrying out the law. The U.S. Court of Appeals, Eighth Circuit, affirmed. The U.S. Supreme Court granted certiorari.

The Court held that a "freedom-of-choice" program was inadequate to eliminate a dual school system. It noted that the plan was similar to the one struck down in *Green*. Instead of creating a unitary school system, the plan placed on parents and children the burden of achieving desegregation, which should have been placed on the school district. The Court noted that because the new school had been substantially completed already, the case should be remanded for consideration of the students' proposal that the new site be used for a completely desegregated high school and that the white high school be converted to a completely desegregated elementary school. Finally, the Court reinforced the observation that federal district courts should oversee school desegregation cases to ensure that a constitutionally acceptable plan is adopted and that it is operated to promote the goal of desegregation. *Raney v. Board of Education*, 391 U.S. 443, 88 S.Ct. 1697, 20 L.Ed.2d 727 (1967).

Where a state perpetuates policies and practices that can be traced to a segregative system and that have segregative effects, the policies will be considered unconstitutional unless there is sound educational justification for them and they cannot, in practicality, be eliminated.

Mississippi maintained a dual system of public education at the university level—one set of universities for whites, and another set for blacks. In 1975, a group of private citizens, who were later joined by the United States, brought suit, charging that state officials had failed to satisfy their obligations under the Fourteenth Amendment's Equal Protection Clause and Title VI of the Civil Rights Act of 1964. In 1981, the State Board of Trustees issued "Mission Statements" classifying the three flagship historically white institutions as "comprehensive" universities, redesignating one of the historically black universities as an "urban" university and characterizing the rest as "regional" institutions. However, the universities remained racially identifiable.

After a trial, the court stated that the affirmative duty to desegregate in the higher education context does not contemplate either restricting student choice or the achievement of racial balance. State policies need merely be racially neutral, developed in good faith, and must not contribute to the racial identifiability of each institution. The court held that Mississippi was currently fulfilling its duty to desegregate. The U.S. Court of Appeals, Fifth Circuit, affirmed. The United States and the private citizens sought review from the U.S. Supreme Court.

The Supreme Court held that the district court had applied the wrong legal standard in ruling that Mississippi had brought itself into compliance with the Equal Protection Clause. If a state perpetuates policies and practices traceable to its prior dual system that continue to have segregative effects, and such policies are without sound educational justification and can be practicably eliminated, the policies violate the clause. This is true even if the state has abolished the legal requirement that the races be separated and has established neutral policies not animated by a discriminatory purpose. The proper inquiry is whether existing racial identifiability is attributable to the state. Because the district court's standard did not ask the appropriate questions, the court of appeals erred in affirming.

Applying the proper standard, several surviving aspects of Mississippi's prior dual system were constitutionally suspect. First, the use of higher minimum ACT composite scores at the HWIs along with the state's refusal to consider high school grade performance was suspect. Second, the unnecessary duplication of programs at HBIs and HWIs was suspect. Third, the mission statements' reflection of previous policies to perpetuate racial separation was suspect. Finally, the state's operation of eight universities had to be examined to determine if it was educationally justifiable. On remand, the state would have to justify all these decisions as sound education policy. *U.S. v. Fordice*, 505 U.S. 717, 112 S.Ct. 2727, 120 L.Ed.2d 575 (1992).

3. Attendance Zones

Another technique used by school districts to achieve racial desegregation was to redraw school attendance zones and increase the number of blacks attending white schools. The Court then

attempted to sort the redrawings that actually desegregated from those that merely appeared to create racial balance within the school district.

A federal district court approved an Oklahoma school district's desegregation plan which included attendance boundary changes. The court also ordered the school district to submit a complete desegregation plan within two months. Students intervened in the lawsuit, and asked the U.S. Court of Appeals, Tenth Circuit, to stay implementation of the boundary changes. The court of appeals vacated the district court's decision, holding that consideration of attendance boundary changes was premature and should be postponed until the school district submitted a full, comprehensive plan. The U.S. Supreme Court reversed, holding that because school districts had the burden of desegregating at once, the school district's attempt to redefine attendance boundaries should have been upheld. The Court remanded the case to the district court. *Dowell v. Board of Education*, 396 U.S. 269, 90 S.Ct. 415, 24 L.Ed.2d 414 (1969).

School districts may draw attendance zones according to race to achieve a unitary school system without violating the Equal Protection Clause.

In 1963, a Georgia county board of education implemented a voluntary program of desegregation. The program, involving only elementary schools in the district, drew geographical attendance zones to achieve a greater racial balance. Black students in five heavily black populated zones had to walk or take a bus to schools in different attendance zones. The result was that black enrollment in each elementary school varied generally between 20 and 40 percent, although two schools had a 50 percent black enrollment. The board's plan was challenged by parents of black students attending the county's elementary schools. They argued that the plan violated the Fourteenth Amendment's Equal Protection Clause and Title IV of the Civil Rights Act of 1964. The parents contended that the plan treated students differently because of their race and that Title IV prohibits school boards from requiring busing to achieve a racial balance. After a trial court upheld the plan, the Georgia Supreme Court reversed, agreeing with the parents' contentions. The U.S. Supreme Court granted certiorari.

The Supreme Court agreed with the trial court's decision upholding the board's plan. It ruled that the board had an affirmative duty to dissolve the dual school system and necessarily drew attendance zones according to race. The board would not have been able to desegregate without assigning the students solely because of their race. The Court also held that Title IV applied only to federal officials, and did not prevent school officials from assigning and busing students. The Court upheld the board's plan. *McDaniel v. Barresi*, 402 U.S. 39, 91 S.Ct. 1287, 28 L.Ed.2d 582 (1971).

However, once a school district had complied with an approved plan, it was not constitutionally required to make adjustments to reach a "no majority" of minority students attendance requirement.

Pasadena, California, high school students and their parents sued their school district for operating a racially segregated school system. The United States intervened in the action. A federal district court ordered the school district to submit a desegregation plan which would assure that there would be no school with a majority of minority students, beginning with the next school year. The school district submitted a plan which the district court approved. Shortly thereafter, school officials filed a motion to modify the district court's earlier order that there be no majority, claiming the term "majority" was ambiguous. The district court denied the modification, holding that because of shifting populations within the school district, several schools had violated the requirement. The court stated that the school district had a continuing duty to abide by the "no majority" requirement. The U.S. Court of Appeals, Ninth Circuit, affirmed but expressed its disapproval of the district court's view that the school district had a lifetime commitment to ensure "no majority" requirements which the district was held in contempt for violating. The U.S. Supreme Court granted certiorari.

The Court vacated the lower court decisions, ruling that the district court had exceeded its authority by approving the board's plan and then requiring it to readjust attendance zones each year. Because the racial makeup of some attendance zones had changed due to people moving, the board was not constitutionally required to make adjustments after it had complied with an approved plan. The school officials had a justifiable grievance as to the ambiguity of the term "no majority," and were entitled to modification of the district court's original order. The Court remanded the case. *Pasadena City Board of Education v. Spangler*, 427 U.S. 424, 96 S.Ct. 2697, 49 L.Ed.2d 599 (1976).

On remand, the revised court order—deleting the "no majority" provision—was upheld.

After the *Pasadena* decision in 1976, the case was remanded to the federal district court, which deleted the "nonmajority" provision of its order. The school officials then sought to stay the district court's order, pending disposition of a petition for a writ of mandamus. The officials claimed that the court's order still had the effect of imposing the standard that there be no school "with a majority of any minority students," which was struck down by the Supreme Court in *Pasadena*. The Supreme Court denied the officials' application, holding that the revised order did not have the same effect since the "no majority" requirement had been deleted. *Vetterli v. United States District Court*, 435 U.S. 1304, 98 S.Ct. 1219, 55 L.Ed.2d 751 (1977).

B. Busing

After *Swann v. Charlotte-Mecklenburg Board of Education*, section IV below, was decided, Justice Powell held that the Education Amendments of 1972 could not be used to stop busing for the purpose of desegregating schools. Only where busing was being used to achieve perfect *racial balance* could it be stopped.

After a plan was adopted for the desegregation of 29 elementary schools in Augusta, Georgia, a challenge was made to the busing required on the grounds that § 803 of the Education Amendments of 1972 required a stay of the judgment where the transportation of students was done for the purpose of achieving *racial balance*. On application to the Supreme Court, Justice Powell held that the desegregation order requiring busing was not entered into for the purpose of achieving a *racial balance*, but was intended to accomplish desegregation—in other words, not necessarily reflecting the racial composition of the school system as a whole, but eliminating dual school systems under *Swann v. Charlotte-Mecklenburg Board of Education*, 402 U.S. 1, 91 S.Ct. 1267, 28 L.Ed.2d 554 (1971). Justice Powell denied the application for a stay of judgment. *Drummond v. Acree*, 409 U.S. 1228, 93 S.Ct. 18, 34 L.Ed.2d 33 (1972).

The busing of students across towns to achieve desegregation was met with resistance by several states. The Supreme Court ordered that busing could not be prohibited, as it often was a viable alternative for school districts in establishing a unitary system.

Because the busing cases involve the authority of federal courts, please see Section IV of this chapter also.

The city of Seattle implemented a desegregation plan which included extensive mandatory busing. Subsequently, a statewide initiative was passed prohibiting school boards from requiring any student to attend a school other than the one geographically nearest to his or her home. The initiative provided exceptions that allowed students to be assigned beyond their neighborhood school if they required special educational programs or if the nearest school was overcrowded, unsafe or it lacked necessary facilities. The Seattle school board challenged the constitutionality of the initiative in a federal district court. The court held that the initiative violated the Fourteenth Amendment's Equal Protection Clause because it allowed busing for nonracial reasons, and disallowed it for racial reasons. The U.S. Court of Appeals, Ninth Circuit, affirmed. The U.S. Supreme Court granted certiorari.

The Court upheld the court of appeals' decision, ruling that the initiative did not allocate governmental power based on any principle other than race, thus imposing a burden on racial minorities. The question of whether to use busing was previously one for the school board. The Court stated that enactment of racially beneficial legislation would be doubly hard if the initiative were allowed to stand. Meaningful and unjustified racial distinctions were not allowed. The Court struck down the initiative. *Washington v. Seattle School District Number 1*, 458 U.S. 457, 102 S.Ct. 3187, 73 L.Ed.2d 896 (1982).

In the case, below, a North Carolina antibusing law was declared unconstitutional.

An ancillary proceeding that grew out of *Swann v. Charlotte-Mecklenburg Board of Education*, see Section IV, below, centered around a North Carolina law which prohibited busing children to achieve racial desegregation. The antibusing legislation was passed in the midst of the *Swann* case. The blacks involved with the *Swann* case sought injunctive and declaratory relief against the statute. A three-judge federal district court declared the antibusing law unconstitutional. The state board of education and school officials sought review by the U.S. Supreme Court.

The Court held that busing based on race was a necessary and legitimate manner in which to carry out desegregation. Although busing would not have to be used by the school district, a flat prohibition against it conflicted with the duty of school officials to implement an effective plan. The district court's decision was upheld. *North Carolina State Board of Education v. Swann*, 402 U.S. 43, 91 S.Ct. 1284, 28 L.Ed.2d 586 (1971).

In 1970, a California court ordered Los Angeles schools to implement a desegregation plan which called for busing over 60,000 students. Public outcry over the desegregation plan resulted in years of litigation, which reached the U.S. Supreme Court three separate times between 1978 and 1982. In *Bustop Inc. v. Board of Education of City of Los Angeles*, the Court refused to grant a stay of the busing order, on the basis that the California Constitution, rather than the U.S. Constitution, controlled.

A California court ordered the Los Angeles Board of Education to implement a desegregation plan which called for reassigning over 60,000 students. The plan paired racially imbalanced white and minority schools, requiring an exchange of students between the paired schools to achieve better racial balance. Parents objected to the plan because they alleged it required some students to ride buses for as long as one and one-half hours per day. The court refused to stay the order, but the California Court of Appeal reversed this decision, basing its decision on *Dayton Board of Education v. Brinkman*, see Section IV, below, and other U.S. Supreme Court cases. The California Supreme Court vacated the court of appeal's decision, basing its decision on the California Constitution rather than on U.S. constitutional grounds.

The parents appealed to the U.S. Supreme Court. The Court refused to grant the stay, finding that the case rested on the California Constitution as the California Supreme Court had found. Under the California Constitution, parties seeking desegregated facilities were not held to the higher standard of showing that the facilities were segregated by state action, known as *de jure* segregation. Under this less stringent standard, state courts could be permitted to achieve desegregation by busing or racial quotas. In this case, the state courts were not forbidden from such measures by the U.S. Constitution. *Bustop Inc. v. Board of Education of City of Los Angeles*, 439 U.S. 1380, 99 S.Ct. 40, 58 L.Ed.2d 88 (1978).

Following the *Bustop* decision, California voters amended the state constitution by a referendum titled Proposition I, which would eliminate independent state grounds as a basis for court-ordered busing. In *Board of Education of Los Angeles v. Superior Court*, the exigencies of an upcoming school year led Justice

Rehnquist to reject another application for a stay of court-ordered busing in Los Angeles schools. For the final disposition by the Supreme Court of this litigation, see *Crawford v. Board of Education*, in Section IV of this chapter.

During remand of the *Bustop* case, above, California voters enacted Proposition I to eliminate independent state grounds as the constitutional basis for court-ordered busing. The Los Angeles School Board argued that the trial court's ten-year-old findings no longer justified a system-wide mandatory busing remedy. However, the trial court again asserted that Los Angeles schools were *de jure* segregated and that the number of mandatorily reassigned students was now between 80,000 and 100,000. The California Court of Appeal ruled against the stay requested by the school board, granting only a partial stay which pertained to the definition of desegregated schools. The California Supreme Court denied the board's appeal and the case came before Supreme Court Justice Rehnquist, sitting as a circuit justice.

According to Justice Rehnquist, Proposition I did not violate the U.S. Constitution. However, he doubted whether four Supreme Court justices would agree to hear the case only a few days before the opening of the 1980-81 school year. Therefore, the application for a stay was again denied. *Board of Education of City of Los Angeles v. Superior Court*, 448 U.S. 1343, 101 S.Ct. 21, 65 L.Ed.2d 1166 (1980).

C. Faculty Desegregation

***Brown I's* desegregation mandate not only required integration of white and black students, but also integration of faculty. The Court set out to eliminate faculty segregation and to establish the conditions necessary to satisfy Fourteenth Amendment requirements.**

Two black students sued in a federal district court to effect pupil and teacher desegregation in an Arkansas school district's high schools. The district court refused to grant the order and held that the students had no standing to challenge desegregation among faculty. The U.S. Court of Appeals, Eighth Circuit, affirmed. During the proceedings, one of the students had graduated and the other had reached the twelfth grade. Two other black high school students petitioned the U.S. Supreme Court to be added as plaintiffs in the suit. The Court granted the motion. It also struck down the assignment of blacks in the district to black high schools. The Court ordered that the black students involved be immediately transferred to the white high school pending implementation of desegregation arrangements. Finally, the Court held that the students also had standing to challenge faculty segregation in the district because it denied them equal opportunities in education and rendered inadequate an otherwise constitutional student desegregation plan soon to be implemented. The Court remanded the case. *Rogers v. Paul*, 382 U.S. 198, 86 S.Ct. 358, 15 L.Ed.2d 265 (1965).

In 1968, a federal district court ordered a school district to achieve a desegregated faculty system whereby the racial makeup would be a ratio of one to six minority to majority.

The Montgomery, Alabama, school district made no effort to desegregate its schools until ten years after *Brown I*. School officials did everything possible to prevent desegregation. In 1964, black students and their parents sued in a federal district court to force the school district to desegregate. The district court concluded that Montgomery had been conducting a dual school system and ordered that certain grades be integrated immediately. Eight black students were finally admitted to the white school. Proceedings continued in the district court in an almost constant interchange between the court and school officials. Finally, in 1968, the district court ordered construction or renovation of schools which would not perpetuate segregation, and the adoption of nondiscriminatory busing routes. It decreed that the ratio of black to white substitute and night school teachers in each school was to be substantially the same as the ratio of black to white teachers in each of these groups for the system as a whole.

Each school with fewer than twelve fulltime teachers was required to have at least two fulltime teachers whose race was different from the majority of faculty, and in schools with twelve or more teachers, the race of one out of six teachers had to be different from the race of the majority of the faculty. The U.S. Court of Appeals, Fifth Circuit, modified the district court's order, ruling that faculty desegregation ratios could approximate the order. It warned against establishing an inflexible mathematical system for faculty integration. The U.S. Supreme Court reinstated the district court's order, observing that over the course of five years, the district court had not hesitated to change its order and allow for experimentation. Given the school district's history of stalling desegregation, the order was reasonable. *U.S. v. Montgomery Board of Education*, 395 U.S. 225, 89 S.Ct. 1670, 23 L.Ed.2d 263 (1968).

The following case also held that the desegregation of faculty must be achieved in conjunction with the desegregation of students.

Mobile, Alabama, is divided by a major highway. Ninety-four percent of the area's black students lived east of the highway, where the schools were 65 percent black and 35 percent white. West of the highway, the schools were twelve percent black and 88 percent white. A school desegregation plan was challenged as inadequate. The plan had been formulated by a federal district court and left 60 percent of the school district's blacks in 19 all-black schools.

The U.S. Court of Appeals, Fifth Circuit, concluded that with respect to faculty and staff, the school board had failed to comply with earlier orders and required the board to establish a faculty and staff ratio in each school substantially the same as that for the entire district. In addition, the court implemented a plan which treated the west and east areas as isolated, with no busing between them. The U.S. Supreme Court granted certiorari. Although it affirmed the court of appeals' faculty and student ratio decision, it reversed its plan for dealing with the east and west areas. The Court concluded that it had not adequately considered all possible techniques to achieve maximum desegregation. The Court remanded the case for formulation of a plan involving the east and west areas. *Davis v. Board of School Commissioners*, 402 U.S. 33, 91 S.Ct. 1289, 28 L.Ed.2d 577 (1971).

The U.S. Supreme Court ruled that faculty allocation plans were entitled to full evidentiary hearings because of the relation of faculty allocation to desegregation.

Parents and students in Virginia challenged desegregation plans for public school systems. They alleged that faculty allocation on a racial basis rendered the plans inadequate under the principles of *Brown I*. However, a federal district court in Virginia approved the plans without inquiring into the challengers' contention. The U.S. Court of Appeals, Fourth Circuit, declined to decide whether the plans were inadequate because no evidentiary hearings had been held, but failed to remand the case for such hearings. After the court of appeals decided that the district court had discretion in assigning hearings on the issue, the U.S. Supreme Court granted certiorari.

The Supreme Court vacated the court of appeals' decision, holding that the challengers were entitled to a full evidentiary hearing on whether the plans allocated faculty on a racial basis. It held that the relation between faculty allocation and desegregation plans was not speculative. It noted that ten years had passed since segregation was declared unconstitutional in *Brown I* and that delays in desegregation were intolerable. The Court remanded the case for an evidentiary hearing. *Bradley v. Richmond School Board*, 382 U.S. 103, 86 S.Ct. 224, 15 L.Ed.2d 187 (1965). (*Bradley I.*)

In further litigation of *Bradley I*, the Court upheld a Congressional statute authorizing attorney's fees awards to those challenging segregation.

A federal district court approved a freedom-of-choice plan by which each pupil was allowed to attend the school of his or her choice. The U.S. Supreme Court's decision in *Green v. County School Board*, see Section III.A.2, above, struck down freedom-of-choice plans where speedier and more effective desegregation methods were available. The school district then conceded that its plan was unconstitutional. The district court finally approved the school district's third plan and awarded the parents the expenses and attorney's fees they had spent on the litigation. In doing so, the district court reasoned that the school district's actions had resulted in an unreasonable delay and that the parents had been acting as private attorneys general. While the U.S. Court of Appeals, Fourth Circuit, was deciding the case, Congress passed a law authorizing the award of attorney's fees in desegregation cases. However, the court of appeals reversed the award, concluding that the statute had not yet gone into effect when the district court made the award. The U.S. Supreme Court granted certiorari.

The Supreme Court reversed the court of appeals' decision, holding that the statute could be applied to attorney's fees awarded before its enactment in situations where the fee award was pending resolution on appeal when the statute became law. Upon examining the parties' nature and identity, the nature of their rights and the impact of the law change on those rights, the Court concluded that applying the statute would not cause injustice. It ruled that the parents had rendered substantial community service by acting as private attorneys general. The Court also stated that the attorney's fees award did not affect any of the school district's rights. The Court upheld the attorney's fees award. *Bradley v. Richmond School Board*, 416 U.S. 696, 94 S.Ct. 2006, 40 L.Ed.2d 476 (1974). (*Bradley II.*)

D. Desegregation in Other Facilities

Desegregation in public schools was just part of *Brown I*'s mandate. Racial segregation in public facilities, such as parks, was also challenged.

A United States senator from Georgia left some land in his will to be used as a park for whites only. The will established a board of managers for the park, which sued the city as a trustee when it refused to prevent blacks from using the park. Several black citizens intervened in the suit, alleging that because racial discrimination was illegal, the city could not be removed as a trustee. A Georgia trial court accepted the city's resignation as a trustee and appointed three private trustees. The Supreme Court of Georgia affirmed. The U.S. Supreme Court granted certiorari.

The Court reversed the lower courts' decisions. It balanced private individuals' freedom of association with the ban on state-sponsored racial inequality. The park had been maintained and supported for years by the city and therefore was subject to the Fourteenth Amendment as a state instrumentality. The Court ruled that appointing private trustees did not negate the park's municipal character. The park could not be segregated if the city continued to maintain it. *Evans v. Newton*, 382 U.S. 296, 86 S.Ct. 486, 15 L.Ed.2d 373 (1966).

Where a board of education and the county grand jury which selected board members were underrepresented by African-Americans, the Court held that the system in place was invalid.

An African-American student and her father brought a class action against the members of a county board of education, among others, challenging the Georgia constitutional and statutory provision which governed school board selection. A federal district court refused to hold the challenged provisions invalid, and appeal was taken to the U.S. Supreme Court. The Court held that there was a substantial disparity between the percentages of African-American residents in the county as a whole and of African-Americans on the newly constituted jury list (the jury selected the board members). Thus, the state statutes had been unconstitutionally applied. Also, the requirement that members of the board be owners of real estate was discriminatory and therefore invalid. *Turner v. Fouche,* 396 U.S. 346, 90 S.Ct. 532, 24 L.Ed.2d 567 (1970).

Exclusive use of city facilities by segregated private schools was struck down in *Gilmore*, below.

Black citizens of Montgomery, Alabama, brought an action in a federal district court to desegregate the city's parks. After the district court granted the order, segregated recreational programs were continued, public swimming pools were closed and facilities in black neighborhoods were not maintained. The black citizens then alleged that the city was permitting racially segregated schools and private groups to use city park facilities. The district court then enjoined the city from allowing any racially segregated private school or any private nonschool club that had a racially discriminatory admissions policy to use park facilities.

The U.S. Court of Appeals, Fifth Circuit, upheld the district court's injunction as it applied to segregated private schools' exclusive use of city facilities. However, it reversed the injunction insofar as it applied to nonexclusive use by segregated private schools and by nonschool groups. It found that there was an insufficient threat to desegregated public education to justify an injunction restraining nonexclusive use by private school groups. Because there was no "symbiotic relationship" between the city and the nonschool groups, the injunction restrained the freedom of association rights of the groups' members. The U.S. Supreme Court granted certiorari.

The Court reversed part of the appellate court's order and remanded the case. It held that the city had properly been enjoined from permitting exclusive use of its facilities by private groups. Such a policy, the Court said, was akin to the "separate but equal" doctrine struck down in *Brown*. The Court further ruled that it could not determine whether private school groups' use of city facilities constituted a violation of the district court's first desegregation order. There was not enough evidence on the record to indicate whether the city was directly involved with private school groups' use of city facilities. The Court remanded the case for a determination on this point. *Gilmore v. City of Montgomery*, 417 U.S. 556, 94 S.Ct. 2416, 41 L.Ed.2d 304 (1974).

In a 1976 public housing desegregation case, the Court shed light on its decision in *Milliken I*, see Section IV, below. The *Milliken I* decision did not create a *per se* rule against interdistrict desegregation plans. It merely excluded school entities which had not participated in unconstitutional segregative policies from federal court jurisdiction in desegregation cases.

Black tenants and applicants for Chicago public housing sued the Chicago Housing Authority and the U.S. Department of Housing and Urban Development (HUD) in a federal district court, alleging that the authority had violated their constitutional rights by locating public housing sites solely in black neighborhoods and by assigning tenants on the basis of race. The tenants prevailed and the court ordered the authority to change its assignment and site selection procedures. However, the court dismissed a similar action against HUD, a decision which was reversed by the U.S. Court of Appeals, Seventh Circuit.

The appeals court ruled that HUD had sanctioned and assisted the authority by knowingly creating segregated public housing. On remand, the district court refused to implement a desegregation plan which would call for incorporating Chicago suburbs into a comprehensive area plan to rectify segregation in city public housing. The appeals court reversed the lower court again, finding that the metropolitan area was a single entity for public housing plan purposes. HUD appealed to the U.S. Supreme Court.

The Supreme Court discussed its decision in *Milliken v. Bradley*, see Section IV, below, in which the Court struck down an interdistrict school desegregation plan in the metropolitan Detroit area. The plan failed because it had not been proven that suburban Detroit districts had not participated in prior constitutional violations. Federal court jurisdiction in desegregation cases extended only to past constitutional violators and, in the absence of such a showing, an interdistrict decree was impermissible. In this case, an interdistrict remedy would not involve federal district court coercion of nonviolating suburban entities, because both HUD and the Chicago Housing Authority had powers to operate beyond city limits. HUD had identified the relevant geographic area as the "Chicago housing market," which extended beyond Chicago city limits. The *Milliken* decision did not create a *per se* rule against interdistrict desegregation remedies. Federal courts were simply forbidden from implementing desegregation decrees which implicated school systems and officials who were not involved in unconstitutional action. *Hills v. Gautreaux*, 425 U.S. 284, 96 S.Ct. 1538, 47 L.Ed.2d 792 (1976).

IV. FEDERAL DISTRICT COURT AUTHORITY

Part of *Brown II's* holding was that federal district courts should oversee school district plans. Subsequently, the Supreme Court has allowed those courts a great deal of discretionary authority over school desegregation plans.

The Louisiana legislature passed a series of laws designed to prevent racial desegregation in New Orleans after a federal court ordered it to desegregate. The federal district court declared the statutes unconstitutional. The state contended that it had exclusive control over education and sought a stay of the statutes' injunction pending determination by the U.S. Supreme Court. The Court denied the stay and dismissed the state's contentions. *Bush v. Orleans School Board*, 364 U.S. 500, 81 S.Ct. 260, 5 L.Ed.2d 245 (1960).

In the Court's 1970 landmark case, *Swann v. Charlotte-Mecklenburg Board of Education*, below, the Court affirmed the broad discretionary powers of federal district courts to implement desegregation plans.

In Charlotte, North Carolina, a geographical zoning plan with free transfer was approved by a federal district court. The plan allowed one-half of the black students to attend 21 nearly all-black schools. After *Green v. County School Board*, see Section III.A.2, above, in which the Court ordered school districts to implement a desegregation plan that would work immediately, the board's plan was challenged in the district court. The court ordered the district to provide a plan for student and teacher desegregation. After the court found an additional plan inadequate, it appointed an expert to arrange a plan. The board and the expert then submitted plans.

The court adopted the district's plan for junior and senior high schools and the expert's plan for elementary schools. The U.S. Court of Appeals, Fourth Circuit, affirmed the district court's order regarding secondary school plans, but vacated the order regarding elementary schools. The court of appeals feared that pairing black and white elementary schools would unduly burden the board and students. The case returned to the district court for reconsideration, and the Supreme Court directed reinstatement of the district court's entire plan pending further proceedings. After the school district acquiesced in the expert's plan, the district court ordered implementation. The U.S. Supreme Court then granted certiorari.

The Court held that where school districts fail in their duty to offer appropriate desegregation remedies, federal district courts have broad discretion to fashion such plans. Therefore, it upheld the district court's decision. Policies with regard to faculty, staff, transportation, extracurricular activities and facilities are good indicators of whether a segregated system exists. The Court identified four considerations when reassigning students to achieve desegregation. First, racial quotas within schools need not reflect the racial composition of the whole system. The district court had properly exercised its discretion by making very limited use of racial quotas. Second, the existence of a one-race school does not necessarily mean the whole system is segregated by law. The courts, however, must determine whether such schools result from the discriminatory conduct of school officials.

Third, the alteration of attendance zones by district courts is permissible. A change in attendance zones does not automatically mean that segregation will end because the change may fail to take into account past discrimination. Finally, the use of busing is an appropriate exercise of district court power. However, busing could not be used if it involved such great distances as to impair children's health or impinge on the educational process. Generally, the Court determined that district courts have broad discretion in ordering desegregation plans. The district court's orders were upheld. *Swann v. Charlotte-Mecklenburg Board of Education*, 402 U.S. 1, 91 S.Ct. 1267, 28 L.Ed.2d 554 (1970).

One hour of travel time was held not to violate the busing limits set out in *Swann*.

Black students and their parents in North Carolina sued their school district in a federal district court to eliminate segregation. At the time, the school district was operating under geographical attendance zones and freedom-of-choice transfer provisions. Of the district's schools, 15 were all black, seven were all white and the remaining schools were less than five percent black. The board submitted a plan calling for satellite zoning and extensive cross-busing, which the district court rejected. The board then modified the plan, retaining geographical zones and a freedom-of-choice transfer provision, but allowing priority majority-to-minority transfers and increasing racial balances in schools.

The district court then approved the modified plan, subject to alterations which prevented minority-to-majority transfers and increased racial contact of students. In addition, the district court ruled that the school district had acted in good faith in devising the attendance zones and in assuring that students could attend the school nearest to their homes when possible. While the case was being appealed to the U.S. Court of Appeals, Fourth Circuit, the Supreme Court handed down its decision in *Swann*, above. In light of the *Swann* holding, the court of appeals remanded the case to the district court for adoption of a new plan which would achieve the greatest degree of desegregation, given the practicalities of the situation. School authorities then adopted a revised pupil assignment plan which required the addition of 157 buses. The school board submitted the plan to the district court under protest, and it was approved. The board then sought to stay the district court's decision until the U.S. Supreme Court could grant a writ of certiorari to hear the case.

Chief Justice Burger, in an opinion in chambers, denied the stay. He determined that the school district had not alleged specific hardships involved in the added bus transportation program. The fact that the district asserted that the average time of travel was one hour did not state a trespass of the busing limits established in *Swann*. Justice Burger found no basis for the argument that school authorities may not be required to employ busing to desegregate schools. Furthermore, the record was inadequate to determine whether the district court had incorrectly read the Court's opinion in *Swann*, so far as its requirements of racial quotas. The stay was denied. *Winston-Salem/Forsyth Board of Education v. Scott*, 404 U.S. 1221, 92 S.Ct. 1236, 31 L.Ed.2d 441 (1971).

In evaluating the response of school officials to desegregation orders, the Court ruled that federal district courts should focus on the effect of proposed action on dismantling the dual segregated education system, rather than on any stated motivation or purpose.

Virginia law defined a "town" as a part of the surrounding county so that town schools included all students who were county residents. However, a "city" incorporated into its school system only those students within city limits. Prior to 1965, a Virginia town maintained white schools within its town boundary, while black students were assigned to schools outside the town boundaries. In 1965, black students sued the school system to end state-enforced segregation. The case eventually reached the U.S. Supreme Court in *Green v. New Kent County School Board*, see Section III.A.2, above. On remand to the federal district court, the court required the county to submit a plan in compliance with the Supreme Court order.

The district court rejected plans submitted by the county and ordered implementation of the plan developed by the students' representatives for the 1969-70 school year. Two weeks later, the town council announced its intent to sever its schools from the county system by virtue of its designation as a "city," which had been accomplished in 1967. Because the severance had the potential effect of restoring racial imbalance between county and city schools, the students' representatives sought an order to prevent the city council and the school board from withdrawing the schools from the county system. The court granted the order, but this decision was reversed by the U.S. Court of Appeals, Fourth Circuit. The students appealed to the U.S. Supreme Court.

The Court stated that under *Green* and other cases, school board actions were to be evaluated according to their effect on dismantling the unconstitutional dual school system. Federal district courts had the power to reject plans which impeded the desegregation process. Although the town council had stated tax revenue reasons for obtaining redesignation as a city, the Court ruled that racial purposes could be imputed where the proposed action was less effective in dismantling the dual system than other proposed plans. The focus was upon the effect rather than the motivation or purpose of the proposed action. The town schools, which had previously been all white, were better equipped and located than the outlying county schools, and withdrawal from the county system would frustrate the district court's desegregation order. The Court ruled for the students, reversing the court of appeals. *Wright v. Council of City of Emporia*, 407 U.S. 451, 92 S.Ct. 2196, 33 L.Ed.2d 51 (1972).

The U.S. Supreme Court ruled that a legislative statute creating a new school district in a city where desegregation was about to take place should be struck down if it hindered the dismantling of segregation.

A North Carolina statute created a new school district in the city of Scotland Neck. The city had previously belonged to a school district in which desegregation was taking place. The United States then sued in a federal district court to enjoin implementation of the statute. It contended that the new school district was a refuge for white students and would promote segregation. After the district court granted the injunction, the U.S. Court of Appeals, Fourth Circuit, reversed. The court of appeals ruled that the statute's effect on desegregation was minimal and, because the statute had been passed by the legislature and not the school board, the statute should not be construed as an alternative to desegregation. The U.S. Supreme Court ruled that the fact that the statute had been passed by the legislature was irrelevant. The statute should be struck down if it hindered the dismantling of segregation in the school district. The Court granted the injunction. *United States v. Scotland Neck Board of Education*, 407 U.S. 484, 92 S.Ct. 2214, 33 L.Ed.2d 75 (1972).

In 1982, the Court made its final pronouncement on busing litigation in Los Angeles. For two earlier rulings, see *Bustop Inc. v. Board of Education of City of Los Angeles* and *Board of Education of City of Los Angeles v. Superior Court*, found in Section III.B., above. In the case which follows, the Court ruled that California's Proposition I facilitated, rather than hindered, the repeal of segregated schools by allowing state adaptability to changing population distribution.

In 1970, a California state court found *de jure* segregation in the Los Angeles Unified School District. It ordered the district to prepare a desegregation plan. The court then approved a desegregation plan that included substantial pupil reassignment and busing. While the trial court was considering alternative plans, California voters ratified Proposition I, which provided that state courts could not order pupil assignment or busing unless a federal court could do so under federal law to remedy an Equal Protection Clause violation. The trial court denied the district's request to stop the desegregation plan, ruling that because it had previously found *de jure* segregation in the district, Proposition I was satisfied. The California Court of Appeal reversed, holding Proposition I constitutional, and banned the district's plan of pupil reassignment and busing. The U.S. Supreme Court granted certiorari.

Before the Court, the students challenging the constitutionality of Proposition I argued that by limiting the state courts' power to desegregate schools, a dual system of state and federal courts had been created. The Court rejected this argument and upheld Proposition I's constitutionality. It concluded that Proposition I was a repeal of segregated schools and was designed to implement, not violate, the Fourteenth Amendment's Equal Protection Clause. The Court rejected the contention that once a state chooses to afford more protection than is required by the constitution, it can never recede. Not allowing such a retraction would destroy the states' ability to experiment with the problems of a heterogeneous population. The Court upheld the court of appeals' decision. *Crawford v. Board of Education*, 458 U.S. 527, 102 S.Ct. 3211, 73 L.Ed.2d 948 (1982).

Detroit's racial composition made effective desegregation plans difficult. The city school district had a 64 percent black population, while the metropolitan area was 81 percent white. A federal district court found that only an interdistrict remedy would bring about desegregation. This required the district court to find that state officials had contributed to segregation by failing to provide funds for busing from the city to the suburbs. The Supreme Court rejected this remedy, citing the *Swann* case, above, for the proposition that the scope of the desegregation remedy is determined by the nature and extent of the constitutional violation. In order to disregard school district boundaries, there must be a showing that the constitutional violator has produced a segregative effect in the other district. An interdistrict remedy is appropriate only when there is an interdistrict violation.

The NAACP filed a lawsuit on behalf of Detroit students in a federal district court, alleging that both Michigan state officials and Detroit school officials operated a dual system of segregated schools. The case was lodged in the courts for several years, and eventually the district court held that the city board's use of optional attendance zones resulted in racially-identifiable schools. The board had also bused black students to predominantly black schools when space was available in white schools which were closer.

The district court ruled that city and state officials were liable for the resulting segregated system and it ordered desegregation efforts which incorporated 54 school districts in the three-county Detroit metropolitan area. It ruled that the racial composition of the area required an area-wide remedy which was permissible because state officials had contributed to the segregated school system. Suburban Detroit school districts were not parties to the litigation. Among other items, the court ordered the state to purchase or lease at least 295 school buses to help implement the plan. The U.S. Court of Appeals, Sixth Circuit, affirmed the portion of the decision requiring interdistrict busing, but vacated the order to obtain new buses. The state officials appealed to the U.S. Supreme Court.

The Court held that while federal district courts could draw upon their equity powers to resolve desegregation cases, the remedy must be refined to meet the constitutional violation. The district court had erred in incorporating outlying school districts which were not constitutional violators into the desegregation order. This was true even though failure to incorporate the suburban school districts could result in schools with black student populations of over 75 percent in Detroit schools. The *Swann* case did not require balance of a metropolitan area's racial composition in each and every classroom. Municipal and school boundaries were not to be disregarded. In the absence of a constitutional violation by the outlying districts, any judicial remedy was limited to the Detroit school district alone. The Court remanded the case for proceedings in the district court to properly formulate a desegregation decree to eliminate dual schools in Detroit. *Milliken v. Bradley*, 418 U.S. 717, 94 S.Ct. 311, 41 L.Ed.2d 1069 (1974). (*Milliken I.*)

In *Milliken II*, below, the Court approved of remedial programs in support of pupil reassignment as an appropriate remedy for prior constitutional violations. Desegregation plans must be properly designed to remedy the prior constitutional violations being addressed.

In *Milliken v. Bradley I*, above, the Supreme Court reversed a district court order which would have required 54 Detroit-area school districts to participate in an interdistrict desegregation plan. The Court held that the order exceeded federal court authority as had been defined in *Swann v. Charlotte-Mecklenburg Board of Education*, above. On remand, the court approved pupil reassignment and magnet school plans to eliminate racially identifiable schools. It also approved a comprehensive, four-part educational program for Detroit schools, including a remedial reading skills program, in-service training for teachers, racially unbiased testing procedures and counseling and career guidance programs. The state of Michigan and the Detroit School Board were to divide costs equally.

The state appealed the portion of the decision requiring it to share the expenses of the four-part remedial program, and the U.S. Supreme Court agreed to hear the appeal. The Court relied on *Swann* and *Milliken I's* requirement that in desegregation cases, the court-ordered remedy is determined by the nature and scope of the constitutional violation. The remedy must be related to the condition which violates the Constitution. The court order must be designed to restore victims of segregation to a position they would occupy absent discriminatory conduct. The federal courts must also take local interests into account in devising desegregation remedies.

In this case, the district court had found that Detroit's *de jure* segregated schools were so completely segregated that both state and local officials were implicated as constitutional violators. Remedial programs which supplemented pupil reassignment were permissible and, as here, were required to eliminate the effects of prior segregation. The proposed plan was properly tailored to remedy previous constitutional violations and the order compelling the state to share future costs did not violate the Eleventh Amendment. *Milliken v. Bradley*, 433 U.S. 267, 97 S.Ct. 2749, 53 L.Ed.2d 745 (1977) (*Milliken II.*)

The U.S. Supreme Court placed the burden on a school district to prove that there was no intent to produce a segregated system.

The U.S. Supreme Court shifted to school authorities the burden of proving that there was no segregative intent in their "neighborhood school policy" although the policy resulted, in fact, in segregated schools. Parents of children attending public schools in Denver sued to remedy alleged segregation. The Supreme Court modified the rulings of the lower courts. It held that purposeful discrimination in a substantial part of a school system would uphold a finding of system wide discriminatory intent unless the district could rebut it. Furthermore, an inference between purpose and racial separation in other parts of the school system could be established. The Supreme Court remanded the case for rehearing consistent with its opinion. *Keyes v. School District No. 1, Denver, Colorado*, 413 U.S. 189, 93 S.Ct. 2686, 37 L.Ed.2d 548 (1973).

Dayton, Ohio, public schools were segregated despite an Ohio law prohibiting separate schools. A federal district court ruled that Dayton school officials had violated the Equal Protection Clause of the Fourteenth Amendment. The ruling was based on the court's finding of "cumulative violations" including racially imbalanced schools and optional attendance zones as well as recent school board actions. The court ordered elimination of the optional attendance zones, new faculty policies, random pupil assignment and busing. The U.S. Court of Appeals, Sixth Circuit, reversed and for five years the parties and courts struggled over the case.

The case came before the U.S. Supreme Court following the court of appeals' approval of a plan which encompassed district-wide racial distribution requirements. The Court held that the final court order was not justifiable in view of the constitutional violations which had been alleged. There was no basis for imposing the order based on cumulative violations. The court vacated the appeals court decision and remanded the case for more specific findings. The district court was to determine whether the school board had taken discriminatory action and to design a remedy to meet the violation. A system wide remedy would only be justified if there was a system wide violation. *Dayton Board of Education v. Brinkman*, 433 U.S. 406, 97 S.Ct. 2766, 53 L.Ed.2d 851. (1977) (*Dayton I.*)

In *Dayton II*, below, the Court held that the school board had failed to meet its responsibility of eradicating the segregated school system.

The Dayton case returned to the district court, where the lawsuit was dismissed for failure to prove a constitutional violation. The U.S. Court of Appeals, Sixth Circuit, reversed, holding that the Dayton school board had perpetuated and failed to eliminate a segregated system which had system wide effects. The school board appealed again to the U.S. Supreme Court, which held that because the Dayton board had operated a segregated system as of the time of *Brown I*, it was under a continuing duty to eradicate the effects of prior segregation. The Dayton board had taken actions after *Brown I* which had actually enhanced segregation in its schools.

After *Brown I*, the measure of the school board's conduct was the effectiveness of its actions in increasing or decreasing the segregation in its schools. The Dayton board failed to meet its affirmative responsibility of eradicating the dual school system by making no attempt to alter the racial characteristics of its schools. The district court had misinterpreted *Dayton I*, above, as requiring complaining students to prove the effect of each individual act of prior discrimination on current segregative matters. The Court affirmed the appellate court's decision for the students. *Dayton Board of Education v. Brinkman*, 443 U.S. 526, 99 S.Ct. 2971, 61 L.Ed.2d 720 (1979). (*Dayton II.*)

The Supreme Court granted an award of attorney's fees against the State of Missouri under 42 U.S.C. § 1988.

In 1977, the Kansas City school district and two students sued the state of Missouri in a federal district court alleging that the state and surrounding school districts had perpetuated a racially segregated school system in the Kansas City metropolitan area. The court ordered interdistrict desegregation remedies, funded by the state and city school district. The complaining parties were represented by a private attorney and the NAACP Legal Defense and Educational Fund. The attorneys billed their clients for over 21,000 attorney hours and over 23,000 hours for paralegals and law clerks. The district court then awarded them $4 million in attorney's fees. The state contested the award, appealing to the U.S. Court of Appeals, Eighth Circuit. The appellate court affirmed the award and the state appealed to the U.S. Supreme Court.

The Supreme Court stated that 42 U.S.C. § 1988 expressly authorized attorney's fees in civil rights litigation as a "cost" against states, irrespective of the Eleventh Amendment. Upward adjustment of the billings was permitted as civil rights litigation tended to be complex, and compensation was generally received several years after services were performed. There was nothing in § 1988 which suggested that paralegal or lawclerk billings should not be taken into account. The attorneys' billings were reasonable according to local standards. The Court affirmed the lower court decisions for the complaining parties. *Missouri v. Jenkins*, 491 U.S. 274, 109 S.Ct. 2463, 105 L.Ed.2d 229 (1989). (*Jenkins I.*)

This case is part of ongoing litigation which seeks to ensure that the Kansas City area schools will be free from segregation. However, in this case, the Supreme Court determined that regardless of a federal district court's power, it could not impose taxes by itself.

The Kansas City, Missouri, School District (KCMSD) and a group of KCMSD students filed a complaint against the state of Missouri, alleging that the state was operating a segregated public school system in the Kansas City metropolitan area. A federal district court transferred KCMSD to the position of defendant, and the court found that segregation had existed. Accordingly, it approved a plan to desegregate the Kansas City schools by utilizing magnet schools to attract white students. However, the court concluded that several provisions of Missouri law would prevent KCMSD from being able to pay its share of the obligation under the desegregation remedy. The court therefore imposed an increase in the property taxes levied by KCMSD to ensure funding for the desegregation of Kansas City's public schools.

The U.S. Court of Appeals, Eighth Circuit, while affirming the actions of the federal district court, held that in the future such action should not be taken. Rather, the court should authorize KCMSD to submit a levy to the state tax collection authorities and use an injunction to forbid the operation of state laws which would hinder KCMSD from adequately funding the remedy. The U.S. Supreme Court then granted the state's petition for certiorari to determine whether the district court's order was lawful.

The Supreme Court held that the federal district court had overstepped its authority by imposing a tax increase. Instead, the district court should have adopted the alternative set forth by the court of appeals—namely, authorizing and directing local government institutions to devise and implement remedies. The Supreme Court further noted that a local government with taxing authority could be ordered to levy taxes in excess of the limit set by state statute where a constitutional obligation required it. Essentially, the Court ruled that a district court could order a local government body to levy taxes beyond state limits; it just could not impose the taxes itself. The Court affirmed the court of appeals' decision insofar as it required the federal district court to modify its funding order, and reversed with respect to the tax increase imposed by the lower court. *Missouri v. Jenkins*, 495 U.S. 33, 110 S.Ct. 1651, 109 L.Ed.2d 31 (1990). (*Jenkins II.*)

The Supreme Court recently stated that supervision of local school districts by federal courts was meant only as a temporary remedy for discrimination. School districts themselves must come forward with plans to ensure the continuation of desegregation.

In 1972, a federal district court issued an injunction imposing a school desegregation plan on Oklahoma City. In 1977, the court found that the school district had achieved unitary status and issued an order terminating the case. In 1984, because of an increase in young black students, which would result in them being bused farther away, the board adopted the Student Reassignment Plan (SRP). The SRP assigned students who were in grades K-4 to their neighborhood schools, but continued busing for grades 5-12. The parents who had brought the original desegregation case filed a motion to reopen the case, claiming that the SRP was a return to segregation. The federal district court refused to reopen the case and held that its 1977 finding that the school district was unitary could not be relitigated.

The parents appealed to the U.S. Court of Appeals, Tenth Circuit, which held that the trial court's 1977 finding was binding, but this did not mean that the 1972 injunction itself was terminated. The case was remanded to determine if the injunction should be lifted. On remand, the trial court found that the SRP was not designed with discriminatory intent and ordered the injunction lifted. The case was again appealed to the U.S. Court of Appeals which reversed the lower court's decision. The school board then petitioned the U.S. Supreme Court for review and its petition was granted.

The Supreme Court first determined that the 1977 order did not dissolve the desegregation decree and that the district court's finding that the school district was unitary was too ambiguous to bar the parents from challenging later actions by the board. However, the Court stressed that supervision of local school districts by the federal courts was meant as a temporary means to remedy past discrimination. The Court remanded the case and instructed the trial court to determine whether the school district had shown sufficient compliance with constitutional requirements when it adopted the SRP. The trial court was to determine whether the school district had complied in good faith and eliminated the "vestiges of past discrimination ... to the extent possible." *Bd. of Educ. of Oklahoma City Public Schools v. Dowell*, 498 U.S. 237, 111 S.Ct. 630, 112 L.Ed.2d 715 (1991).

In *Freeman v. Pitts*, the Court held that federal courts may use an incremental approach when analyzing desegregation cases. Where a school district has become unitary in some areas, but not others, courts may relinquish control in those unitary areas so that more concentrated efforts can be made in the areas that are still segregated.

The Dekalb County Georgia School System (DCSS) was found to be unlawfully segregated in 1969 and was placed under judicial supervision. Various measures were taken toward becoming unitary, and DCSS asked that the judicial control be removed. A federal district court found that unitary status had been achieved to the extent practicable with respect to four of the six factors set out in *Green v. New Kent County School Bd.*, above. The four factors for which a unitary system had been established were student assignments, transportation, physical facilities, and extracurricular activities.

The two factors for which unitary status had not yet been achieved were faculty assignments and resource allocation (which the court examined in relation to a non-*Green* factor: the quality of education). The district court then relinquished control in the areas which it had found were unitary, and retained control of the others. On appeal, the U.S. Court of Appeals disagreed that the "incremental" approach should be used. Instead it held that unitary status in some categories could not lead to relinquished judicial control until all facets under consideration were unitary at the same time. The U.S. Supreme Court granted certiorari.

The Court indicated that the *Green* framework does not need to be applied as construed by the court of appeals. Through relinquishing control in areas deemed to be unitary, a court and school district may thus more effectively concentrate on the areas in need of further attention. The Court held that the "incremental" approach was constitutional, and that a court may declare that it will order no further remedy in any area which is found to be unitary. The order of the court of appeals was reversed, and the case was remanded to the district court. *Freeman v. Pitts*, 503 U.S. 467, 112 S.Ct. 1430, 118 L.Ed.2d 108 (1992).

In the continuing litigation of *Missouri v. Jenkins,* the Supreme Court held that the remedial orders fashioned by the federal district court had exceeded its authority. First, the across-the-board salary increases designed to improve the "desegregative attractiveness" of the school district were part of an interdistrict goal that went beyond the intradistrict problem. Also, the lower court should not have placed so great an emphasis on student achievement levels when it required the state to continue funding certain quality education programs.

In 1977, the Kansas City, Missouri, School District (KCMSD), its school board and a group of resident students sued the State of Missouri and a number of suburban Kansas City school districts in the U.S. District Court for the Western District of Missouri, claiming that the state had caused and perpetuated racial segregation in Kansas City schools. Following realignment of the parties to make the KCMSD a nominal defendant, the district court conducted a lengthy trial resulting in a ruling that the state and KCMSD were liable for an intradistrict constitutional violation. The defendants were ordered to eliminate all vestiges of state-imposed segregation.

Because the district's student population was almost 70 percent African-American, the district court ordered a wide range of quality education plans which converted every high school and middle school, and some elementary schools, into magnet schools to attract white students from adjoining suburbs. This action was based upon the court's finding that KCMSD student achievement levels still lagged behind national averages in some grades. The state contested its court-ordered responsibility to help fund capital improvements for KCMSD schools. It also contested district court orders requiring it to share in the cost of teacher salary increases and quality education plans.

The U.S. Court of Appeals, Eighth Circuit, affirmed the district court orders, and the state appealed to the U.S. Supreme Court. The Court observed that the district court's remedial plan had been based on a budget that exceeded KCMSD's authority to tax. There was a lack of evidence in the district court record to substantiate the theory that continuing lack of academic achievement in the district was the result of past segregation. The Court determined that the district court had exceeded its authority by ordering the construction of a superior school system to attract white students from suburban and private schools. Its mandate was to remove the racial identity of KCMSD schools, and the interdistrict remedy went beyond the intradistrict violation. The magnet district concept of KCMSD schools could not be supported by the existence of white flight and the district court orders for state contribution to salary increases, quality education programs and capital improvements were reversed. *Missouri v. Jenkins*, 515 U.S. 70, 115 S.Ct. 2038, 132 L.Ed.2d 63 (1995). (*Jenkins III.*)

CHAPTER TWO

Private Schools

I. **PRIVATE SCHOOLS AND THE CONSTITUTION—
    FORMULATION OF THE RULES**

Many of the cases in this chapter are of no less significance to
public educators than they are to private educators. Before the
proliferation of education law cases in U.S. courts after World War
II, the U.S. Supreme Court's most significant education cases
pertained to state laws which attempted to restrain parochial
schools by requiring uniform instruction. See *Meyer v. Nebraska*
and *Pierce v. Society of Sisters*, below. In addition to the impact of
these cases on private school law, they are important in the Court's
developing doctrine of constitutional protection for individual
privacy rights. The U.S. Constitution does not expressly protect
individual rights to privacy, family life, or personal freedom except

in that these concepts are embodied by the Due Process Clauses of the Fifth and Fourteenth Amendments. The Due Process Clauses guarantee against government deprivation of life, liberty and property without due process of law. The *Meyer* and *Pierce* cases below help to define the scope of personal privacy rights.

The state of Nebraska convicted a parochial school teacher of violating a state statute which prohibited instruction in any language other than English in grades one through eight. The teacher had conducted classes in German. The teacher appealed his conviction to the U.S. Supreme Court.

The Court considered the Due Process Clause of the U.S. Constitution's Fourteenth Amendment. The concept of due process as a protection of personal liberty interests involved "not merely freedom from bodily restraint, but also the right of the individual to contract, to engage in any of the common occupations of life, to acquire useful knowledge, to marry, establish a home and bring up children, to worship God according to the dictates of his own conscience, and generally, to enjoy those privileges long recognized at common-law as essential to the orderly pursuit of happiness by free men." Accordingly, the teacher's right to teach German was a liberty interest protected by the U.S. Constitution. Parents of children attending the school also had a constitutionally-protected interest in hiring the teacher. The Court summarized the statute as arbitrary, and with no reasonable relation to any legitimate state purpose. There could be no justification for abolishing the right to teach foreign languages. *Meyer v. Nebraska*, 262 U.S. 390, 43 S.Ct. 625, 67 L.Ed. 1042 (1923).

Two years after considering the *Meyer* case, the Court heard *Pierce v. Society of Sisters*, a case arising in Oregon after the state passed a statute requiring parents to send their children ages eight through 16 to public schools. Private schools were not expressly banned; however, the statute required instruction through grades eight at public schools only. The Court agreed with the Catholic school and military academy which brought suit to enjoin enforcement of the statute. According to the Court, the statute as applied forced private schools out of business. Parents have a right to be free of unreasonable state interference in the upbringing and education of their children. States were forbidden from standardizing resident children by forcing their attendance at public schools only.

supplying them free of cost to private school students in the state. The citizens claimed that the act violated the state Constitution and § 4 of Article 4 of the federal Constitution, as well as the Fourteenth Amendment. Louisiana courts refused to issue an injunction and the citizens appealed to the U.S. Supreme Court. The Supreme Court stated that no federal question arose under § 4 of Article 4 which guaranteed a republican form of government to its citizens, since this was a political, not a judicial, matter. The Court also stated that the purchases of the books did not constitute a taking of private property for a private use in violation of the Fourteenth Amendment. The books were purchased for the children, not for the schools themselves. The Court also stated that the students only used the books, thereby remaining the property of the state. *Cochran v. Louisiana State Board of Education*, 281 U.S. 370, 50 S.Ct. 335, 74 L.Ed. 913 (1930).

Under the U.S. Constitution, a state may permissibly provide bus transportation to and from school for parochial school children. Although the Constitution does not *require* this transportation, some states have enacted transportation statutes which grant this benefit to all students regardless of where they attend school. The principle that transportation may be provided to parochial school students without violating the First Amendment was established in the 1947 U.S. Supreme Court case *Everson v. Board of Education*.

A New Jersey law reimbursed parents of children attending nonprofit religious schools for costs incurred by the children in using public transportation to travel to and from school. The law's stated purpose was to provide transportation expenses for all students, regardless of where they attended school, as long as the school was nonprofit. The Supreme Court's analysis was as follows:

[1.] New Jersey cannot consistently with the "establishment of religion" clause of the First Amendment contribute tax-raised funds to the support of an institution which teaches the tenets and faith of any church. [2.] On the other hand, other language of the amendment commands that New Jersey cannot hamper its citizens in the free exercise of their own religion. [3.] Consequently, it cannot exclude individual Catholics, Lutherans, Mohammedans, Baptists, Jews, Methodists, Non-believers, Presbyterians, or the members of any other faith, *because of their faith, or lack of it*, from receiving the benefits of public welfare legislation. While we do not mean to intimate that a state could not provide transportation only to children attending public schools, we must be careful to be sure that we do not inadvertently prohibit New Jersey from extending its general state law benefits to all citizens without regard to their religious belief. Measured by these standards, we cannot say that the First Amendment prohibits New Jersey from spending tax-raised funds to pay the bus fares of parochial school pupils as a part of a general program under which it pays the fares of pupils attending public and other schools.

The Supreme Court analogized free transportation to other state benefits such as police and fire protection, connections for sewage disposal, and public roads and sidewalks, which also benefited parochial school children. It was not the purpose of the First Amendment to cut off religious institutions from all government benefits. Rather, the state was only required to be neutral toward religion. *Everson v. Board of Education*, 330 U.S. 1, 67 S.Ct. 504, 91 L.Ed. 711 (1947).

Any cooperation between public school systems and parochial schools must pass stringent constitutional examination. Cooperative efforts, such as leasing of public or private school classrooms, must avoid the appearance of government approval of religion and must not constitute government aid to, or excessive government entanglement with, religious schools or organizations.

The first type of release time program to be declared unconstitutional by the U.S. Supreme Court was a Champaign, Illinois, program in which public school students were given religious instruction in the public schools. Jewish, Catholic and Protestant community leaders formed the Champaign Council on Religious Education and obtained permission to offer classes to students in grades four through nine. The three religious groups each taught their own classes. The classes were conducted in public school classrooms and were composed of pupils whose parents had given permission for them to attend. Each religious group offered one 30-45 minute class per week.

Although the council supplied religious education teachers at no cost to the school district, the superintendent of schools exercised supervisory powers over them. Only students whose parents released them for religious study attended the religion classes held at the public school. Attendance was monitored by the religion teachers and absences were reported to the public school authorities. Students in the religious education program were released from regular class study while they attended the religion classes. However, the students not released for religious study were not released from regular class study.

A taxpayer in the Champaign school district sued the school board claiming that the release time program violated the Establishment Clause of the First Amendment. The U.S. Supreme Court agreed. It noted that public school authorities engaged in close cooperation with the religious council and its religious education program and taxpayer-supported public school buildings were made available for various religions to propagate their faiths. Further, the Illinois compulsory attendance law helped provide a captive audience of pupils for the religious education classes.

"This is beyond all question a utilization of the tax-established and tax-supported public school system to aid religious groups," said the Court. "[T]he First Amendment has erected a wall between Church and State which must be kept high and impregnable. "According to the Court, it was irrelevant whether the Champaign release time program aided only one religion or aided all religions. The critical fact was that the program aided *religion*, and that was unacceptable. *McCollum v. Board of Education*, 333 U.S. 203, 68 S.Ct. 461, 92 L.Ed. 649 (1948).

In 1952, the Supreme Court upheld a New York time release program in which students could obtain permission to receive time to attend religious instruction off public school grounds. The Court approved the program because no religious indoctrination was taking place in public school buildings, there was no expenditure of public funds for religious training, and religious instruction took place off school grounds.

New York City schools permitted students to leave school during the day to attend their religious centers for instruction or devotional exercises. The time release program required parental permission and those who were not released stayed in classrooms. Religious organizations bore all costs for the program, and no religious instruction took place on public school grounds. Resident taxpayers whose children attended public schools filed a lawsuit in New York courts, ultimately leading to a decision by the New York Court of Appeals that the law was constitutional. The taxpayers appealed to the U.S. Supreme Court.

The Court found no evidence that any element of coercion was involved in the program. Although the First Amendment required separation of church and state, this concept should not be pressed to the extreme. Otherwise, the Constitution could be construed to deprive religious entities of police and fire protection, and other unintended consequences. Cooperation by public teachers and schools in adjusting their schedules to the religious needs of students was permissible so long as it was neutral and noncompulsory. Failure to adjust schedules for religious instruction would amount to a preference for atheism, which was nowhere present in the Constitution. The Court upheld the New York City time release program. *Zorach v. Clauson*, 343 U.S. 306, 72 S.Ct. 679, 96 L.Ed. 954 (1952).

The Court considered *Board of Education v. Allen*, a New York textbook loan case, in 1968. The Court drew an important distinction between the free loaning of textbooks to students, which was authorized by the statute, and state support of private schools, which was forbidden. Because the statute required public school authorities to approve the textbooks, only secular books would be loaned. This safeguard brought the New York statute within the constitutional requirements of the First Amendment religion clauses.

In 1965, a New York law was amended to require local public school authorities to lend textbooks free of charge to all students grades seven through twelve in their districts, including parochial school students. The statute required private schools to comply with state compulsory education law, and required public school authorities to approve all textbooks. A board of education brought suit in a New York trial court against the state commissioner of education, alleging that the law violated the state and federal Constitutions. The trial court ruled that the statute was unconstitutional and the commissioner appealed to a state appellate division court. The appellate division court reversed, finding that the statute did not violate the Constitution. This decision was appealed to New York's highest court. The New York Court of Appeals held that the law did not violate either the state or federal constitution, and the U.S. Supreme Court granted review.

The Court considered most of the early cases in this chapter, drawing particular importance from the *Everson* and *Pierce* cases, above. The statute did not authorize the distribution of religious books, nor did it give direct support to religious schools. The Court stated that the law had the secular purpose of furthering the educational opportunities available to students. Since the law only allowed free secular books to be distributed to parochial school students, there was no danger that the state would be advancing the religious mission of the parochial schools. The statute did not violate the Establishment Clause. Because the statute had no coercive effect, it did not violate the Free Exercise Clause, and the Court affirmed the New York Court of Appeals' decision. *Board of Education v. Allen*, 392 U.S. 236, 88 S.Ct. 1923, 20 L.Ed.2d 1060 (1968).

II. TAXPAYER STANDING—CHALLENGES TO STATE SUPPORT OF PRIVATE SCHOOLS

As federal support of education grew in the 1960s, taxpayers brought an increasing number of lawsuits to challenge aid which went to private schools. The Court had long relied on the procedural requirement of *standing* to limit such suits by federal taxpayers. The standing doctrine states that no person may challenge the constitutionality of a government action or law unless the person suffers a tangible injury. From 1923 until 1968, the Court ruled that federal taxpayers were without standing to challenge federal statutes on constitutional grounds. In 1968, the Court established a new test for granting taxpayers standing in cases alleging violation of the religion clauses in the landmark case of *Flast v. Cohen*, below. The test relaxed the standing requirement by expressly permitting religion clause lawsuits where the taxpayers could establish a logical link between the legislation and their status as taxpayers. Next, taxpayers were required to show a nexus between taxpayer status and the precise nature of the alleged constitutional violation.

A group of taxpayers filed suit in a New York federal district court seeking to enjoin the federal Department of Health, Education and Welfare from expending funds under Titles I and II of the Elementary and Secondary Education Act of 1965. The taxpayers claimed that federal funds were being appropriated to finance instruction in reading, arithmetic and other subjects in religious schools and to purchase textbooks and other instructional materials in such schools. The taxpayers claimed that such expenditures violated the Establishment and Free Exercise Clauses of the First Amendment. The district court dismissed the case on the grounds that the taxpayers lacked standing to maintain the action. The taxpayers appealed directly to the Supreme Court, which reversed the district court's dismissal.

On appeal, the government argued that taxpayers were absolutely barred from suing government entities over the validity of federal spending programs. The Court disagreed, finding no absolute bar to federal taxpayer suits. It established a two-part test for determining when taxpayers had standing to challenge expenditures of federal funds on the grounds that such expenditures violated the Establishment and Free Exercise Clauses of the First Amendment. In order to do so, taxpayers needed to establish a logical link between their status as taxpayers and the type of legislation which they attacked. Secondly, the taxpayers were required to establish a nexus between their status as taxpayers and the precise nature of the constitutional infringement alleged. Under this test, a taxpayer will be a proper party to allege the unconstitutionality of congressional actions under the Taxing and Spending Clause of Article I, § 8, of the Constitution when the specific constitutional limitations imposed on congressional taxing and spending powers are exceeded. In this case, the taxpayers had satisfied both parts of the nexus test in support of their claim, having alleged that tax revenues were being spent in violation of a specific constitutional provision. The Court reversed the district court's decision. *Flast v. Cohen*, 392 U.S. 83, 88 S.Ct. 1942, 20 L.Ed.2d 947 (1968).

In 1982, the Supreme Court ruled that a Pennsylvania taxpayer group lacked standing to challenge a governmental conveyance of surplus property to a private religious college. The Court ruled that the group could show no injury to itself or any of its members as a result of the conveyance.

Congress enacted the Federal Property and Administrative Services Act, 40 U.S.C. § 471 *et seq.*, to dispose of surplus property and authorize its transfer to public or private entities. This statute authorized the education secretary to dispose of surplus real property for schools. The secretary was permitted to take into account any benefit accruing to the U.S. from any new use of the transferred property. In 1973, the secretary of defense and general services administration declared a Pennsylvania army hospital site surplus property. In 1976, the education secretary conveyed part of the property to a Christian college.

Although the appraised value of the property was $577,500, the secretary computed a 100 percent public benefit allowance, permitting the college to acquire the property for no cost. A taxpayer group advocating the separation of church from state learned of the conveyance and sued the college and federal government in a federal district court, claiming that the conveyance violated the Establishment Clause. The court dismissed the complaint, ruling that the taxpayers lacked standing under the Supreme Court's decision in *Flast v. Cohen*. The U.S. Court of Appeals, Third Circuit, reversed the district court's decision and the Supreme Court agreed to hear an appeal by the college and federal government.

The Court stated that Article II of the federal Constitution limited the judicial power of courts to cases and controversies. Litigants were entitled to bring a lawsuit only by showing some actual or threatened injury. Without such a showing, lawsuits were to be dismissed for lack of standing. In this case, the taxpayers had alleged injury from deprivation of fair and constitutional use of their tax dollars. This allegation was insufficient to confer standing in federal courts. Under *Flast*, taxpayers were proper parties only to allege the unconstitutionality of congressional actions under the Taxing and Spending Clause and were required to show that the action went beyond the powers delegated to Congress. Courts were not available to taxpayers to vent generalized grievances of government conduct or spending. The complained of statute arose under the Property Clause and therefore the taxpayers had no standing to complain about the property transfer. As the taxpayers had failed to allege any personal injury, the Court reversed the court of appeals' decision. *Valley Forge Christian College v. Americans United for Separation of Church and State*, 454 U.S. 464, 102 S.Ct. 752, 70 L.Ed.2d 700 (1982).

III. DEFINING THE ESTABLISHMENT CLAUSE— THE *LEMON* TEST

The First Amendment to the U.S. Constitution provides in part that "Congress shall make no law respecting an establishment of religion, or prohibiting the free exercise thereof . . . ." The courts have consistently held that this constitutional provision requires the separation of church and state at all levels of government. In *Lemon v. Kurtzman*, below, the U.S. Supreme Court established a three-part test for determining whether government aid to religious schools violates the First Amendment. The elements of the "Lemon" test are as follows: "First, the statute must have a secular legislative purpose, second, its principal or primary effect must be one that neither advances nor inhibits religion, ... finally, the statute must not foster 'an excessive government entanglement with religion.'" If a statute or government program fails any of these three tests, it is unconstitutional.

In *Lemon v. Kurtzman*, the U.S. Supreme Court invalidated a Pennsylvania statute which provided state money to finance the operation of parochial schools. At the same time, the Court also considered *Early v. DiCenso*, a Rhode Island case involving a state statute which called for a 15 percent salary supplement to parochial school teachers who taught nonreligious subjects also offered in the public schools using only public school teaching materials. The Pennsylvania statute authorized payment of state funds to parochial schools to help defray the cost of teachers' salaries, textbooks and other instructional materials. Reimbursement was limited, however, to the costs of secular subjects which were also taught in the public schools.

The Supreme Court evaluated the Rhode Island and Pennsylvania programs using its now famous three-part test. "First, the statute must have a secular legislative purpose; second, its principal or primary effect must be one that neither advances nor inhibits religion, ... finally, the statute must not foster 'an excessive government entanglement with religion.'" Applying this test to the two state programs, the Court held that the legislative purpose of the programs was a legitimate, secular concern with maintaining high educational standards in both public and private schools. The Court did not reach the second inquiry under the three-part test because it concluded that the state programs failed to pass muster under the third inquiry.

The Rhode Island salary supplement program excessively entangled the state with religion because of the highly religious nature of the Roman Catholic parochial schools which were the primary beneficiaries of the program. The teachers who received the salary supplements provided instruction in classrooms and buildings containing religious symbols such as crucifixes. In such an atmosphere, even a person dedicated to remaining religiously neutral would probably allow some religious content to creep into the ostensibly secular instruction. Similar defects were found in the Pennsylvania program. The Court also observed that in order to ensure that the state-funded parochial school teachers did not inject religious dogma into their instruction, the state would be forced to extensively monitor the parochial school classrooms. This would result in excessive state entanglement with religion.

The Court also found the danger of a different type of entanglement in the Pennsylvania program: politics and religion would inexorably tend to be mixed. In communities with large numbers of parochial school students, candidates for political office might be elected on the basis of their degree of support for financial aid to parochial schools. "Ordinarily political debate and division, however vigorous or even partisan, are normal and healthy manifestations of our democratic system of government, but political division along religious lines was one of the principal evils against which the First Amendment's Establishment Clause was intended to protect . . . The potential divisiveness of such conflict is a threat to the normal political process . . ." Consequently, the salary supplement programs were held to violate the First Amendment. *Lemon v. Kurtzman, Early v. DiCenso*, 403 U.S. 602, 91 S.Ct. 2105, 29 L.Ed.2d 745 (1971). (*Lemon I.*)

**was also unconstitutional, because of its potential effect of support-
ing religiously-affiliated schools.**

Shortly after the Supreme Court announced *Lemon v. Kurtzman*, the
Pennsylvania legislature enacted the Parent Reimbursement Act for
Nonpublic Education, which reimbursed partial private school tuition
expenses. Like the New York statute considered in *Committee for
Public Education and Religious Liberty v. Nyquist*, above, the act
reimbursed qualified parents for a portion of their tuition expenses for
dependents who were enrolled in private schools. However, the reimbursements were funded from cigarette tax revenues, administered by
a state agency. The legislation stated its intent to further a secular
purpose—reducing the burden on public schools by encouraging private school attendance. The legislative findings in support of the
legislation stated that if the 500,000 private school students in the state
were transferred to public schools, the state's operating expenses would
increase $400 million, with over $1billion in added capital costs. A
Pennsylvania taxpayer group sued the state treasurer for an order
declaring the statute unconstitutional. A federal district court ruled for
the taxpayers, and the treasurer appealed to the U.S. Supreme Court.

The Court again examined the act's effect in view of *Lemon v.
Kurtzman*. There was no distinction between the Pennsylvania statute
and the New York reimbursement statute invalidated in *Nyquist*.
Regardless of its stated intentions, the act had the effect of supporting
religiously-affiliated schools. Having held the act unconstitutional on
Establishment Clause grounds, the court rejected an Equal Protection
Clause argument by parents of students attending nonsectarian schools
as spurious and affirmed the district court's decision. *Sloan v. Lemon*,
413 U.S. 825, 93 S.Ct. 2982, 37 L.Ed.2d 939 (1973).

**In *Hunt v. McNair*, decided at the same time the Court an-
nounced the *Sloan*, *Nyquist*, and *Levitt* decisions, the Court upheld
a program for state aid to private colleges. Because religious
indoctrination was not a fundamental purpose of church-related
colleges, state support to them was less likely to cause religious
entanglement than state support for religiously-affiliated primary
and secondary schools. State aid may not go to institutions that are
so pervasively sectarian that secular activities cannot be separated
from sectarian ones.**

The South Carolina legislature enacted its Educational Facilities
Authority Act, which established a state agency that was authorized to

issue revenue bonds to higher education institutions to finance building construction projects with low-interest loans. The act prohibited use of revenues for any facility used for sectarian purposes. No state general revenues were expended under the act, and bonds were not governmental obligations. A Baptist college in the state applied for funds. A state agency was to issue bonds and make bond proceeds available to the college, which would then be obligated to convey the project being funded to the state agency at no cost. The agency was then to lease back the property until the college repaid the full amount of the revenue bonds, when title would revert to the college.

A South Carolina taxpayer sued officials in a state trial court, claiming that the statute violated the Establishment Clause. The Court ruled for the state officials and this decision was affirmed by the South Carolina Supreme Court. The U.S. Supreme Court vacated the judgment in view of its then-recent decision in *Lemon v. Kurtzman*. The state supreme court reaffirmed its holding and the case returned to the U.S. Supreme Court. Applying the three-part *Lemon* test, the Court found that the statute served a secular purpose which did not have the primary effect of advancing or inhibiting religion without unconstitutional entanglement between the state and the college.

According to the Court, state aid to private colleges presented less opportunity for entanglement between states and religious institutions. This was because church-related colleges were less likely than primary and secondary schools to inculcate religious instruction. State aid may not go to institutions that are so pervasively sectarian that secular activities cannot be separated from sectarian ones. If secular activities are severable, they alone may be funded. The Court reaffirmed the state supreme court's decision for the state officials. *Hunt v. McNair*, 413 U.S. 734, 93 S.Ct. 2868, 37 L.Ed.2d 923 (1973).

Pennsylvania law provided for aid to nonpublic schools in the form of auxiliary services, loans of textbooks acceptable for use in public schools and loans of other instructional materials and equipment useful to the education of nonpublic school children. In this lawsuit challenging the constitutionality of the law, the Supreme Court restated the three-part *Lemon* test for determining the validity of state laws which provide such aid.

In *Meek v. Pittenger*, the U.S. Supreme Court ruled unconstitutional most of a Pennsylvania program providing various types of state aid to parochial schools. This was a new program enacted by the state legislature after the Supreme Court in *Lemon v. Kurtzman* (above) invalidated Pennsylvania's direct funding of parochial school operations. The state's new program provided that: 1) textbooks would be loaned to private school students in grades K-12; 2) classroom equipment such as periodicals, photographs, maps, charts, tapes, records, films, projectors and lab equipment would be "loaned" to private schools; and 3) "auxiliary services" such as counseling, testing, and speech and hearing therapy would be provided on private school premises by public school personnel.

The Supreme Court upheld the textbook loans but the remainder of the program was invalidated. The loaning of classroom equipment was found to present a danger that public funds would advance religion since there was no guarantee that the maps, projectors and the like would not be used for religious lessons. Unlike the loaned textbooks, which had a nonreligious content and presumably could not readily be used for religious indoctrination, maps and other equipment could easily be put to religious uses. Because maps and the like could be used to advance religion the state could not "loan" such items to parochial schools.

The Supreme Court also struck down the "auxiliary services" on the ground of excessive entanglement. The Court once again stated that the political divisiveness of the Pennsylvania program caused politics and religion to mix, thus entangling the state in religion. It also emphasized that because the auxiliary services were to be provided by public school employees on the grounds of parochial schools, there was a danger that public employees might transmit or advance religious doctrines in the course of their employment. *Meek v. Pittenger*, 421 U.S. 349, 95 S.Ct. 1753, 44 L.Ed.2d 217 (1975).

In a 1976 case involving Maryland state assistance to colleges with religious affiliations, the Court determined that the colleges were not pervasively religious and that disbursements to the colleges did not risk church and state entanglement.

Maryland education law authorized annual noncategorical grants to religiously-affiliated colleges, subject to a restriction that the funds not go to sectarian purposes. Four resident taxpayers sued the state in a federal district court for a declaration that the statute was unconstitutional and an order prohibiting state payments to the colleges. They also sought a declaration that the state be entitled to recover funds already paid to the colleges. The court ruled that the statute was constitutional and refused to grant any of the taxpayers' requested orders. The Supreme Court agreed to consider the case.

The Court held that scrupulous neutrality was the proper policy in cases involving the separation between church and state. "And religious institutions need not be quarantined from public benefits that are neutrally available to all." Under *Hunt v. McNair*, above, state aid may not be constitutionally given to institutions that are so pervasively sectarian that secular activities cannot be separated from sectarian ones. If secular activities are severable, they alone may be funded. In this case, the colleges were not pervasively sectarian despite their strong religious affiliations. This was because each college's secular activities could be separated from sectarian activities, and in each case state funds had gone only to the secular side. The Court's three-part Establishment Clause test forbade only "excessive" entanglement between church and state, which Maryland's statute avoided. There was no error in the district court's decision and the Court affirmed its judgment. *Roemer v. Board of Public Works*, 426 U.S. 736, 96 S.Ct. 2337, 49 L.Ed.2d 179 (1976).

The Court affirmed parts of an Ohio statute authorizing state funding for private school testing and scoring, diagnostic and therapeutic services for private school students and textbook loans to students. However, parts of the same statute which permitted state funding for loans of equipment and materials were unconstitutional because the loaned equipment could be stored in sectarian facilities. Funding for field trips was unconstitutional because the presence of sectarian teachers presented the risk of religious indoctrination.

The Ohio legislature enacted an education statute involving several forms of assistance to private schools. The statute authorized the state to provide books, instructional materials and equipment, standardized testing and scoring, diagnostic services, therapeutic services and field trip transportation for private school students. An Ohio taxpayer group sued state officials in a federal district court, which found the statute constitutional in all respects. On appeal, the Supreme Court considered each aspect of the statute. The diagnostic services were to consist of speech, hearing and psychological evaluations performed on the parochial school premises by public employees and physicians. Any treatment rendered as a result of the diagnostic evaluations would take place off parochial school premises. The Court upheld this part by distinguishing diagnostic services from teaching or counseling.

"The nature of the relationship between the diagnostician and the pupil," said the Court, "does not provide the same opportunity for the transmission of sectarian views as attends the relationship between teacher and student or that between counselor and student." Accordingly, it made no difference whether the diagnostic services were provided on or off the parochial school grounds.

The provision of therapeutic services, such as guidance counseling and remedial services, was also upheld because the services were provided to parochial school students off the parochial school premises. As long as the services were rendered at a "religiously neutral" site, said the Court, there was no danger of public employees transmitting religious views to the students. Although the Court conceded that some minimal level of monitoring would be necessary to ensure that religious views were not transmitted by the counselors to the students, this monitoring would not result in excessive entanglement: "It can hardly be said that the supervision of public employees performing public functions on public property creates an excessive entanglement between church and state." The textbook program withstood constitutional scrutiny because the books were the same as those used in public schools and were approved by state education officials. The testing and scoring expenditures were also acceptable because they were made to evaluate private school student progress in secular subjects and test content was controlled by the state.

However, the Court ruled that the expenditures for instructional materials and equipment were unconstitutional because the materials and equipment could be stored by the schools. This had the primary effect of loaning materials and equipment to sectarian schools. Field trip expenditures were also unconstitutional because of the role played by teachers. Their presence on location presented an unacceptable risk that religious doctrine would be discussed where teachers worked for sectarian schools. Accordingly, the Court affirmed parts of the Ohio statute, but reversed the district court judgment concerning funds for materials, equipment and field trips. *Wolman v. Walter*, 433 U.S. 229, 97 S.Ct. 2593, 53 L.Ed.2d 714 (1977).

The New York state legislature responded to the Court's decision in *Committee for Public Education and Religious Liberty v. Levitt*, by enacting a statute which permitted parochial schools to recover expenses denied to them by the district court's decision in the *Levitt* case. A New York academy sued the state under the amended statute, seeking reimbursement for its performance of state-mandated services. The state argued that the statute was unconstitutional, and a New York trial court agreed. The academy appealed to a New York appellate division court, which ruled for

the state, but the New York Court of Appeals reversed and remanded the case for a determination of the amount due the academy. The state appealed to the U.S. Supreme Court, which agreed to consider the case.

The Court considered the case in light of its *Lemon II* decision, in which the Court ruled that district courts maintained flexibility under equitable principles to consider even remote possibilities of constitutional harm. In this case, the state legislature had taken action which was inconsistent with the federal district court's order by passing the amended statute. State legislatures were without power to modify federal court injunctions because the authority of federal courts would be undermined each time they ruled state statutes unconstitutional. The modified statute simply consolidated claims for reimbursement to one payment per school, but was substantively the same as the statute previously ruled unconstitutional. Because state aid was still being dispersed without any check on sectarian activity, the risk for impermissible religious indoctrination was present and the statute did not comply with the constitutional guarantee against separation of church and state. Because the potential for excessive entanglement between church and state existed, the statute was unconstitutional and the Court reversed and remanded the decision of New York's highest court. *New York v. Cathedral Academy*, 434 U.S. 125, 98 S.Ct. 340, 54 L.Ed.2d 346 (1977).

The New York legislature succeeded in enacting a private school reimbursement statute which complied with the U.S. Constitution following the Supreme Court's decision in the *Levitt* case. The statute was constitutional because of its incorporation of auditing and recordkeeping to ensure that only secular services were reimbursed out of state funds.

The New York legislature enacted a new statute following the Supreme Court's decision in *Levitt v. Committee for Public Education*, above. The new statute reimbursed private schools for their costs in implementing state-required testing, reporting and recordkeeping. However, the statute implemented an audit system for state funding to ensure that only actual costs were reimbursed for only secular services. A taxpayer group sued state officials to prevent them from making the reimbursements, claiming the statute still violated the Establishment Clause. A federal district court ruled that the new statute was constitutional and the taxpayers appealed to the U.S. Supreme Court.

The Supreme Court noted that the act called for tests which were prepared by state education officials dealing only with secular academic matters, which were graded by private school personnel who had no control over the test contents. There was no substantial risk that the test could be used for any religious educational purpose. The act satisfied the three-part *Lemon* test, as it had a secular legislative purpose, whose principal effect neither enhanced nor inhibited religion without risk of excessive government entanglement with religion. Although the recordkeeping and reporting services reimbursed by the state pertained to private school student and faculty information, it could not be used for any part of the teaching process in support of a particular ideological outlook.

The fact that the statute called for direct cash payments to nonpublic schools did not invalidate the act because there was no primarily religious effect in recordkeeping and reporting functions. There were adequate safeguards to prevent excess subsidies or misdirected reimbursements. In upholding the statute, the Court interpreted its decision in *Meek v. Pittenger* to permit this type of limited reimbursement to sectarian schools. The *Meek* case should not be interpreted to forbid this type of support to religious schools. *Committee for Public Education v. Regan*, 444 U.S. 646, 100 S.Ct. 840, 63 L.Ed.2d 94 (1980).

The U.S. Supreme Court invalidated a shared time program where the school district leased classrooms from religious schools and offered remedial and enriched education to private school students. The reasoning used in this case was overruled by *Agostini v. Felton*, 521 U.S. 203, 117 S.Ct. 1997, 138 L.Ed.2d 391, (1997), below.

A Michigan school district adopted a program called "shared time" by which full-time public school teachers offered instruction in remedial courses during the regular school day at parochial schools. A significant number of these teachers were former parochial school employees. The district also operated a "community education" program where remedial courses were offered at the close of the day at parochial schools. Unlike their counterparts in the shared time program, community education teachers were full-time employees of private schools who were considered part-time public school employees. In both programs, the instruction was offered on the premises of the parochial schools and the classes were attended only by parochial school students. All religious symbols were removed from any classroom where shared time or community education programs took place.

A group of Michigan taxpayers brought suit in U.S. district court seeking to enjoin continuation of the programs. The court granted their request. The school district appealed to the U.S. Court of Appeals, 6th Circuit, which upheld the injunction. The school district appealed to the U.S. Supreme Court.

The Supreme Court again relied on its three-part analysis for Establishment Clause cases, first announced in *Lemon v. Kurtzman*. The Michigan programs violated the Establishment Clause of the U.S. Constitution by impermissibly aiding religion in three ways. First, most teachers in the program were either former or present employees of religious schools and it was likely that they would subtly allow religious indoctrination to creep into their classes. Second, the fact that the government provided such services on the premises of a religious school building threatened to convey the message of state approval of religion. Third, the programs subsidized religion by taking over a substantial portion of each school's duty to provide a comprehensive education. Although the programs served a secular purpose, there was an unacceptable risk that the state would be sponsoring the parochial schools' religious missions. Because the programs had a primary or principal effect of advancing religion, they violated the Establishment Clause and the Court affirmed the court of appeals' decision for the taxpayers. *Grand Rapids School District v. Ball*, 473 U.S. 373, 105 S.Ct. 3216, 87 L.Ed.2d 267 (1985).

In a companion case to *Grand Rapids School District v. Ball* that was also overruled by the Court in *Agostini v. Felton*, below, the Court ruled unconstitutional New York City's use of Title I funds to pay public school teacher salaries for instruction taking place on parochial school grounds. The New York City program violated the Establishment Clause of the Constitution because it required ongoing state oversight which constituted excessive entanglement of church and state.

A group of New York City taxpayers filed a lawsuit in a federal district court to challenge a city program in which public school teachers taught secular subjects on parochial school grounds. The City utilized federal funds from Title I of the Elementary and Secondary Education Act. Title I funds were intended to help educationally-deprived children from low-income families. The teachers taught remedial reading and mathematics and English as a second language. They also provided guidance services. The district court upheld the use of federal funds for this program and the taxpayers appealed to the U.S.

Court of Appeals, Second Circuit. New York education officials appealed to the U.S. Supreme Court following reversal by the court of appeals.

The Court found the case indistinguishable from *Grand Rapids School District v. Ball*, above. The program required New York public school system administrators to establish an ongoing presence at participating schools to monitor public school teachers and parochial school classrooms to ensure that there was no overt religious presence in Title I funded classes. This necessarily involved excessive entanglement between church and state officials, which violated the third part of the Court's Establishment Clause test. Despite the program's good intentions it did not withstand constitutional scrutiny and the Court affirmed the court of appeals' decision. *Aguilar v. Felton*, 473 U.S. 402, 105 S.Ct. 3232, 87 L.Ed.2d 290 (1985).

The Court upheld an Illinois statute which established child care licensing requirements. The act was upheld because it complied with constitutional requirements for specificity and was rationally related to a legitimate state purpose.

An association of two hundred Illinois nonsectarian child care facilities challenged the state child care act, claiming that its requirements for issuing, renewing and revoking licenses for child care facilities was unconstitutional. The association also complained that requiring child care facility operators to undergo examinations to screen out previous child abusers was unconstitutional. The association sued the Illinois Department of Children & Family Services in an Illinois circuit court. In addition to challenging the act's requirements, the association claimed that exemptions under the act for sectarian child care facilities were unconstitutional. The association prevailed at the circuit court level. The Illinois Supreme Court reversed the decision holding that the exemptions for sectarian child care facilities satisfied the three-part test outlined by the U.S. Supreme Court in the *Lemon v. Kurtzman* decision.

The association petitioned the U.S. Supreme Court to review the case. The Supreme Court summarily dismissed the appeal because the act was rationally related to legitimate state ends. The Illinois legislature could rightfully require child care facilities to be adequately staffed. The act did not violate the association members' equal protection rights. The Illinois Supreme Court had correctly ruled that the act served a secular purpose, did not advance religion, did not entangle government with religion and did not violate the Establishment Clause.

The act's regulations were sufficiently specific to apprise the association members of the conduct expected of them and were not unconstitutionally vague. The provisions of the child care act were upheld. *Pre-School Owners Association of Illinois v. Illinois Department of Children and Family Services*, 487 U.S. 1212, 108 S.Ct. 2861, 101 L.Ed.2d 897 (1988).

Two nonschool cases suggest the direction of future Supreme Court analysis under the *Lemon* test. The refined test developed by Justice O'Connor would limit the prohibition on government endorsement of religion to intentional endorsement.

In *Lynch v. Donnelly*, 465 U.S. 668, 104 S.Ct. 1355, 79 L.Ed.2d 604 (1984), citizens challenged a city's display of religious symbols in a holiday display. The Court upheld the challenged action utilizing the familiar three-pronged *Lemon* test. In her concurring opinion, Justice O'Connor expressed concern over the present formulation of the Lemon test and offered an alternative, or refinement, of the test. Justice O'Connor stated that the "purpose prong" of the *Lemon* test should be interpreted to prohibit intentional endorsement of religion by government. The "primary effects" prong should be interpreted to prohibit government action which may not intentionally endorse religion, but which communicates to the public an endorsement of religion. The "excessive entanglement prong" should be interpreted as before, except that it should not include political divisiveness as a factor, as it has in many state-aid-to-private-school cases. The reformed rule under the *Lynch* analysis is: 1) The government action may not have the objective purpose of endorsing religion; 2) the government action may not have the subjective purpose of endorsing religion; 3) the government action may not involve excess entanglement with religion.

The Supreme Court adopted the *Lynch v. Donnelly* variant of the *Lemon* test in the following case, holding that a city government's display of a creche and menorah violated the Establishment Clause as an improper government endorsement of religion.

The city of Pittsburgh and Allegheny County maintained two recurring holiday displays located on public property in downtown Pittsburgh. The first was a nativity scene which was placed on the "Grand Staircase" of the county courthouse. The creche was donated by a Catholic group and bore a sign to that effect. The second was an 18-foot Chanukah menorah, which was placed outside the "City-County" building next to the city's 45-foot Christmas tree and a textual statement declaring the city's "salute to liberty." The menorah was owned by a Jewish group, but was stored and maintained by the city. The American Civil Liberties Union and seven local residents brought suit to permanently enjoin the county and city from displaying the creche and menorah as violations of the Establishment Clause. A federal district court denied relief, relying on *Lynch v. Donnelly*, above. The Court of Appeals for the Third Circuit reversed, and the matter was appealed to the U.S. Supreme Court.

The Court stated that the display of the creche violated the Establishment Clause, but that the display of the menorah did not. In doing so the Court adopted the analytical framework of Justice O'Connor's concurrence in *Lynch v. Donnelly*. The Court stated that the Establishment Clause forbids the government from appearing to take a position on religious belief or from making adherence to a religion relevant in any way to a person's standing in the community. This is an impermissible endorsement of religion. The Court found that when viewed in its overall context the creche violated the Establishment Clause because the creche endorsed a patently Christian message. In contrast to the creche in *Lynch*, there were no Santa Clauses or reindeer to detract from its religious message. Although the city may recognize Christmas as a cultural phenomenon, it may not endorse it as a Christian holy day.

The Court continued, however, that the menorah, given its particular physical setting, did not violate the Establishment Clause. Its combined display with a Christmas tree and the "salute to liberty," did not impermissibly endorse the Jewish faith. In recognizing Chanukah as a cultural phenomenon, the lack of a more secular alternative detracted from the government's message of endorsement. Similarly, the size of the city's Christmas tree clearly made it, and not the menorah, the center of the display. *County of Allegheny v. American Civil Liberties Union*, 492 U.S. 573, 109 S.Ct. 3086, 106 L.Ed.2d 472 (1989).

The Supreme Court held that the provision of a sign language interpreter to a parochial high school student did not violate the Establishment Clause. Under the Individuals with Disabilities Education Act, this was nothing more than the neutral provision of benefits as part of a general program. It was not the advancement of religion.

An Arizona student attended a school for the deaf from grades one through five and a public school from grades six through eight. During his public school attendance, a sign language interpreter was provided by the school district. The student's parents enrolled him in a parochial high school for ninth grade, and requested the school district to continue providing a sign language interpreter. The school district refused, and the student's parents then sued the school district in the U.S. District Court for the District of Arizona under the Individuals with Disabilities Education Act (IDEA), 20 U.S.C. § 1400 *et seq.*

The court granted the school district's summary judgment motion, finding that "the interpreter would act as a conduit for the religious inculcation" of the student — thereby promoting his religious development at government expense. On appeal, the U.S. Court of Appeals, Ninth Circuit, affirmed the district court decision, applying the test found in *Lemon v. Kurtzman,* in determining that the furnishing of a sign language interpreter to a parochial school student had the primary effect of advancing religion in violation of the Establishment Clause of the U.S. Constitution.

The court of appeals stated that the placement of a public school employee in a parochial school would create the appearance that the government was a joint sponsor of the private school's activities. The U.S. Supreme Court granted the parents' petition for a writ of certiorari. On appeal, the school district cited 34 CFR § 75.532(a)(1), an IDEA regulation, as authority for the prohibition against using federal funds for private school sign language interpreters.

The Supreme Court stated that the Establishment Clause did not completely prohibit religious institutions from participating in publicly-sponsored benefits. If this were the case, religious groups would not even enjoy police and fire protection or have use of public roads and sidewalks. Government programs which neutrally provide benefits to broad classes of citizens are not subject to Establishment Clause prohibition simply because some religiously affiliated institutions receive "an attenuated financial benefit."

Providing a sign language interpreter under the IDEA was part of a general program for distribution of benefits in a neutral manner to qualified students. The provision of the interpreter provided only an indirect economic benefit to the parochial school and was a neutral service which was part of a general program that was not "skewed" toward religion. A sign language interpreter, unlike an instructor or counselor, was ethically bound to transmit everything said in exactly the same way as it was intended. Because the Establishment Clause did not prevent the school district from providing the student with a sign language interpreter under the IDEA, the Supreme Court reversed the court of appeals' decision. *Zobrest v. Catalina Foothills School Dist.,* 509 U.S. 1, 113 S.Ct. 2462, 125 L.Ed.2d 1 (1993).

In 1997, the Supreme Court overruled its earlier decision in *Aguilar v. Felton*, above. The Court held that a federally funded program providing supplemental, remedial instruction to disadvantaged children on a neutral basis was not invalid under the Establishment Clause, even though the instruction was given on sectarian school grounds by public employees.

Title I of the Elementary and Secondary Education Act of 1965 provides federal funding through states to local educational agencies to provide remedial education, guidance and job counseling to at-risk students and students residing in low-income areas. Title I requires that funding be made available for all eligible students, including those attending private schools. Local agencies retain control over Title I funds and materials. The New York City Board of Education attempted to implement Title I programs at parochial schools by allowing public employees to instruct students on private school grounds during school hours. The U.S. Supreme Court, in *Aguilar v. Felton*, above, agreed with a group of taxpayers that this violated the Establishment Clause.

On remand, a federal district court ordered the city board to refrain from using Title I funds for any plan or program under which public school teachers and counselors furnished services on sectarian school grounds. In response to *Aguilar*, local education boards modified Title I programs by moving classes to remote sites including mobile instructional units parked near sectarian schools. However, the city board and a new group of parents and parochial school students filed motions seeking relief from the permanent order.

The district court denied the motions, and the U.S. Court of Appeals, Second Circuit, affirmed the decision. On further appeal, the U.S. Supreme Court agreed with the city board and students that recent Supreme Court decisions required a new ruling on the question of government aid to religious schools. For example, the provision of a sign language interpreter by a school district at a private school was upheld in *Zobrest v. Catalina Foothills School Dist.*, above. The Court held that it would no longer presume that the presence of a public school teacher on parochial school grounds creates a symbolic union between church and state. The provision of Title I services at parochial schools resembled the provision of a sign language interpreter under the IDEA. New York City's Title I program was constitutionally permissible because it did not result in government indoctrination, define funding recipients by reference to religion or create excessive entanglement between education officials and religious schools. The Court reversed the lower court judgments. *Agostini v. Felton*, 521 U.S. 203, 117 S.Ct. 1997, 138 L.Ed.2d 391 (1997).

The Religious Freedom Restoration Act of 1993 was enacted to substantially limit the government's power to burden a person's exercise of religion even where the burden resulted from a rule of general applicability. However, the Supreme Court held that the RFRA was unconstitutional because it exceeded Congress' enforcement power under § 5 of the Fourteenth Amendment.

A Catholic archbishop in San Antonio applied for a building permit to enlarge a 70-year-old church. City authorities denied the permit on the ground that the church building was part of a historical district. The archbishop brought suit against the city in a federal district court, asserting in part that the denial of the permit violated the Religious Freedom Restoration Act of 1993 (RFRA) which prohibited government from substantially burdening a person's exercise of religion even if the burden resulted from a rule of general applicability unless the government could demonstrate that the burden furthered a compelling governmental interest in the least restrictive way. The district court determined that the RFRA exceeded the scope of Congress' authority under § 5 of the Fourteenth Amendment, but the U.S. Court of Appeals, Fifth Circuit, reversed, finding the RFRA to be constitutional. The U.S. Supreme Court granted certiorari.

The Supreme Court held that the RFRA was unconstitutional. It altered the Free Exercise Clause's meaning by granting greater protections than the Constitution itself provided. The RFRA's sweeping coverage ensured its intrusion at every level of government. The law was not simply remedial or preventive of unconstitutional behavior, but proscribed state conduct that the Fourteenth Amendment did not even prohibit. The Court noted that when the exercise of religion has been burdened by a law of general applicability, it does not follow that the persons affected have been burdened any more than other citizens or that they have been burdened because of their religious beliefs. Since the RFRA contradicted vital principles necessary to maintain separation of powers and the federal-state balance, it was unconstitutional. *City of Boerne, Texas v. Flores*, 521 U.S. 507, 117 S.Ct. 2157, 138 L.Ed.2d 624 (1997).

IV. PRIVATE SCHOOLS AND GOVERNMENT REGULATION

The Supreme Court ruled that state and local education officials were required to develop comparable programs for public and private school students in order to receive funds under Title I of the Higher Education Facilities Act of 1963.

Parents of children attending nonpublic schools in Kansas City, Missouri, claimed that the state of Missouri had failed to provide "comparable" aid programs for public and nonpublic school students as required by Title I. They contended that on-the-premises teacher instruction was being given public school students but was denied to private school students. The state of Missouri contended that the Missouri Constitution prohibits the state from providing on-the-premises instruction in private schools. The Supreme Court held that under Title I, state and local public educational officials are responsible for developing programs which are "comparable" for public and nonpublic students. Further, "comparable" did not mean identical. Thus, if the state of Missouri determined that on-the-premises instruction violated the Missouri Constitution it became necessary for state educational officials to devise means of implementing "comparable" aid programs, though not necessarily identical, to public and nonpublic school students. For a case involving Title I funding and private colleges, please see *Tilton v. Richardson*, above. *Wheeler v. Barrera*, 417 U.S. 402, 94 S.Ct. 2274, 41 L.Ed.2d 159 (1974).

In *Norwood v. Harrison*, the U.S. Supreme Court ruled that private schools with racially discriminatory admissions policies were not entitled to participate in a Mississippi textbook loan program.

Private non-Catholic schools in Mississippi increased from only 17 in 1963-64 to 155 in 1970. During this time, major public school desegregation efforts were begun. Enrollment at the private schools grew from 2,362 to 42,000. During the 1970-71 school year, 34,000 students in 107 all-white private schools received books valued at over $490,000. The books were loaned under a 1942 Mississippi legislative amendment extending the textbook distribution program to all students in the state. County education superintendents distributed the books until 1970, but in that year a state education regulation was modified to send books directly to private schools which requested textbooks for free distribution to their students.

Parents of Mississippi public school students filed a class action suit in a federal district court to obtain an injunction against the lending program. They claimed that since all-white private schools excluded black students on the basis of race, the program constituted direct state support of racially segregated schools. The district court dismissed the complaint, noting that the statute predated the Supreme Court's decision in *Brown I* and that textbook loans to private secular school students had been approved by the Court in *Board of Education v. Allen*. The parents appealed to the U.S. Supreme Court.

The Court first considered the applicability of its decision in *Pierce v. Society of Sisters*, ruling that although there was a parental right to enroll children in private schools, there was no constitutional right for private schools to receive state aid. States were not required to support private schools without regard to their discriminatory conduct. The Court stated that private schools practicing discriminatory admissions policies communicated a message that segregation in education was desirable. Although private bias was not barred by the Constitution, schools which practiced discriminatory policies could not call upon the Constitution to demand state aid. Private schools could not invoke the Free Exercise Clause if they were not seeking to protect religious beliefs.

"Invidious private discrimination may be characterized as a form of exercising freedom of association protected by the First Amendment, but it has never been accorded affirmative constitutional protections." The Court vacated the case and remanded it to the district court, giving the lower court guidelines for a proper injunction. The district court was directed to require schools seeking textbooks for their students to become certified by the state textbook purchasing board. Certification would require an affirmative statement of admissions policies and practices, including the number of minority students in attendance. *Norwood v. Harrison*, 413 U.S. 455, 93 S.Ct. 2804, 37 L.Ed.2d 723 (1973).

Following the Civil War, Congress enacted antidiscrimination statutes known as the Reconstruction Civil Rights Statutes, 42 U.S.C. § 1981 *et seq*. Section 1981 of the act prohibits racial discrimination in the making and enforcement of contracts. In *Runyon v. McCrary*, the U.S. Supreme Court applied § 1981 to a private school, ruling that the act outlawed racial discrimination in private schools.

The parents of two black children answered advertisements for two private schools in Virginia and sought to enroll their children. The schools rejected the applications because of the students' race. The students sued the schools in a federal district court under 42 U.S.C. § 1981, which states that all persons in the U.S. have equal rights to make and enforce contracts. The students sought an order to prevent racial discrimination by the schools in their admissions policies as well as declaratory relief and damages. The district court granted the requested order and enjoined the schools from discriminating on the basis of race, holding that § 1981 made racially-discriminatory admissions policies illegal. The district court's decision was affirmed by the U.S. Court of Appeals, Fourth Circuit, and the U.S. Supreme Court agreed to hear the schools' appeals.

According to the Court, both schools maintained admissions policies which were "classic" violations of § 1981. There was no merit to the schools' argument that § 1981 did not extend to private discriminatory acts. Congress had intended § 1981 to prohibit private discriminatory acts, and the statute was constitutional under § 2 of the Thirteenth Amendment. However, the Court narrowed its holding to private schools whose potential clientele was more public than private. Because the school had solicited its students from the public at large, the Court was not confronted by the question of whether a purely private club or organization would also be prohibited from using such discriminatory admissions policies.

The Court also ruled that § 1981 did not violate the rights of parents of white students to freely associate with persons of their choice. The statute did not conflict with parental rights to direct the educations of their children. Constitutional rights of association did not extend to racially exclusionary practices. Privacy rights were not unreasonably interfered with by the statute, and parents had the option to send their children to schools of their choice. The Court did not extend its holding to religious schools that practiced racial exclusion on religious grounds. The Court affirmed the injunction against the schools. *Runyon v. McCrary*, 427 U.S. 160, 96 S.Ct. 2586, 49 L.Ed.2d 415 (1976).

The U.S. Supreme Court held that parochial schools with no separate legal existence from churches or religious associations were exempt from payment of unemployment compensation taxes under the Federal Unemployment Tax Act (FUTA).

FUTA was part of the 1935 Social Security Act and established cooperative federal and state programs for benefits to unemployed workers. Amendments during the 1960's and 1970's excluded FUTA taxes for all services performed for religious, charitable or educational organizations which were tax exempt under the Internal Revenue Code. By definition, nonprofit church-related schools were exempt from the tax. A 1970 amendment narrowed the broad exemption for nonprofit organizations by requiring state coverage for employees of nonprofit organizations, hospitals and higher education institutions. A 1976 amendment left the exceptions for religious employment unchanged, but deleted reference to employees of institutions of higher education.

The U.S. Secretary of Labor announced that the 1976 amendment was intended to result in state coverage of church-related schools, and notified states to begin collecting unemployment taxes from church-related schools. Two South Dakota schools which were operated by churches and had no separate legal existence from religious organizations appealed the state department of labor's proposal to tax them. The state unemployment insurance division's referee ruled that the schools' employees were performing employment under the act and that they were not eligible for an exemption. The schools appealed to a South Dakota trial court, which reversed the decision as clearly erroneous. The South Dakota Supreme Court reversed the trial court's decision, ruling that the schools were subject to unemployment compensation taxes. The U.S. Supreme Court agreed to hear the schools' petition.

The Court ruled that the 1970 amendment to FUTA exempted schools without separate legal existence from a church from unemployment compensation taxes. Religiously affiliated schools came within the meaning of the word "church," and their employees were church employees. The 1976 amendment to the act did not alter or repeal this exemption. The Court reversed the South Dakota Supreme Court's decision, ruling the schools to be exempt from FUTA taxes. *St. Martin's Evangelical Lutheran Church v. South Dakota*, 451 U.S. 772, 101 S.Ct. 2142, 68 L.Ed.2d 612 (1981).

Until 1970, the Internal Revenue Service granted tax-exempt status to private schools regardless of their admissions policies. Taxpayers were also entitled to charitable deductions for making contributions to private schools. In 1970, the IRS issued a revenue ruling stating that private schools with racially discriminatory admissions policies were not charitable. Two private religious colleges with racially discriminatory admissions policies sued the IRS for tax refunds, and the IRS counterclaimed for unpaid taxes. The Supreme Court upheld the IRS's ruling, stating that institu-

tions with tax-exempt status must serve a public purpose and not be contrary to public policy.

Until 1970, the Internal Revenue Service (IRS) granted tax-exempt status to private schools regardless of their admission policies, and taxpayers were permitted to take charitable deductions for contributing to these schools. When the IRS issued a revenue ruling revoking tax exempt status to private schools with racially discriminatory policies and disallowing charitable deductions for contributing to them, two nonprofit Christian schools filed for tax refunds. One school's policy permitted black admissions, but prohibited interracial dating, while the other school accepted only whites. Both schools sued the IRS for nominal tax refunds.

The IRS countersued for unpaid taxes in the amount of almost $490,000 plus interest for one school and over $160,000 plus interest and penalties for the other. Both schools filed appeals in federal district courts, where one school was successful and the other lost. However, the U.S. Court of Appeals, Fourth Circuit, concluded in both cases that the institutions were not charitable because their admissions policies ran contrary to public policy. The U.S. Supreme Court agreed to hear both cases and consolidated them on appeal.

According to the Court, Congress intended tax-exempt status for institutions which were beneficial to society. Racial discrimination in education violated fundamental constitutional principles and served no national public policy. The Court ruled that the IRS's ruling was consistent with the common law concept that racially discriminatory private schools were not charitable. The Court also rejected the schools' arguments that the IRS ruling violated their rights to freely exercise their religion under the First Amendment. It also rejected one school's contention that its policy prohibiting racial intermarriage was not racially discriminatory. The Court ruled that the policy based on racial affiliation and association was also a form of racial discrimination. The Court affirmed the rulings by the IRS and the court of appeals. *Bob Jones University v. U.S.*, 461 U.S. 574, 103 S.Ct. 2017, 76 L.Ed.2d 157 (1983).

The U.S. Supreme Court upheld a Minnesota state income tax deduction for tuition, nonsecular textbooks and transportation. The deduction uniformly applied to taxpayers with dependents in public and private schools.

Minnesota allowed state taxpayers to claim deductions for education expenses for dependents attending elementary and secondary schools. The deduction was available to both public and private school students' parents. A group of Minnesota taxpayers sued the commissioner of the state department of revenue and several parents who had taken the deduction for their expenses in sending their children to parochial schools. The court ruled for the commissioner and the taxpayers appealed to the U.S. Court of Appeals, Eighth Circuit, which affirmed the district court's decision. The U.S. Supreme Court granted certiorari.

The Supreme Court rejected the taxpayers' argument that the deduction violated the Establishment Clause. The Court cited many of the cases in this chapter, placing its primary reliance on the *Lemon* test. The tax deduction served a secular purpose in support of both public and private education. The existence of private schools relieved public schools of a great burden, as ten percent of Minnesota students attended private schools. The statute did not have the primary effect of advancing any religion as it was available to all parents and helped to equalize the tax burden. This was distinguished from the statute struck down in *Nyquist*, see Section III above, in which public assistance was provided only to parents of private school students.

Although taxpayers enjoyed a financial benefit from the deduction, individual parental choice controlled how much of the benefit flowed to parochial schools. Despite evidence that 96 percent of the students in private schools attended religiously-affiliated institutions, any unequal effect was to be considered as a return for the benefits accruing to state taxpayers from the existence of parochial schools. As the deduction did not excessively entangle the state in religion, it passed constitutional scrutiny and the Court affirmed the lower court decisions. *Mueller v. Allen*, 463 U.S. 388, 103 S.Ct. 3062, 77 L.Ed.2d 721 (1983).

In 1984, the Court required a private college, which had an "unbending policy" of refusing all forms of government assistance, to comply with Title IX antidiscrimination requirements because its students participated in the direct federal Basic Educational Opportunity Grants program which was administered by the Federal Department of Education. The Court required the college to submit compliance information regarding administration of its financial aid program in order to receive its grants.

A private liberal arts college in Pennsylvania sought to preserve institutional freedom by refusing state and federal assistance. However, many of its students received Basic Educational Opportunity Grants (BEOG's) which were administered by the Federal Department of Education's Alternate Disbursement System. Title IX of the Education Amendments of 1972, 20 U.S.C. § 1681(a) prohibits sex discrimination in educational programs which receive federal financial assistance. The education department was authorized to secure compliance by terminating assistance for noncomplying programs. The college refused to execute a compliance assurance form issued by the department, and the department began proceedings to declare the college and its students ineligible for BEOGs.

The department prevailed in an administrative proceeding and the college and four of its students sued the department in a federal district court. The court ruled for the students and college and the department appealed to the U.S. Court of Appeals, Third Circuit. The appeals court determined that BEOGs resembled non-earmarked aid to the college; therefore, the college was a program participant. According to the court of appeals, the department could appropriately terminate federal financial aid to students and the college without any evidence of actual sex discrimination. The U.S. Supreme Court agreed to hear the appeal of the college and its students.

According to the Court, there was a distinction between direct government assistance to schools, and aid which was received directly by students. However, as the college received federal funds indirectly through student tuition payments, it was a recipient of federal financial assistance. The college was required to execute an assurance of compliance with the department of education. The assurance of compliance was limited to those educational programs or activities which actually received federal financial assistance through the BEOG program. Failure to execute the appropriate program-specific assurance of compliance would justify termination of student financial aid. The Court affirmed the court of appeals' decision. *Grove City College v. Bell*, 465 U.S. 555, 104 S.Ct. 1211, 79 L.Ed.2d 516 (1984).

The Supreme Court rejected claims by parents of black public school children seeking a court order to require the IRS to adopt more stringent standards for determining tax-exempt status for private schools with racially discriminatory admissions policies. The Court ruled that the parents had no standing in the courts to challenge IRS standards as none of the children had sought enrollment in any of the private schools.

Parents of black students in public schools alleged that the IRS employed insufficient standards for denying tax-exempt status to racially discriminatory schools. They sought to prove that failure by the IRS to deny tax-exempt status to these schools harmed the students directly by interfering with their opportunity to receive quality education in desegregated facilities. They also argued that while their school districts were undergoing the transition from segregated dual systems to unitary desegregated systems, racially segregated private schools flourished. The achievement of tax-exempt status constituted federal aid to private schools which thwarted desegregation efforts. The parents sued the Secretary of the Treasury in the U.S. District Court for the District of Columbia, which dismissed the case for lack of standing by the parents. The District of Columbia Court of Appeals reversed and remanded the case, and the secretary appealed to the U.S. Supreme Court, which agreed to hear the case.

The Court reviewed IRS standards for obtaining tax-exempt status and found that the regulations required institutions to admit students of all races and forbade racial discrimination in school admissions, loan programs and athletic programs. Schools were required to make an affirmative showing that they had adopted nondiscriminatory policies and to make them publicly known. The parents had failed to allege that their children were victims of any discriminatory exclusion by the private schools, and had no interest in enrolling them in private schools. Because the students' parents had failed to allege an injury to themselves which was traceable to the actions of the private schools or the IRS, they were without standing to challenge their policies in the courts. The Court rejected as speculative the parents' theory that denial of tax-exempt status to such schools would result in greater white student enrollment in the public schools. Accordingly, the Court upheld the appeals court's decision for the secretary. *Allen v. Wright*, 468 U.S. 737, 104 S.Ct. 3315, 82 L.Ed.2d 556 (1984).

The Supreme Court ordered a private university to allow access to peer review materials for the purpose of determining whether an individual has been discriminated against.

The University of Pennsylvania, a private institution, denied tenure to a female associate professor. The professor filed a charge with the Equal Employment Opportunity Commission (EEOC) alleging discrimination based on race, sex and national origin in violation of Title VII of the Civil Rights Act of 1964. During its investigation, the EEOC issued a subpoena seeking disclosure of the professor's tenure-review file and the tenure files of five male faculty members identified as having received more favorable treatment. The university refused to produce a number of the tenure-file documents and asked the EEOC to modify the subpoena to exclude "confidential peer review information." The EEOC refused and successfully sought enforcement of its subpoena through a federal district court. The U.S. Court of Appeals, Third Circuit, affirmed and rejected the university's claim that policy consideration and the First Amendment principles of academic freedom required recognition of a qualified privilege or the adoption of a balancing approach that would require the EEOC to demonstrate a showing of need to obtain peer review materials. The U.S. Supreme Court then agreed to hear the case.

The Supreme Court held that a university does not enjoy a special privilege requiring a judicial finding of necessity prior to access of peer review materials. The Court was reluctant to add such a privilege to protect "academic autonomy" when Congress had failed to do so in Title VII. The Court also stated that "academic freedom" could not be used as the basis for such a privilege. The university's assertion that the quality of instruction and scholarship would decline as a result was too speculative. The Court affirmed the lower court decisions. *Univ. of Pennsylvania v. EEOC*, 493 U.S. 182, 110 S.Ct. 577, 107 L.Ed.2d 571 (1990).

The owner of a private school in Texas, who was held to have had his civil rights violated, but who was only awarded $1 in nominal damages, was not entitled to recover his attorney's fees because the degree of success he had obtained was so minimal.

A Texas man owned and operated a school for delinquent, disabled, and disturbed teens. After one of the school's students died in 1973, a county grand jury returned a murder indictment charging the owner with wilful failure to administer proper medical treatment and failure to provide timely hospitalization. The state of Texas obtained a temporary injunction that closed the school. The lieutenant governor of Texas participated in events leading to the permanent closing of the school. The owner sued the lieutenant governor, the judge involved in the closing, a county attorney, and the director and two employees of the Department of Public Welfare for monetary and injunctive relief under 42 U.S.C. §§ 1983 and 1985. The complaint ultimately asked for damages of $17 million. The owner died in 1983, and the administrators of his estate continued the case. The case was tried before a jury, which found that although the defendants had committed acts that deprived the owner of a civil right, this deprivation was not the proximate cause of any damages. Therefore, it held that the owner's estate should take nothing.

The U.S. Court of Appeals for the Fifth Circuit affirmed in part and reversed in part. The court affirmed the failure to award compensatory or nominal damages against the conspirators because the complainants had not proven an actual deprivation of a constitutional right. Because the jury found that the lieutenant governor had deprived the owner of a civil right, however, the court remanded for entry of judgment against the lieutenant governor for $1 in nominal damages. The owner's estate then sought attorney's fees under 42 U.S.C. § 1988, which allows prevailing parties in civil rights actions to be awarded reasonable attorney's fees. The district court entered an award ordering the estate to be paid $280,000 in fees, $27,000 in expenses, and $10,000 in prejudgment interest. A divided Fifth Circuit panel reversed the fee award stating that an award of $1 was insufficient to justify an award as a prevailing party. The U.S. Supreme Court granted review.

The Supreme Court held that a plaintiff who wins nominal damages is a prevailing party under § 1988. A plaintiff prevails when actual relief on the merits of his claim materially alters the legal relationship between the parties by modifying the defendant's behavior in a way that directly benefits the plaintiff. Here, the estate was entitled to nominal damages because it was able to establish liability for denial of procedural due process. The prevailing party inquiry does not turn on the magnitude of the relief obtained or whether a nominal damages award is a technical, insignificant victory.

However, even though the estate was the prevailing party it was not entitled to a fee award. While the technical nature of nominal damages does not affect prevailing party inquiry, it does bear on the fees awarded under § 1988. The most critical factor in determining a fee award's reasonableness is the degree of success obtained, since a fee based upon the hours expended on the litigation as a whole may be excessive if a plaintiff achieves only partial or limited success. Since the estate failed to prove the essential element of its claim for monetary relief, the only reasonable fee was no fee at all. *Farrar v. Hobby*, 506 U.S. 103, 113 S.Ct. 566, 121 L.Ed.2d 494 (1992).

In the following tax case, the Court held that nonprofit status does not exclude private school entities from Commerce Clause coverage. Nonprofit institutions are subject to real estate taxation, federal antitrust regulation and other laws regulating commerce.

A Maine nonprofit corporation operated a summer camp for children of the Christian Science faith. Activities included supervised prayer, meditation and church services, and the weekly tuition for the camp was roughly $400. A Maine statute exempted charitable institutions from real estate and personal property taxes. However, institutions that were operated primarily for the benefit of nonresidents were only entitled to a more limited tax benefit, and then only if the weekly charge of services did not exceed $30 per person. Because most of the campers were not residents of the state and weekly tuition was over $30, the corporation was ineligible for any tax exemption. It petitioned the town for a refund of the taxes it had paid, arguing that the exemption violated the Commerce Clause of the U.S. Constitution. The petition was denied and the corporation sued the town in a state trial court which ruled in the corporation's favor. The Maine Supreme Judicial Court reversed this decision and the U.S. Supreme Court granted certiorari.

The Court noted that the Commerce Clause was designed to override restrictive and conflicting state commercial regulations that fostered local interests and prejudiced nonresidents. The town argued that the Commerce Clause was inapplicable because the campers were not articles of commerce and therefore, interstate commerce was not implicated. The Court disagreed, finding that the camp was engaged in commerce not only as a purchaser, but also as a provider of goods and services. The town then argued that the Commerce Clause did not apply because a real estate tax was at issue.

The Court, however, held that a real estate tax, like any other tax, could impermissibly burden interstate commerce and noted that if the exemption applied to for-profit entities, there would be no question of a Commerce Clause violation. It found no reason why an entity's nonprofit status should exclude it from Commerce Clause coverage and noted that nonprofit institutions are subject to other laws regulating commerce as well as federal antitrust laws. Finally, the Court found that the town did not defend the statute by showing that it advanced a legitimate purpose which could not be obtained by reasonable, nondiscriminatory alternatives. The Court reversed the state supreme court's decision. *Camps Newfound/Owatonna, Inc. v. Town of Harrison, Maine,* 520 U.S. 564, 117 S.Ct. 1590, 137 L.Ed.2d 852 (1997).

CHAPTER THREE

Student Rights

I. ADMISSIONS, ATTENDANCE, AND TUITION

The U.S. Constitution makes no specific mention of a right to a free public education. However, such a right, once established by state law, may be enforced through the Equal Protection Clause of the Fourteenth Amendment. Among other things, the Fourteenth Amendment guarantees that "no state shall make or enforce any law which abridges the privileges or immunities of citizens of the United States; nor shall any state deprive any person of life, liberty, or property, without due process of law; nor deny to any person within its jurisdiction the equal protection of the laws."

While the Equal Protection Clause does not mandate a program of free education, every state has enacted legislation for the establishment and enforcement of education laws. The Equal Protection Clause requires that once a program of free education has been established, the law must be applied equally to any person within the jurisdiction. Thus children of illegal aliens, disabled and mentally retarded children, minority children, etc., are all entitled to equal protection of the laws. School administrators may, within certain limits, establish health regulations, make minimum age requirements, and otherwise reasonably regulate the school environment.

It has long been recognized that the state may require mandatory schooling of the children within its jurisdiction. The reach of this mandate is not without limit, however. Here, the U.S. Supreme Court held that while the state could require all children to attend school, it could not force them to attend public schools exclusively.

In 1922, the voters of the state of Oregon enacted by initiative a law requiring that all school-age children attend public schools. A Catholic parochial school and a military academy challenged the law in federal court. An injunction was granted to the private schools preventing enforcement of the law, and the state of Oregon appealed to the U.S. Supreme Court. Affirming the lower court's injunction, the Supreme Court held that while the state has a strong interest in educating its citizens, parents have a strong interest in directing the upbringing of their children. The Court resolved the conflict between these competing interests by declaring that "[t]he child is not the mere creature of the State." Although states may require children to attend school, requiring attendance at public schools only is an infringement of parents' constitutional rights. *Pierce v. Society of Sisters*, 268 U.S. 510, 45 S.Ct. 571, 69 L.Ed. 1070 (1925).

The Supreme Court made an exception to the general requirements of state compulsory attendance laws when it considered the case of Old Order Amish who had been convicted of violating Wisconsin's compulsory attendance law. Because of the order's sincerely-held religious beliefs, the state could not compel attendance by the Amish without violating their First Amendment rights.

Wisconsin's compulsory school-attendance law required all residents to attend school until age 16. Old Order Amish conducted their own vocational and religious instruction of their children until age 14 or 15. Wisconsin education officials sought compliance and convicted Amish parents of violating the law. The evidence showed that the Amish provided continuing informal vocational education to their children designed to prepare them for life in the rural Amish community. The parents sincerely believed that high school attendance was contrary to Amish beliefs. The Wisconsin Supreme Court reversed the convictions, and state officials appealed to the U.S. Supreme Court.

The U.S. Supreme Court tempered the general rule stated in *Pierce v. Society of Sisters*, above, ruling that states could require some form of school attendance of all children. The Court stated that the state's interest in universal education needed to be balanced against the traditional interests of parents and the Free Exercise Clause of the First Amendment. The Supreme Court held that Wisconsin's interest in compelling Amish children to attend school after the eighth grade was minimal, and accordingly it upheld the state supreme court's reversal of the parents' criminal convictions. The Court cautioned that its holding was limited to children residing in traditionally discrete and isolated communities such as the Amish. *Wisconsin v. Yoder*, 406 U.S. 205, 92 S.Ct. 526, 32 L.Ed.2d 15 (1972).

Although a state may validly classify students in its university system as "resident" and "nonresident," the means by which it does so is subject to challenge. In this case, the Court struck down a statute which created an irrebuttable presumption of nonresidency. The Court held that students must be allowed to present evidence rebutting any presumption of nonresidence.

Connecticut required nonresidents enrolled in the state's university system to pay tuition and other fees at a higher rate than state residents. It also created an irreversible and irrebuttable statutory presumption that if the legal address of a student, if married, was outside the state at the time of application for admission or, if single, was outside the state at some point during the preceding year, the student remained a nonresident as long as the student remained enrolled in Connecticut schools. Two students, one married, one single, who were both residents of Connecticut, challenged the presumption, claiming that it violated the Fourteenth Amendment's guarantee of due process and equal protection. A three-judge district court panel upheld the students' claim and the matter was appealed to the U.S. Supreme Court.

The Court held that the Due Process Clause does not permit the states to deny a student the opportunity to present evidence that the student is a bona fide resident of the state, and thus entitled to in-state tuition rates, on the basis of an irrebuttable presumption of nonresidence. Such a presumption is not necessarily true and the state had reasonable alternatives in making residency determinations. *Vlandis v. Kline*, 412 U.S. 441, 93 S.Ct. 2230, 37 L.Ed.2d 63 (1973).

One of the difficulties faced by students and school officials seeking judicial resolution of disputes is the amount of time it takes a case to move through the court system. By the time a case reaches its final appeal, depending on the nature of relief sought, there may well be no reason for the court to decide the issue. In these situations, the case is considered *moot* and dismissed. In this case, a student sought a final court order mandating admission to law school, but by the time the case reached the Supreme Court it was the eve of the student's graduation. The Court dismissed the case.

A student applied for admission to a state-operated law school in Washington. The size of the incoming class was limited, and the school accepted less than ten percent of those who applied. The student was among those rejected by the school. He sued the school, claiming that its policy of giving favorable status to certain minority students in admission decisions discriminated against him on the basis of his race in violation of the Equal Protection Clause of the Fourteenth Amendment. The student brought suit on behalf of himself and not as the representative of any class. He sought an injunction ordering the school to admit him as a member of the first-year class. A Washington state trial court agreed with his claim and granted the requested relief. The student entered the school and began his legal studies. The Washington Supreme Court reversed and held that the admissions policy did not violate the Constitution. By this time, the student was in his second year.

The student petitioned the U.S. Supreme Court for review and received a stay of the Washington Supreme Court's judgment pending the final disposition of the U.S. Supreme Court. When the case was finally argued before the Court, the student was in his final quarter of law school and the Court determined that the question was moot. The Court stated that since the student had only brought the action for his own behalf and had already been granted the relief he had sought, the controversy between the school and himself was at an end. Furthermore, there was no immediate danger that the student might be subjected to the "gauntlet" of law school admissions again. The Court dismissed the case. *DeFunis v. Odegaard*, 416 U.S. 312, 94 S.Ct.1704, 40 L.Ed.2d 164 (1974).

Reiterating the general rule of *Vlandis v. Kline*, above, the Court, in this case, held that the right to rebut a presumption of nonresidence extends even to aliens with visas living in-state. (See also *Toll v. Moreno*, below.)

The University of Maryland granted "in-state" tuition status only to students domiciled in Maryland, or, if a student was financially dependent on the student's parents, to students whose parents were domiciled in Maryland. The university could also deny in-state status to individuals who did not pay the full spectrum of Maryland state taxes. The university refused to grant in-state status to a number of students, each of whom was dependent on a parent who held a "G-4 visa" (a nonimmigrant visa granted to officers and employees of international treaty organizations and members of their immediate family).

The university stated that the holder of a G-4 visa could not acquire Maryland domicile because the holder was incapable of showing an essential element of domicile—the intent to live permanently or indefinitely in Maryland. After unsuccessful appeals at the administrative level, the students brought a class action in federal court seeking declaratory and injunctive relief. The students alleged that university policy violated the Equal Protection Clause. The district court granted relief, stating that the G-4 visa could not create an irrebuttable presumption of nondomicile. The Court of Appeals affirmed.

On appeal, the Supreme Court refused to decide the matter and certified the question to Maryland's highest court, the Maryland Court of Appeals, for a determination. The Court stated that the case was controlled by the principles announced in *Vlandis v. Kline*, above, that when a state purports to be concerned with domicile, it must provide an individual with the opportunity to present evidence bearing on that issue. Federal law allows aliens holding a G-4 visa to acquire domicile in the United States. However, the question of whether such domicile could be acquired in Maryland was a question of state law. Since no controlling precedent had been decided by the state's highest court, the Supreme Court declined to rule and certified the question to the Maryland high court. *Elgin v. Moreno*, 435 U.S. 647, 98 S.Ct. 1338, 55 L.Ed.2d 614 (1978).

The Fourteenth Amendment provides that no state shall deny to any person within its jurisdiction the equal protection of the laws. The Supreme Court, in this case, decided that this protection extended to illegal aliens who sought to attend the Texas public schools.

In May 1975, the Texas legislature revised its education laws to withhold from local school districts any state funds for the education of children who were not legally admitted into the United States. It also authorized local school districts to deny enrollment in their public schools to children not legally admitted into the country. The legislation was challenged by numerous groups. One group filed a class action on behalf of certain school-age children of Mexican origin who could not establish that they had been legally admitted into the United States. The action complained of the exclusion of the children from public school.

A federal district court enjoined the school district from denying a free education to the children, and the U.S. Court of Appeals, Fifth Circuit, upheld the decision. The legislation was also challenged by numerous other plaintiffs whose cases were consolidated and heard as a single action before a federal district court. The district court held that the law violated the Equal Protection Clause of the Fourteenth Amendment and the Fifth Circuit summarily affirmed. The Supreme Court consolidated the two cases and granted review.

The state claimed that undocumented aliens were not persons within the jurisdiction of Texas, and that they therefore were not entitled to equal protection of its laws. The Court rejected this argument, stating that whatever an alien's status under the immigration laws, an alien is surely a person in any sense of the term. The term "within its jurisdiction" was meant as a term of geographic location and the Equal Protection Clause extends its protection to all persons within a state, whether citizen or stranger. The Court stated that the discrimination contained in the statute could not be upheld unless it rationally furthered some substantial goal of the state. The Court stated that the Texas statute imposed a lifetime hardship on a discrete class of children not account-able for their disabling status. The argument that the statutory classifi-cation furthered the state's interest in its limited resources for education of its lawful residents does not suffice since there was no evidence to show that exclusion of the children would improve the overall quality of education in the state. *Plyler v. Doe*, 457 U.S. 202, 102 S.Ct. 2382, 72 L.Ed.2d 786 (1982).

Federal law supersedes, or preempts, state law when both deal with the same subject matter and the state law attempts to impose burdens not contemplated by Congress. In the follow-up to *Elgin v. Moreno,* above, the Court struck down a university policy which imposed additional restrictions on an alien's right to acquire domicile in a state and thus qualify for in-state tuition.

The University of Maryland's student fee schedule policy denied students whose parents held nonimmigrant alien visas (those visas issued to officers or employees of certain international organizations and their families) in-state status, even if they were domiciled in the state, thus denying them preferential fee and tuition schedules. The U.S. Supreme Court found the policy to be in violation of the Supremacy Clause of the U.S. Constitution which states, "This Constitution, and the laws of the United States which shall be made in Pursuance thereof; and all Treaties made, or which shall be made, under the Authority of the United States, shall be the supreme Law of the Land." The Court stated that the university's policy conflicted directly with the will of Congress as expressed in the Immigration and Nationality Act of 1952. In passing the Immigration and Nationality Act, Congress explicitly decided not to bar nonimmigrant aliens such as these the right to acquire domicile in the United States. The university's policy denying these aliens "in-state" status, solely on the basis of their immigration status, amounted to an ancillary burden not contemplated by Congress in admitting them to the United States. Thus, the University of Maryland's student fee schedule as applied to these aliens was held to be unconsti-tutional. *Toll v. Moreno*, 458 U.S. 1, 102 S.Ct. 2977, 73 L.Ed.2d 563 (1982).

The Equal Protection Clause of the Fourteenth Amendment is not violated when a person is subjected to differential treatment under state law if that differential treatment is rationally related to a substantial state interest. In contrast to *Plyler v. Doe*, above, the Court here upheld a Texas statute limiting free school attendance

to *bona fide* residents of the state. The statute was held to advance the state's substantial interest in assuring that state services are enjoyed only by state residents.

The Texas Education Code permitted school districts to deny free admission to public schools for minors who lived apart from a "parent, guardian, or the person having lawful control of him" if the minor's primary purpose in being in the district was to attend public free schools. A minor left his parent's home in Mexico to live with his sister in a Texas town for the purpose of attending school there. When the school district denied his application for tuition-free admission, his sister sued the state in federal court, alleging that the law was unconstitutional. The district court held for the state, finding that the state's interest in protecting and preserving the quality of its educational system and the rights of its *bona fide* residents to attend school on a preferred tuition basis was legitimate. The Court of Appeals affirmed.

The Supreme Court of the United States upheld the Texas residency requirement. The Court noted that a *bona fide* residence requirement, appropriately defined and uniformly applied, furthers a substantial state interest in assuring that services provided for its residents are enjoyed only by residents. Such a requirement with respect to attendance in public schools does not violate the Equal Protection Clause of the Fourteenth Amendment. Residence, said the Court, generally requires both physical presence and intention to remain. Here, Texas merely requires that as long as the child is not living in the district for the sole purpose of attending school, he satisfies the statutory test. The Court held that this was a *bona fide* residency requirement and that the Constitution permits a state to restrict eligibility for tuition-free education to its *bona fide* residents. *Martinez v. Bynum*, 461 U.S. 321, 103 S.Ct. 1838, 75 L.Ed.2d 879 (1983).

In the following case, the Supreme Court stated that federal assistance may be based on compliance with federal laws. The Court held that a statute mandating compliance with the Selective Service System's requirements as a prerequisite to federal aid did not violate the Fifth Amendment's protection from self-incrimination since no student is compelled to apply for federal aid.

Section 12(f) of the Military Selective Service Act denied federal financial assistance under Title IV of the Higher Education Act to male students between the ages of 18 and 26 who failed to register for the draft. Applicants for assistance were required to file a statement with their institutions attesting to their compliance with the Selective Service Act. A group of students who had not registered for the draft sued the selective service system to enjoin enforcement of § 12(f). A federal district court held that the act was a bill of attainder because it singled out an identifiable group that would be ineligible for Title IV aid based on their failure to register. The district court also held that the compliance requirement violated the Fifth Amendment's privilege against compelled self-incrimination.

On appeal, the Supreme Court rejected the claims that the law was a bill of attainder; i.e., a law which imposes a penalty without a trial, and the Court upheld the law. The law clearly gave nonregistrants 30 days after receiving notice of ineligibility for federal financial aid to register for the draft and thereby qualify for aid. Furthermore, the bill of attainder prohibition in the Constitution applies only to statutes which inflict punishments on specified groups or individuals such as "all Communists." The Court also held that the denial of aid based on these requirements was not "punishment." The Court stated that if students wish to further their education at the expense of their country, they cannot expect the benefits without accepting their fair share of governmental responsibility. Finally, the law did not violate the Fifth Amendment because there was nothing forcing students to apply for federal aid. *Selective Service System v. Minnesota Public Interest Research Group*, 468 U.S. 841, 104 S.Ct. 3348, 82 L.Ed.2d 632 (1984).

In a Rehabilitation Act lawsuit brought by a former student against the U.S. Merchant Marine Academy, the Court held that Congress had not waived the government's sovereign immunity against monetary damages awards for violations of § 504(a).

A first-year student at the U.S. Merchant Marine Academy was diagnosed with diabetes. He was separated from the Academy on the grounds that his diabetes was a disqualifying condition. He filed suit in federal district court against the Secretary of the Department of Transportation and others, alleging that they violated § 504(a) of the Rehabilitation Act (Act). He requested reinstatement, compensatory damages, attorney's fees and costs. The district court granted the student summary judgment, finding that his separation from the Academy violated the Act, and ordered him reinstated.

The government disputed the compensatory damages award, contending that it was protected by sovereign immunity. The district court disagreed and found that the student was entitled to damages. Soon after, the U.S. Court of Appeals, District of Columbia Circuit, held in another case that the government had not waived its immunity against monetary damages for violations of § 504(a). The district court then vacated part of its prior decision and denied compensatory damages. The student appealed and the D.C. Circuit Court of Appeals granted the government's motion for summary judgment.

The U.S. Supreme Court granted certiorari to determine whether Congress has waived the government's sovereign immunity against monetary damage awards for violations of § 504(a). The Court found that a waiver of sovereign immunity must be clearly expressed in the statutory text. The Court found no such language in the text of § 504(a). The student argued that section 505(a)(2) of the Act states that the remedies set forth in Title VI of the Civil Rights Act of 1964 are "available to any person aggrieved by any act. . . by any recipient of Federal assistance or Federal provider of such assistance under [§ 504]." Because Title VI provides for monetary damages, the student claimed that read together, § 505(a)(2) and § 504(a) establish a waiver of the government's immunity against monetary damages.

The Court, however, found that this was not an unequivocal expression of a waiver of immunity. It also found that the Department of Transportation is not a provider of financial assistance to the Academy because it manages the Academy. Because there is no clear expression of the government's intent to waive its sovereign immunity, monetary damage awards are not allowed under § 504(a) of the Act. The court of appeals' decision was affirmed. *Lane v. Pena*, 518 U.S. 187, 116 S.Ct. 2092, 135 L.Ed.2d 486 (1996).

The Supreme Court held that the categorical exclusion of women from the Virginia Military Institute—a public school—denied equal protection to women despite the fact that the state offered them a parallel program at a private college.

The U.S. Attorney General's office filed a complaint against the Commonwealth of Virginia and Virginia Military Institute (VMI) on behalf of a female high school student seeking admission to the male-only college. The U.S. District Court for the Western District of Virginia found that because single gender education conferred substantial benefits on students and preserved the unique military training offered at VMI, the exclusion of women did not violate the Equal Protection Clause. The U.S. Court of Appeals, Fourth Circuit, vacated the district court judgment, ruling that Virginia had failed to state an adequate policy justifying the men-only program.

On remand, the district court found that the institution of coeducational methods at VMI would materially affect its program. It approved the commonwealth plan for instituting a parallel program for women even though the program differed substantially from VMI in its academic offerings, educational methods and financial resources. The court of appeals affirmed the district court decision, and the attorney general's office appealed to the U.S. Supreme Court.

The Court stated that parties seeking to defend gender-based government action must demonstrate an exceedingly persuasive justification that is genuine and not invented as a response to litigation. Virginia had failed to show an exceedingly persuasive justification for excluding women from VMI. There was evidence that some women would be able to participate at VMI, and the court of appeals had improperly relied on the district court judgment that most women would not gain from the adversative method employed by the college. The remedy proposed by Virginia left its exclusionary policy intact and afforded women no opportunity to experience the rigorous military training offered at VMI. The parallel women's program was substantially limited in its course offerings, and participants would not gain the benefits of association with VMI's faculty, stature, funding, prestige and alumni support. The proposal did not remedy the constitutional violation, and the Court reversed and remanded the case. *U.S. v. Virginia*, 518 U.S. 515, 116 S.Ct. 2264, 135 L.Ed.2d 735 (1996).

II. ESTABLISHMENT OF RELIGION IN PUBLIC SCHOOLS

The Establishment Clause of the U.S. Constitution's First Amendment provides that "Congress shall make no law respecting an establishment of religion." The Establishment Clause applies to all state government entities, including school districts and universities, through the Fourteenth Amendment.

In *Lemon v. Kurtzman*, 403 U.S. 602, 91 S.Ct. 2105, 29 L.Ed.2d 745 (1971), the U.S. Supreme Court devised a three-part test which has been used in subsequent cases to determine if government action violates the Establishment Clause. The *Lemon* test requires that 1) a government practice or enactment must have a secular purpose, 2) its principal or primary effect must be one that neither advances nor inhibits religion, and 3) it must not foster an excessive government entanglement with religion. Claims of Establishment Clause violations in public schools have, until recently, been decided on the basis of the *Lemon* test. However, courts have found the test difficult to apply and there has been much confusion in this regard.

The Supreme Court recently decided a case in which it used the "endorsement test" to analyze whether an Establishment Clause violation had occurred with respect to placing a cross on public property. Under this test, only when the government itself has expressed a religious message, or discriminated in favor of private religious expression, is there an Establishment Clause violation. In other words, where the government has promulgated neutral policies that happen to benefit religion, no violation will be found. See *Capitol Square Review and Advisory Bd. v. Pinette,* 515 U.S. 753, 115 S.Ct. 2440, 132 L.Ed.2d 650 (1995).

Long-standing Supreme Court doctrine has held that to maintain a lawsuit the party bringing the action must have suffered an injury of some kind. Here, the Supreme Court dismissed a constitutional challenge to a New Jersey statute since the plaintiff could show no injury.

A taxpayer and a parent sued their board of education seeking a declaration that a New Jersey statute providing for the reading, without comment, of five verses from the Old Testament at the opening of each school day was unconstitutional. The Supreme Court of New Jersey held that the statute did not violate the Establishment Clause. The U.S. Supreme Court, however, dismissed the case without deciding the constitutional question. The Court stated that there was no assertion that either party suffered any injury. The student could have been excused during Bible reading, but no such excuse was requested. The Court also stated that there was no evidence to support a taxpayer grievance. No information was given to support any claim that Bible reading increased the taxpayer's out-of-pocket expenses. *Doremus v. Board of Education,* 342 U.S. 429, 72 S.Ct. 394, 96 L.Ed.2d 475 (1952).

In a pre-*Lemon* decision, the Supreme Court struck down the use of a prayer which had been composed by state officials. Moving away from the *dicta* of *Doremus*, which had stated that where the religious activity is not mandatory there is no injury, the Court stated that neither the denominational neutrality nor the lack of state compulsion freed the prayer from the limitations of the Establishment Clause.

A New York board of education directed the school district's principal to have a prayer read aloud by each class in the presence of a teacher at the beginning of each school day. This procedure was adopted on the recommendation of the state board of regents, an agency established to supervise public schools in the state. These state officials had composed the prayer and published it as part of their "Statement on Moral and Spiritual Training in the Schools." The parents of ten pupils sued in New York state court insisting that use of this official prayer in the public schools was contrary to the beliefs, religions, and religious practices of both themselves and their children. They claimed that the state action violated the Establishment Clause of the First Amendment. The New York Court of Appeals upheld the use of the prayer as long as the schools did not compel any pupil to join in the prayer over the student's parents' objections.

On appeal, the Supreme Court held that the practice was wholly inconsistent with the Establishment Clause. The Court stated that there could be no doubt that the classroom invocation was a religious activity. Neither the fact that the prayer was denominationally neutral nor that its observance was voluntary served to free it from the limitations of the Establishment Clause. *Engel v. Vitale*, 370 U.S. 421, 82 S.Ct. 1261, 8 L.Ed.2d 601 (1962).

Following the decision in *Engel v. Vitale*, the Supreme Court furthered the idea that religious activities performed by school officials violate the Establishment Clause, even if students are not required to take part. The Court struck down two laws which required scripture reading and prayer at the opening of the school day. In doing so, it formulated the "primary purpose and effects" test, which would later become the first two prongs of the *Lemon* test.

Pennsylvania law required that "[a]t least ten verses from the Holy Bible shall be read, without comment, at the opening of each public school on each school day. Any child shall be excused from such Bible reading, or attending such Bible reading, upon written request of his parents or guardian." A family sued to enjoin enforcement of the statute as violative of the First Amendment. A three-judge district court panel held that the statutes violated the Establishment Clause and granted injunctive relief. Similarly, the school commissioner of Baltimore had adopted a rule which mandated that at the opening of the school day a chapter of the Bible or the Lord's Prayer would be read without comment. The rule was challenged in the Maryland state court system which eventually reached the conclusion that the rule did not violate the First Amendment.

On appeal, the Supreme Court held that both rules violated the Establishment Clause. The Court reiterated the premise of *Engel v. Vitale*, above, that neither the state nor the federal government can constitutionally force a person to profess a belief or disbelief in any religion. Nor can it pass laws which aid all religions as against nonbelievers. The Court used a test, which later was to become the first two prongs of the *Lemon* test. The Court stated that the primary purpose of the state requirement that the Bible be read or the Lord's Prayer be recited was religious. The Court also noted that it was intended by the state to be a religious ceremony. The compulsory nature of the ceremonies was not mitigated by the fact that students may absent themselves from the ceremonies, for that fact furnishes no defense to a claim of unconstitutionality under the Establishment Clause. *Abington School District v. Schempp*, 374 U.S. 203, 83 S.Ct. 1560, 10 L.Ed.2d 844 (1963).

In a 1964 Florida case, the Supreme Court held that a state law which required devotional Bible reading and prayer in public schools was unconstitutional.

A group of students in Florida brought suit in state court seeking to stop certain religious practices in the Dade County public schools. State law required daily readings from the Bible, the recitation of the Lord's Prayer, the singing of religious hymns, religious and sectarian baccalaureate programs, and other religious practices. The trial court denied relief to the students, and the Florida Supreme Court affirmed that decision. The U.S. Supreme Court vacated the judgment and remanded the case, 374 U.S. 487, 83 S.Ct. 1864, 10 L.Ed.2d 1043. The Supreme Court of Florida again affirmed the lower court. On appeal again, the U.S. Supreme Court reversed with respect to the issues of devotional Bible reading and the constitutionality of prayer. The Court dismissed the other issues before it as not properly presented. *Chamberlin v. Dade County, Board of Public Instruction*, 377 U.S. 402, 84 S.Ct. 1272, 12 L.Ed.2d 407 (1964).

While the Court will normally give deference to the secular legislative purpose advanced by a government body in support of its action, that purpose must not be a sham. In this case, the Court struck down a statute mandating the posting of the Ten Commandments in public classrooms despite the secular purpose advanced by the Kentucky legislature.

A Kentucky statute required the posting of the Ten Commandments, purchased with private contributions, on the wall of each public classroom in the state. A group of citizens sought an injunction against the statute's enforcement claiming that it violated the First Amendment's Establishment and Free Exercise Clauses. The Kentucky state courts upheld the statute, finding that its purpose was secular, not religious, and that the statute would neither advance nor inhibit any religion, nor involve the state excessively in religious matters.

Utilizing the three-part test first announced in *Lemon v. Kurtzman*, the U.S. Supreme Court struck down the statute. The Court concluded that the posting of the Ten Commandments had no secular purpose. Kentucky state education officials insisted that the statute in question served the secular purpose of teaching students the foundation of Western Civilization and the Common Law. The Court stated, however, that the pre-eminent purpose was plainly religious in nature. The Ten Commandments undeniably came from a religious text despite the legislative recitation of a secular purpose. The Court stated that the text here was not integrated into a course or study of history, civilization, ethics, or comparative religion, but simply posted to induce children to read, meditate upon, and perhaps, to venerate and obey them. The Court also stated that it made no difference that the cost of posting the Commandments was paid for through private funds and that they were not read aloud. *Stone v. Graham*, 449 U.S. 39, 101 S.Ct. 192, 66 L.Ed.2d 199 (1981).

Legislatures have tried to avoid the stigmatizing effect of compulsory school prayer by enacting "period of silence" laws, allowing students to meditate or engage in voluntary prayer. The Supreme Court has held, however, that such laws are constitutionally invalid under the purpose and effect prongs of the *Lemon* test. In this case, the Court struck down two Alabama statutes, stating that their primary purpose had been to affirmatively reestablish prayer in the public schools.

The father of three grade school children sued in U.S. district court challenging the validity of two Alabama statutes: a 1981 statute that allowed a period of silence for "meditation or voluntary prayer"; and a 1982 statute authorizing teachers to lead "willing students" in a nonsectarian prayer composed by the state legislature. The district court declared that the First Amendment to the U.S. Constitution did not prohibit the state of Alabama from establishing a state religion.

The father appealed to the U.S. Court of Appeals, Fifth Circuit, which reversed the district court's ruling and held that both statutes were unconstitutional. The state of Alabama then appealed to the U.S. Supreme Court, which agreed to review only that portion of the court of appeals' decision which invalidated the 1981 statute allowing "meditation or voluntary prayer." The Supreme Court reviewed the legislative history of the 1981 statute and concluded that the intent of the Alabama legislature was to affirmatively reestablish prayer in the public schools. The inclusion of the words "or voluntary prayer" in the statute indicated that it had been enacted to convey state approval of a religious activity and violated the first prong of the *Lemon* test and the First Amendment Establishment Clause. *Wallace v. Jaffree*, 472 U.S. 38, 105 S.Ct. 2479, 96 L.Ed.2d 29 (1985).

In 1987, the Court struck down a Louisiana statute which attempted to encourage the teaching of creation science instead of the theory of evolution. The statute violated the Establishment Clause of the First Amendment because it had no clear secular purpose.

In 1981, the Louisiana legislature passed a statute called "Balanced Treatment for Creation-Science and Evolution-Science in Public School Instruction." The statute called for equal time instruction in creation science when evolution theory was taught. The statute specified the development of curriculum guides and supplied research services for creation science only. The statute's stated purpose was to protect academic freedom. A group of Louisiana parents, teachers and religious leaders challenged the act in a federal district court, claiming it violated the U.S. Constitution's Establishment Clause. They sought an injunction against Louisiana state education officials as well as declaratory relief. The court ruled the statute unconstitutional and the state education officials appealed to the U.S. Court of Appeals, Fifth Circuit. The appeals court affirmed, ruling that the statute did not protect academic freedom and attempted to discredit evolutionary theory by substituting religious instruction in the form of creationism. The U.S. Supreme Court agreed to hear the case.

Applying the Establishment Clause test first described in *Lemon v. Kurtzman*, see Chapter Two, Section III, above, the Supreme Court held that the statute failed to pass constitutional standards. The Supreme Court noted that the statute called for sanctions against teachers who would not teach creation science. It did not further its stated purpose of protecting academic freedom, and had no evident secular purpose.

There was no legitimate state interest in protecting a particular religious view from an antagonistic scientific view. The statute clearly had the purpose of advancing a religious doctrine and state legislators who had enacted the statute were seeking to restructure the state's public school science curriculum to conform with the doctrine. Because the primary purpose of the statute endorsed a particular religious doctrine, it impermissibly furthered religion in violation of the Establishment Clause. The Court affirmed the lower court decisions. *Edwards v. Aguillard*, 482 U.S. 578, 107 S.Ct. 2573, 96 L.Ed.2d 510 (1987).

The U.S. Supreme Court dismissed the appeal of a 1987 case involving New Jersey's "minute of silence" law for procedural reasons, without reaching the underlying substantive issue. However, in doing so it let stand the Third Circuit's earlier decision invalidating the law as a violation of the Establishment Clause.

A 1983 New Jersey law allowed public school teachers to hold a one-minute period of silence at the beginning of each school day. After a legal challenge by interested students, parents and teachers, a U.S. district court held that the minute of silence law violated the First Amendment. The U.S. Court of Appeals, Third Circuit, agreed with the lower court, finding that the law was unconstitutional because the New Jersey legislature's intent in passing the law was to give public school students a chance to pray. The Supreme Court agreed to review the court of appeals' decision.

The Supreme Court avoided the question of whether the minute of silence law violated the First Amendment and chose instead to decide the case on jurisdictional grounds. The Court pointed out that after the minute of silence law was passed, the New Jersey Attorney General had declined to defend the statute in federal court. This forced New Jersey legislative leaders to intervene in the case to defend the minute of silence law. After the court of appeals rendered its decision upholding the district court's invalidation of the law, the legislators lost their posts, and the new legislators refused to appeal the case. The Supreme Court's decision to hear the case was based upon an appeal filed with the Court by the former legislative leaders.

After hearing arguments in the case, the Supreme Court held that because the former legislative leaders had lost their posts they were not entitled to appeal the court of appeals' ruling. Thus the Supreme Court had no jurisdiction over the case, requiring dismissal. The Court declared that despite the former legislative leaders' inability to pursue an appeal of the court of appeals' decision in the case, that court's ruling invalidating the minute of silence law would stand as valid legal precedent. *Karcher v. May*, 484 U.S. 72, 108 S.Ct. 388, 98 L.Ed.2d 327 (1987).

Even though government may accommodate the free exercise of religion, that accommodation is subject to the limitations imposed by the Establishment Clause. In the following case, the Court held that school officials could not direct the performance of a formal religious exercise.

The principals of public middle and high schools in Providence, Rhode Island, were permitted to invite members of the clergy to give invocations and benedictions at their schools' graduation ceremonies. One principal invited a rabbi to offer such prayers at a middle school graduation. A student's parent sought to block the prayer in federal court, but was unsuccessful. The prayer was given at the ceremony, and the parent was in attendance. He then sought a permanent injunction barring Providence public school officials from inviting clergy to give prayers at future graduations. The district court enjoined the practice and the U.S. Court of Appeals, First Circuit, affirmed. The principal sought review from the U.S. Supreme Court.

The Supreme Court held that including clergy members who offer prayers as part of an official public school graduation ceremony is forbidden by the First Amendment's Establishment Clause. The government may not coerce anyone to support or participate in religion or its exercise, or otherwise act in any way which establishes a state religion or religious faith, or tends to do so. In this case, state officials directed the performance of a formal religious exercise. The principal decided that a prayer should be given, he selected the religious partici-pant, and through a pamphlet which provided guidelines, directed and controlled the prayer's content.

The school district's supervision and control of a high school graduation ceremony places subtle and indirect public and peer pres-sure on attending students to stand as a group or maintain respectful silence during the invocation and benediction. The state may not force a student dissenter to participate or protest. The argument that the ceremony is voluntary also is unpersuasive. A student is not truly free to be absent from the exercise in any real sense of the term voluntary. *Lee v. Weisman*, 505 U.S. 577, 112 S.Ct. 2649, 120 L.Ed.2d 467 (1992).

III. DUE PROCESS AND EQUAL PROTECTION

At the center of the American system of law is the notion that all laws will be equally enforced and that all persons subject to the law will be treated fairly. The equality of protection and the elements of fair play, known as *due process of law*, are guaranteed by the U.S. Constitution. The Fourteenth Amendment provides that "No state shall make or enforce any law which shall abridge the privileges or immunities of citizens of the United States; nor shall any State deprive any person of life, liberty, or property, without due process of law; nor deny to any person within its jurisdiction the equal protection of the laws." The Fifth Amendment, similarly, guarantees that the federal government must provide due process to all citizens.

The concept of *equal protection of the law* simply means that all persons or classes of persons enjoy the same protection of law given to all others similarly situated. As noted in the introductory material to Section One of this Chapter, the Equal Protection Clause does not mandate a program of free education. However, once established by a state, such a program must treat all those similarly situated equally. If there is disparate treatment of a class of persons, then that treatment must have some rational relationship to a substantial governmental interest in order to withstand constitutional scrutiny.

In the simplest cases, due process is accorded an individual when the governmental body affords the individual notice of the charges against him and an opportunity to respond, usually at an impartial hearing. There are many variations and the courts do not always agree on what constitutes due process of law.

As the following case points out, school districts have a duty to provide some form of equal opportunity to students who do not speak English. The precise nature of this duty, however, was not discussed.

The San Francisco school system was integrated in 1971 as a result of a federal decree. There were nearly 3,000 students of Chinese ancestry in the school system who did not speak English. Only 1,000 were given supplemental courses in English. Chinese students brought a class action suit against the San Francisco school district seeking relief against the unequal educational opportunities. The students did not ask for any specific form of relief. A federal district court denied any form of relief and the U.S. Court of Appeals for the Ninth Circuit affirmed this denial.

On appeal, the U.S. Supreme Court found that the inequality violated § 601 of the Civil Rights Act of 1964, 42 U.S.C. § 2000d (Title VI). That section prohibits discrimination based "on the ground of race, color, or national origin," in "any program or activity receiving Federal financial assistance." The Department of Health, Education and Welfare had issued regulations requiring school districts that were federally funded to rectify the language deficiency in order to open instruction to all students. Since the San Francisco school district used federal funds, the lower court judgments were reversed. *Lau v. Nichols*, 414 U.S. 563, 94 S.Ct. 786, 39 L.Ed.2d 1 (1974).

In this case, the Supreme Court upheld disparate treatment in unemployment status between those attending school in the day and those attending school at night. The treatment bore a rational relationship to the state's goal of providing unemployment benefits only to those who were not full-time students.

Idaho law provided that "no person shall be deemed to be unemployed while attending a regular established school excluding night school." A woman enrolled in summer school and attended classes from 7 a.m. to 9 a.m. Monday through Friday prior to her regular job as a retail clerk. When she lost this job, the Idaho Department of Employment held that she was ineligible for state unemployment insurance benefits. She sued in state court alleging that the law violated the Equal Protection Clause of the Fourteenth Amendment. The Idaho Supreme Court agreed, but the U.S. Supreme Court reversed.

The Court stated that it was rational for the Idaho legislature to conclude that daytime employment is far more plentiful than night work and, consequently, that attending school in the daytime imposes a greater restriction upon obtaining full-time employment than does attending night school. Moreover, the classification serves as a predictable and convenient means for distinguishing between those who are likely to be students primarily and part-time workers only secondarily, and those who are primarily full-time workers and students only secondarily. *Idaho Department of Employment v. Smith*, 434 U.S. 100, 98 S.Ct. 327, 54 L.Ed.2d 324 (1977).

While achieving a diverse student body may be a worthy goal, the means chosen to achieve that goal must comport with the Equal Protection Clause. In this case, the U.S. Supreme Court held that a special admissions program which reserved close to one-sixth of the available spots in a medical school each year for minority students,

was unnecessary to achieve that goal and violated the Equal Protection Clause.

The Medical School of the University of California at Davis had two admission programs for its entering class of 100 students. Under the regular procedure, candidates whose overall undergraduate grade point averages fell below 2.5 on a scale of 4.0 were summarily rejected. The special admissions policy, designed to assist minority or other disadvantaged applicants, reserved 16 of the 100 openings each year for medical school admission based upon criteria other than that used in the general admissions program. Special admission applicants did not need to meet the 2.5 or better grade point average of the general admission group nor were their Medical College Admission Test scores measured against general admission candidates.

A white male brought suit to compel his admission to medical school after he was twice rejected for admission even though candidates with lower grade point averages and lower test score results were being admitted under the special admissions program. The plaintiff alleged that the special admissions excluded him from medical school on the basis of his race in violation of the Equal Protection Clause of the Fourteenth Amendment, the California Constitution, and Title VI of the 1964 Civil Rights Act. Title VI of the Civil Rights Act provides that no person shall on the ground of race or color be excluded from participating in any program receiving federal financial assistance. The Equal Protection Clause states that no state shall deny to any person within its jurisdiction the equal protection of the law. The California Supreme Court concluded that the special admissions program was not the least intrusive means of achieving the state's goals of integrating the medical profession under a strict scrutiny standard.

On appeal to the U.S. Supreme Court, the Court ruled that while the goal of achieving a diverse student body is sufficiently compelling to justify considerations of race in admissions decisions under some circumstances, the special admissions program, which foreclosed consideration to persons such as the plaintiff, was unnecessary to achieve this compelling goal and was therefore invalid under the Equal Protection Clause. Since the school could not prove that the plaintiff would not have been admitted even if there had been no special admissions program, the Court ordered that he be admitted to the medical school. *Regents of the University of California v. Bakke*, 438 U.S. 265, 98 S.Ct. 2733, 57 L.Ed.2d 750 (1978).

Although federal law or regulations may prohibit certain actions, it is not always clear whether Congress intends to allow private citizens to bring lawsuits for violations of those laws or regulations. Many times a cessation of federal funding or other punitive measure is intended to be the sole remedy for violation, depriving the private citizen of *standing* to bring suit. In this case, the Supreme Court upheld a woman's right to bring suit under federal education law despite the fact that the law created no express cause of action in the person injured.

Section 901(a) of Title IX of the Education Amendments of 1972 prohibits any educational program or activity receiving federal funds from discriminating on the basis of sex. After being denied admission to two medical schools, a woman sued in federal court alleging that she had been excluded from participation in these private university programs on the basis of her gender, and that these universities were receiving federal funding at the time of this exclusion. The district court granted the universities' motion to dismiss since Title IX did not expressly authorize a private right of action by a person injured by a violation of § 901. The court also held that no private remedy should be inferred.

The U.S. Court of Appeals for the Seventh Circuit agreed. The court of appeals concluded that Congress intended the remedy of § 902, which allowed termination of federal funding, to be the exclusive means of enforcement, and that Title VI of the Civil Rights Act of 1964 did not include an implied private cause of action. On appeal, the U.S. Supreme Court reversed, holding that the woman could maintain her lawsuit despite the lack of any express authorization in Title IX.

The Court stated that before concluding that Congress intended to make a remedy available to a special class of litigants the following four factors must be analyzed: 1) whether the statute was enacted for the benefit of a special group of which the plaintiff is a member; 2) whether there is any indication of legislative intent to create a private remedy; 3) whether implication of such remedy is consistent with the underlying purposes of the legislative scheme; and 4) whether implying a federal remedy is inappropriate because the subject matter is basically a concern of the states. The Court stated that all four factors were satisfied here. Title IX expressly conferred a benefit on those discriminated against on the basis of sex, and the woman clearly fell into that class. Title IX was patterned after Title VI which had been construed to create a private remedy. The implication of a private remedy was consistent with the legislative scheme since it provided better protection against discrimination. And since the Civil War, the Federal Government has been the primary protector of citizens from discrimination of any sort. *Cannon v. University of Chicago*, 441 U.S. 677, 99 S.Ct. 1946, 60 L.Ed.2d 560 (1979).

Gender-based distinctions in the schools must pass constitutional scrutiny. Here, Justice Stevens, sitting as a Circuit Justice, found that gender-based distinctions in high-school sports are probably justifiable.

When an Illinois school district denied a talented eleven-year-old girl a tryout with the boys' basketball team, the girl filed suit in a U.S. district court. The district court ruled that the girl had a constitutionally protected interest in developing her skills to the fullest and ordered the school to allow her the tryout. The school district postponed the tryouts long enough to appeal the court order to the U.S. Court of Appeals where the order was stayed. The girl immediately filed a counter-appeal to the U.S. Supreme Court. Mr. Justice Stevens of the U.S. Supreme Court, sitting as Circuit Justice, heard the girl's appeal.

Justice Stevens found that the school had implemented a gender-based classification for contact-sports eligibility, a classification suggested by HEW guidelines. He determined that there was a sufficient showing by the school that the rule denying female participation on an all-boys contact sports team was probably justifiable. Justice Stevens deferred the judgment of his colleagues on the court of appeals which stayed the district court's order. His decision permitted the school to refuse female participation on an all-boys' contact sports team based on the HEW's suggested gender-based guidelines. *O'Connor v. Board of Education of School District 23*, 449 U.S. 1301, 101 S.Ct. 72, 66 L.Ed.2d 179 (1980).

In contrast to the *O'Connor* case, above, gender-based distinctions in academic fields will generally not withstand constitutional scrutiny. Here, the Supreme Court held that a Mississippi university could not justify a policy which denied men the opportunity to enroll for credit.

The policy of the Mississippi University for Women, a state-supported university, was to limit its enrollment to women. The university denied otherwise qualified males the right to enroll for credit in its School of Nursing. One male, who was denied admission, sued in federal court claiming that the university's policy violated the Fourteenth Amendment's Equal Protection Clause. The lower federal courts agreed and the school appealed to the U.S. Supreme Court. In the view of the Supreme Court, the university's discriminatory admission policy against men was not substantially and directly related to an important governmental objective. The school argued that women enrolled in its School of Nursing would be adversely affected by the presence of men. However, the record showed that the nursing school allowed men to attend classes in the school as auditors, thus fatally undermining the school's claim that admission of men would adversely affect women students. The Court held that the policy of the university, which limited enrollment to women, violated the Equal Protection Clause. *Mississippi University for Women v. Hogan*, 458 U.S. 718, 102 S.Ct. 3331, 73 L.Ed.2d 1090 (1982).

In *Cannon v. University of Chicago*, above, the Supreme Court recognized an implied cause of action under Title IX. Thirteen years later, the Court held that money damages would be available in private lawsuits brought under Title IX, and that this option ought to be explored before equitable relief is granted.

A high school student was repeatedly sexually abused and harassed by a teacher. The student brought suit against the teacher and the school under Title IX of the Education Amendments of 1972. The teacher resigned upon condition that all matters against him be dropped. A federal district court then dismissed the suit against the school, because it held that Title IX does not allow an award of damages. The U.S. Court of Appeals, Eleventh Circuit, affirmed, and the student appealed to the U.S. Supreme Court.

Though Title IX does not expressly create a cause of action, an implied cause of action has been recognized in earlier judicial decisions. The issue in this case was whether the available remedies for an implied right of action were limited, and thus precluded damage awards. The Court noted that when Title IX was passed, "the traditional assumption in favor of all available remedies was firmly established [in the judiciary]." Further, Congress made no attempt to alter that presumption upon amending Title IX. An award of damages was ruled to be allowable. In closing, the Court noted that an award of damages is a legal remedy, which any court is bound to explore before resorting to equitable remedies. The dismissal was reversed. *Franklin v. Gwinnett County Public Schools*, 503 U.S. 60, 112 S.Ct. 1028, 117 L.Ed.2d 208 (1992).

In examining whether Title IX creates a cause of action for peer sexual harassment, the Supreme Court held that school districts may be liable for deliberate indifference to known acts of peer sexual harassment under Title IX in cases where the response of school administrators is clearly unreasonable under the circumstances.

A Georgia student complained to her teacher of sexual harassment by a male student. The teacher did not immediately notify the principal of the harassment. Although the harasser was eventually charged with sexual battery, school officials took no action against him. The student sued the school board in federal district court under Title IX of the Education Amendments of 1972, which prohibit sex discrimination by education programs receiving federal funding. The district court dismissed the case and the student appealed to the U.S. Court of Appeals, Eleventh Circuit. The circuit court reversed the judgment but granted the board's petition for rehearing. On rehearing, the circuit court observed that if it adopted the student's argument, a school board must immediately isolate an alleged harasser to avoid a Title IX lawsuit. Because Congress did not discuss student-on-student harassment during consideration of the Title IX amendments, there was no merit to this assertion. The circuit court affirmed the dismissal.

The Supreme Court reversed, holding that school districts may be liable for deliberate indifference to known acts of peer sexual harassment under Title IX in cases where the response of school administrators is clearly unreasonable under the circumstances. A recipient of federal funds may be liable for student-on-student sexual harassment where the funding recipient is deliberately indifferent to known student sexual harassment and the harasser is under the recipient's disciplinary authority. In order to create Title IX liability, the harassment must be so severe, pervasive and objectively offensive that it deprives the victim of access to the funding recipient's educational opportunities or benefits. The Supreme Court stated that the harassment alleged by the student was sufficiently severe to avoid pretrial dismissal, thus reversing and remanding the case. *Davis v. Monroe County Board of Education,* 119 S.Ct. 1661, 143 L.Ed.2d 839 (1999).

In another Title IX case, the Supreme Court concluded that the National Collegiate Athletic Association (NCAA) was not a recipient of federal funds, and therefore, could not be sued under Title IX.

A college graduate who had played intercollegiate volleyball at a private college for two years before enrolling in postgraduate programs at other colleges sought a waiver of the NCAA's Postbaccalaureate Bylaw. Under the Postbaccalaureate Bylaw, postgraduate student-athletes can compete in intercollegiate sports only at the institution from which they received an undergraduate degree. When the NCAA denied the student's request for a waiver, she filed suit in a federal district court, claiming the NCAA's decision discriminated against her on the basis of gender in violation of Title IX. The complaint also alleged that the NCAA granted more waivers to male students than female students. The district court dismissed the case, and denied the student's request to add as parties to her suit the two colleges that she had attended after receiving her undergraduate degree. Both colleges received Title IX funds. The U.S. Court of Appeals, Third Circuit, allowed the student to bring the colleges into the suit, ruling that the student had made a legally sufficient claim that the NCAA received Title IX funds through the dues paid by member institutions, such as the two colleges.

The Supreme Court disagreed with the circuit court, holding that entities receiving federal financial assistance are covered by Title IX, but those that only benefit economically from federal financial assistance are not. While entities that receive federal funding in a direct or indirect manner may be sued under Title IX, the NCAA did not receive federal funds through its receipt of dues from member institutions. The NCAA only received an indirect economic benefit, which did not trigger Title IX coverage. The Supreme Court limited its decision to the question of whether an entity which receives dues payments from recipients of federal funding is considered a recipient of federal funds for Title IX applicability purposes, refusing to address the student's other arguments regarding the applicability of Title IX to the NCAA. The circuit court decision was vacated and remanded to the district court for further proceedings. *National Collegiate Athletic Assn. v. Smith*, 119 S.Ct. 924, 142 L.Ed.2d 929 (1999).

IV. FREEDOM OF SPEECH AND RELIGION

The First Amendment provides that Congress shall make no law prohibiting the free exercise of religion or abridging the freedom of speech. These prohibitions, like most other portions of the Bill of Rights, have been made applicable to the states and state entities through the Fourteenth Amendment. While the language of the First Amendment seems absolute, the Supreme Court has recognized limits to each of these liberties when exercised in the educational environment.

For example, student speech is generally protected if it does not disrupt classroom activities, infringe on the rights of others, or endanger the health or welfare of others. However, high school or elementary school administrators may exercise prior restraint over student publications if the administrator reasonably believes the publication would disrupt the school environment. Administrators may also punish students who engage in "offensively lewd or indecent" speech. Likewise, a student's right to free exercise of religion may also be restricted where such restrictions serve an overriding public interest. Usually this involves compliance with mandatory attendance laws or state health laws.

A. Freedom of Speech

In order for the state to justify prohibition of a particular expression of opinion in the schools, it must show that the expression would materially interfere with the requirements of appropriate school discipline or school operation. Here, students' expressive act of wearing black armbands in protesting the Vietnam War could not be restrained by school officials.

In December 1965, a group of adults and high school students, determined to publicize their objections to the hostilities in Vietnam and their support for a truce, wore black armbands during the holiday season and fasted on December 16 and New Year's Eve. Three students and their parents had previously engaged in similar activities and they decided to participate in this program. The principals of the Des Moines schools became aware of the plan and adopted a policy that any student wearing an armband to school would be asked to remove it, and if he refused, he would be suspended until he returned without the armband. The three students wore their armbands and were all suspended until they agreed to come back without the armbands. They did not return to school until the planned protest period had ended. The students sued the school district under 42 U.S.C. § 1983 for an injunction restraining school officials from disciplining the students and for nominal damages. A federal district court dismissed the complaint and the Eighth Circuit Court of Appeals summarily affirmed.

On appeal to the U.S. Supreme Court, the decision was reversed and remanded. The Court stated that neither students nor teachers shed their constitutional rights to freedom of speech or expression at the schoolhouse gate. In order for the state to justify prohibition of a particular expression of opinion, it must be able to show something more than a mere desire to avoid the discomfort and unpleasantness that always accompany an unpopular viewpoint. Where there is no evidence that an expression would materially interfere with the requirements of appropriate discipline in the operation of the school, the prohibition cannot be sustained. The expressive act of wearing black armbands did not interrupt school activities, nor intrude in school affairs or the lives of others. The Court stated that the Constitution did not permit school officials to deny this form of expression. *Tinker v. Des Moines Community School District*, 393 U.S. 503, 89 S.Ct. 733, 21 L.Ed.2d 733 (1969).

Under the Fourteenth Amendment's Equal Protection Clause, there may be legitimate reasons why the government may subject similar activities to differential treatment. However, that differential treatment must be supported by an appropriate governmental interest. In this case, the Court struck down a statute which allowed peaceful labor picketing within 150 feet of a school, but forbade other peaceful picketing because there was no appropriate governmental interest in denying expression of "less favored views."

A federal postal employee picketed Jones Commercial High School in Chicago for seven months. During school hours and usually by himself, he would walk the public sidewalk adjoining the school carrying a sign which read: "Jones High School practices black discrimination. Jones High School has a black quota." His picketing was always peaceful, orderly and quiet. After seven months, the city of Chicago posted an ordinance prohibiting picketing within 150 feet of any school building while the school was in session and one-half hour before and after the school was in session. The ordinance did not apply to peaceful picketing of any school involved in a labor dispute.

As a result of the ordinance, the postman voluntarily ceased his picketing. He sued, seeking injunctive relief, claiming that the ordinance violated the First Amendment by punishing protected free speech and the Fourteenth Amendment by exempting only peaceful labor picketing. A federal district court dismissed the complaint and the U.S. Court of Appeals, Seventh Circuit, reversed, holding that the ordinance was overbroad and patently unconstitutional. The U.S. Supreme Court granted certiorari.

The Court held that the ordinance was unconstitutional since it made an impermissible distinction between labor picketing and other peaceful picketing, in violation of the Fourteenth Amendment's Equal

Protection Clause. The Court stated that there was not an appropriate governmental interest suitably furthered by the differential treatment. Government may not grant the use of a forum to people whose views it finds acceptable, but deny use to those wishing to express less favored views. Since the ordinance focused on the subject matter of the picketing, rather than its time, place and manner, it was unconstitutional. *Police Department of Chicago v. Mosley*, 408 U.S. 92, 92 S.Ct. 2286, 33 L.Ed.2d 212 (1972).

Content-based regulation of speech implicates both the free speech guarantee of the First Amendment, and the Equal Protection Clause of the Fourteenth Amendment. In general, such regulations will not withstand constitutional scrutiny, although content-neutral regulations may.

A protester was convicted for his part in a demonstration outside a senior high school in Illinois. The protest had been organized when school administrators took no action on grievances of black students at the school. Approximately 200 people gathered for the demonstration. The protester's brother and twin sisters attended the school. Forty demonstrators were arrested and charged with violating two city ordinances which prohibited picketing within 150 feet of any school and making noise which disrupts a school session. The protester claimed that the ordinances were unconstitutionally vague and overbroad. The Supreme Court of Illinois disagreed and the protester appealed to the U.S. Supreme Court.

The Court held that the antipicketing ordinance was unconstitutional, but that the antinoise ordinance was valid. The Court noted that the antipicketing ordinance was virtually identical to the one invalidated as violative of equal protection in *Police Department of Chicago v. Mosley*, above, and was likewise invalid. The Court stated, however, that the antinoise ordinance was not vague since, with fair warning, it prohibited only actual, imminent and willful interference with normal school activity. The ordinance was not overbroad since it did not infringe on the free speech rights of the protester; it only prohibited activity disruptive of classwork. *Grayned v. City of Rockford*, 408 U.S. 104, 92 S.Ct. 2294, 33 L.Ed.2d 222 (1972).

In the following case, the Supreme Court held that students' rights to freedom of association may not be disregarded. Nor may those rights be limited solely on the basis of the philosophy underlying the students' desire to associate.

A group of students desired to form a local chapter of Students for a Democratic Society (SDS) at a state-supported college. They were, however, denied recognition as a campus organization. Recognition would have allowed the student organization to use campus facilities for meetings and to use the campus bulletin board and school newspaper. The president had denied recognition because he was not satisfied that the group was independent of the national SDS, which he concluded had a philosophy of disruption and violence in conflict with the college's declaration of student rights. The students sued for declaratory and injunctive relief.

The district court first ordered an additional administrative hearing, at which the college president reaffirmed his prior decision. It then held that the students had failed to show that they could function independently of the national SDS and that the college's refusal to recognize the group, in light of the disruptive and violent nature of the national organization, was justifiable. The U.S. Court of Appeals for the Second Circuit affirmed, stating that the students had failed to avail themselves of the due process of law accorded to them and had failed to meet their burden of complying with the prevailing standards for recognition.

The U.S. Supreme Court held that the lower courts erred in disregarding the First Amendment interest in freedom of association that the students had in furthering their personal beliefs. It also held that putting the burden on the students (to show entitlement to recognition) rather than on the president (to justify nonrecognition) was also in error. The Court stated that insofar as the denial of recognition was based on the group's affiliation with the national SDS, or as a result of disagreement with the group's philosophy, the president's decision violated the students' First Amendment rights. A proper basis for nonrecognition might have been that the group refused to comply with a rule requiring them to abide by reasonable campus regulations. Since it was not clear that the college had such a rule, and whether the students intended to observe it, the case was remanded to the district court for resolution. *Healy v. James*, 408 U.S. 169, 92 S.Ct. 2338, 33 L.Ed.2d 266 (1972).

Following the ruling in *Healy v. James*, above, the Supreme Court held that, at the collegiate level, the conduct of students and the dissemination of ideas—no matter how offensive, could not be curtailed based solely on the "conventions of decency."

A graduate student at the University of Missouri was expelled for distributing on campus a newspaper which allegedly violated the bylaws of the university's curators since it contained forms of "indecent speech." The newspaper was found objectionable for two reasons. First, on the front cover was a political cartoon of policemen raping the Statue of Liberty and the Goddess of Justice with a caption that read ". . . with Liberty and Justice for All." Secondly, the issue contained an article entitled "Mother Fucker Acquitted," which discussed the trial and acquittal on an assault charge of a New York youth. The expelled student sued the university in a federal district court, alleging that the university's action was improperly premised on activities protected by the First Amendment. The district court denied relief, and the Eighth Circuit Court of Appeals affirmed.

On appeal, the U.S. Supreme Court, in a per curiam opinion, held that the student should be reinstated. The Court stated that while a university has an undoubted prerogative to enforce reasonable rules governing student conduct, it is not immune from the sweep of the First Amendment. The Court continued that *Healy v. James*, above, makes it clear that the mere dissemination of ideas—no matter how offensive to good taste—may not be shut off in the name of "conventions of decency" alone. *Papish v. University of Missouri*, 410 U.S. 667, 93 S.Ct. 1197, 35 L.Ed.2d 618 (1973).

One of the difficulties inherent in litigating student free speech issues is that by the time a lawsuit works its way through the system, any relief the Court might grant would be moot since the students involved will have graduated. In this case, a group of students sought a permanent injunction forbidding school officials from blocking distribution of a student newspaper. By the time the case reached the Supreme Court, the students had all graduated and the case was moot.

A group of six students brought suit against the Indianapolis Board of School Commissioners. The students had been involved in the publication and distribution of a student newspaper, and they alleged that certain of the rules and regulations of the board interfered with their First and Fourteenth Amendment rights. They prevailed on the merits of their action at the district court level and the U.S. Court of Appeals affirmed. By the time the action reached the U.S. Supreme Court, however, all the students had graduated from the Indianapolis school system. The Supreme Court, therefore, held that the case was moot and dismissed the action. The Court also ordered the district court to vacate its judgment granting a permanent injunction against the board since it was uncertain who the injunction was meant to protect. *Board of School*

Commissioners v. Jacobs, 420 U.S. 128, 95 S.Ct. 848, 43 L.Ed.2d 74 (1975).

In the following case, the U.S. Supreme Court recognized that the right to receive information and ideas is an "inherent corollary of the rights of free speech and press" embodied in the First Amendment. Thus, a decision to remove books from a school library is unconstitutional if it is motivated by school officials' intent to deny students access to ideas with which the school officials disagree.

A local board of education ordered certain books, which it characterized as "anti-American, anti-Christian, and anti-Semtic[sic] and just plain filthy," to be removed from high school and junior high school libraries. A group of students brought an action for injunctive and declaratory relief under 42 U.S.C. § 1983 against the board and board members, alleging that the board's action violated their First Amendment rights. The district court granted summary judgment to the school board. The U.S. Court of Appeals reversed and ordered a trial on the merits of the student's claim. On appeal, the U.S. Supreme Court affirmed the court of appeals' decision.

The Court stated that the First Amendment imposes limitations upon a local school board's exercise of its discretion to remove books from school libraries. While a local school board must have broad discretion in the management of school affairs, such discretion must be exercised in a manner that comports with the transcendent imperatives of the First Amendment. Although the board may have absolute discretion in the area of curriculum, that absolute discretion does not extend into the school library and the "regime of voluntary inquiry that there holds sway." Since a genuine issue surrounded the board's exclusion of the books removed, the students' claims would be remanded for a trial. *Board of Education v. Pico*, 457 U.S. 853, 102 S.Ct. 2799, 73 L.Ed.2d 435 (1982).

While students may have the right to advocate unpopular viewpoints, the U.S. Supreme Court has ruled that students may be punished for engaging in lewd or indecent speech. Here, the Court upheld the suspension of a student whose use of sexual innuendo was said to have violated legitimate standards of civil and mature conduct.

A male high school student in Bethel, Washington, delivered a speech nominating a fellow student for elective student office before an assembly of over 600 peers, many of whom were 14-year-olds. All students were required to attend the assembly as part of the school's self-government program. In his nominating speech, the student referred to his candidate in terms of an elaborate, explicit sexual metaphor, despite having been warned in advance by two teachers not to deliver it. During the speech a counselor observed students' reactions, which included laughter, graphic sexual gestures, hooting, bewilderment and embarrassment. Further, a teacher reported that she had to use class time the next day to discuss the speech. The morning after the assembly, the student was called into the assistant principal's office and notified that he had violated a school rule prohibiting obscene language or gestures. When he admitted to the assistant principal that he had deliberately used sexual innuendo in his speech, he was informed that he would be suspended for three days and that his name would be removed from the list of candidates for student speaker at graduation.

The student brought suit against the school in a U.S. district court, claiming that his First Amendment right to freedom of speech had been violated. The district court agreed and awarded him $278 as compensation for deprivation of his constitutional rights (since he served two days of his suspension) and $12,750 in litigation costs and attorney's fees. The court also ordered the school district to allow the student to speak at graduation. The U.S. Court of Appeals, Ninth Circuit, rejected the school district's appeal and held that the district had failed to prove that the speech had interfered with or disrupted the educational environment. On further appeal by the school district, the U.S. Supreme Court ruled that while public school students have the right to advocate unpopular and controversial views in school, that right must be balanced against the schools' interest in teaching socially appropriate behavior. A public school, as an instrument of the state, may legitimately establish standards of civil and mature conduct. The Court observed that such standards would be difficult to convey in a school which tolerated the "lewd, indecent and offensive" speech and conduct which the student exhibited. *Bethel School District v. Fraser*, 478 U.S. 675, 106 S.Ct. 3159, 92 L.Ed.2d 549 (1986).

Although students do not relinquish their free speech rights while attending school, high school or elementary school administrators may exercise prior restraint over student publications if a reasonable basis exists for the belief that a publication would materially disrupt classwork, involve substantial disorder or in-

vade the rights of others. In this case, the Supreme Court held that since a school newspaper was not an open forum for voicing student speech, the principal's deletion of two articles was reasonable.

This case involved a Missouri high school student newspaper. The school's principal objected to two articles dealing with pregnancy and divorce which had been prepared for publication in the paper. Because the principal believed that there was no time to edit the articles as the end of the school year was at hand, he deleted the two pages on which the articles appeared. Former high school students who were members of the newspaper's staff filed a lawsuit against the school district and school officials alleging that their First Amendment rights were violated when the pages were removed from the newspaper before publication. A U.S. district court ruled in favor of the school district. The U.S. Court of Appeals, Eighth Circuit, reversed, holding that the newspaper was a public forum "intended to be and operated as a conduit for student viewpoint." The school district filed for review by the U.S. Supreme Court, which agreed to hear the case.

The U.S. Supreme Court noted that school facilities, including school sponsored newspapers, become public forums only if school authorities have intentionally opened those facilities for indiscriminate use by either the general public "or by some segment of the public, such as student organizations." The Court determined that since the school district allowed a large amount of control by the journalism teacher and the principal, it had not intentionally opened the newspaper as a public forum for indiscriminate use in voicing student speech.

The Court determined that school officials can exercise "editorial control over the style and content of student speech in school-sponsored expressive activities so long as their actions are reasonably related to legitimate [educational] concerns." The Court ruled that the principal's conclusion that the pregnancy and divorce articles were not suitable for publication could not be rejected as unreasonable. Because his decision to delete the two full pages from the newspaper was reasonable under the circumstances, no violation of the First Amendment had occurred. *Hazelwood School Dist. v. Kuhlmeier*, 484 U.S. 261, 108 S.Ct. 562, 98 L.Ed.2d 592 (1988).

The Supreme Court has held that restrictions on commercial free speech need not be subjected to as rigorous an analysis to determine the restrictions' reasonableness. As long as the restriction is reasonable, it will be upheld.

The State University of New York (SUNY) prohibited private commercial enterprises from operating in SUNY facilities. Campus police prevented a housewares manufacturer from demonstrating and selling its products at a party hosted in a student dormitory. The manufacturer and a group of students sued SUNY in a federal district court, stating that the policy violated the First Amendment. The court held for SUNY, stating that the student dormitories did not constitute a public forum for purposes of commercial activity, and that the restrictions were reasonable in light of the dormitories' purpose. The manufacturer dropped out of the lawsuit and the students appealed to the U.S. Court of Appeals, Second Circuit. The court of appeals reversed, stating that it was unclear whether the policy directly advanced SUNY's interest and whether it was the least restrictive means of achieving that interest. The court of appeals remanded the case to the district court, but the U.S. Supreme Court granted review of the case.

The Supreme Court stated that the court of appeals erred in requiring the district court to apply a least restrictive means test. The Court stated that regulations on commercial speech require only a reasonable "fit" between the government's ends and the means chosen to accomplish those ends. The Supreme Court reversed and remanded the case. *Bd. of Trustees of the State Univ. of New York v. Fox*, 492 U.S. 469, 109 S.Ct. 3028, 106 L.Ed.2d 388 (1989).

B. Freedom of Religion

It has not always been clear whether the First Amendment free speech guarantee prohibits the government from compelling speech from students. Although overruled only three years later, the following case held that students could be forced to recite the pledge of allegiance despite religious objections.

A brother and sister were expelled from a Pennsylvania school district for refusing to participate in a pledge of allegiance to the national flag as part of a daily school exercise. The local board of education required both teachers and pupils to participate in this ceremony. The students' family was affiliated with the Jehovah's Witnesses. The children had been brought up to believe that such a gesture of respect for the flag was forbidden by scripture. The children were of an age for which Pennsylvania made school attendance mandatory. Their father brought suit, seeking to enjoin the authorities from continuing to force participation in the flag salute ceremony as a precondition to his children's attendance at school. A federal district court granted relief and the U.S. Court of Appeals for the Third Circuit affirmed.

On appeal, the Supreme Court reversed. The Court stated that although the law could not reach the affirmative pursuit of one's convictions and beliefs, a strong government should be able to promote some great common good. The Court reasoned that the religious liberty which the Constitution protects has never excluded legislation of general scope not directed against doctrinal loyalties of particular sects. National unity, the Court continued, is the basis of national security and the legislature had the right to select appropriate means for its attainment. The Court stated that compelling students to recite the pledge of allegiance presented a totally different order of problem from that of the propriety of cleaning littered streets by limiting free expression through the prohibition of distributing handbills. *Minersville School District v. Gobitis*, 310 U.S. 586, 60 S.Ct. 1010, 84 L.Ed. 1375 (1940).

In this case, the Supreme Court, overruling *Minersville School District v. Gobitis*, accepted the notion that the First Amendment prohibits compelled belief or speech.

Following the Supreme Court's decision in *Minersville School District v. Gobitis*, above, the West Virginia legislature amended its laws to require all schools to teach courses on history, civics and the state and federal constitutions "for the purpose of teaching, fostering, and perpetuating the ideals, principles and spirit of Americanism, and increasing the knowledge of the organization and machinery of the government." The law also required private schools to teach courses "similar to those required for the public schools."

The state board of education adopted a resolution containing recitals taken largely from the *Gobitis* opinion, ordering that the salute of the flag become "a regular part of the program of activities in the public schools" and that all teachers and pupils "shall be required to participate in the salute honoring the Nation represented by the Flag." Failure to salute the flag was to be considered an act of insubordination, to be dealt with by expulsion until the student complied. Meanwhile, the student would be considered unlawfully delinquent. A group of Jehovah's Witnesses brought suit in federal district court seeking an injunction to prevent enforcement of the statute against them. They claimed that the law and regulations were an unconstitutional denial of religious freedom, freedom of speech, and equal protection. The district court restrained enforcement of the statute.

On direct appeal to the U.S. Supreme Court, the Court held that the law exceeded the limitations of the First Amendment. As a result, the Court overruled its three-year-old decision in *Minersville School District v. Gobitis*. The Court stated that while the state may teach history and the organization of government, which may inspire patriotism, it may not compel students to declare a belief. The Court stated that the Fourteenth Amendment, as applied to the states, protects the citizen against the state itself and all its creatures—boards of education not excepted. The means chosen by the board of education and the state of West Virginia to achieve national unity were impermissible. "If there is any fixed star in our constitutional constellation, it is that no official, high or petty, can prescribe what shall be orthodox in politics, nationalism, religion, or other matters of opinion or force citizens to confess by word or act their faith therein." *West Virginia Board of Education v. Barnette*, 319 U.S. 624, 63 S.Ct. 1178, 87 L.Ed. 1628 (1943).

While the Establishment Clause prohibits the state from partaking in or motivating religious activities, it does not prevent private citizens from using public facilities for religious purposes. In fact, if the public body makes its facilities available to the general public, the Free Exercise and Free Speech clauses of the First Amendment prohibit it from excluding religious groups from using those facilities based solely on the religious nature of the groups. Here the Supreme Court struck down a rule which did just that.

The University of Missouri at Kansas City, a state university, made its facilities available for the general use of registered student groups. A registered student religious group that had previously received permission to conduct its meetings in university facilities was informed that it could no longer do so because of a university regulation that prohibited use of its facilities for the purposes of religious worship or teaching. Members of the group brought suit, alleging that the regulation violated their First Amendment rights to free exercise of religion and freedom of speech. A U.S. district court upheld the school's regulation, but the U.S. Court of Appeals, Eighth Circuit, reversed, stating that the regulation was discriminatory against religious speech and that the Establishment Clause does not bar a policy of equal access in which facilities are open to groups and speakers of all kinds.

The Supreme Court agreed with the court of appeals' assessment, stating that the university policy violated the fundamental principle that a state regulation of speech must be content-neutral. It is obligatory upon the state to show that the regulation is necessary to serve a compelling state interest and that it is narrowly drawn to achieve that end. The state was unable to do that here. The state's interest in achieving greater separation of church and state than is already ensured under the Establishment Clause was not sufficiently "compelling" to justify content-based discrimination against religious speech of the student group in question. *Widmar v. Vincent*, 454 U.S. 263, 102 S.Ct. 269, 70 L.Ed.2d 400 (1981).

In the following case, a high school religious group asked the federal courts to determine whether they could pray on school grounds. Following a favorable result in the district court, the school board, with the exception of a single member, voted to allow the students to pray on school grounds. The U.S. Supreme Court held that the single board member lacked standing to appeal the district court's decision.

A group of high school students formed a club called "Petros" for the purpose of promoting "spiritual growth and positive attitudes" in the lives of its members. The group asked the principal of their high school for permission to meet on school premises during student activity periods scheduled on regular school days. The principal allowed the group to hold an organizational meeting which was attended by approximately 45 students. At the meeting, students prayed and read passages of Scripture. The principal then informed the group that they could not hold any further meetings until he had discussed the matter with the school superintendent, who denied the group permission after discussions with the school district's attorney. The students then sued, alleging that the refusal to allow the group to meet on the same basis as other student groups because of its religious activities violated the First Amendment. A federal district court held for the students and the school district took no appeal. Thereafter, the school district allowed the student meetings as requested. A member of the school board did appeal, however. No one questioned his standing to appeal, and the U.S. Court of Appeals for the Third Circuit held in his favor.

On appeal, the U.S. Supreme Court held that the board member had no standing to appeal in his individual capacity, and therefore the court of appeals had no jurisdiction to hear the appeal. Although the lawsuit was brought against the board, there was nothing else in the complaint or record to indicate that relief was sought or awarded against any school board member in his individual capacity. The board member had no personal stake in the outcome of the litigation. The Supreme Court thus vacated the court of appeals' judgment and ordered the case dismissed for lack of jurisdiction. *Bender v. Williamsport Area School District*, 475 U.S. 534, 106 S.Ct. 1326, 89 L.Ed.2d 501 (1986).

If a school allows its students to join extracurricular organizations, it cannot then deny students the right to meet for religious purposes. Any such restriction might be a violation of the Equal Access Act.

A Nebraska high school student wanted permission to begin a Christian Club. The high school permitted its students to join, on a voluntary basis, a number of groups and clubs which met after school. The school required that each of these clubs have faculty sponsors. However, the student who wished to start the Christian Club did not have a faculty sponsor. The principal and superintendent both denied the request of the student because the student did not have a sponsor and because a religious club at the school would violate the Establishment Clause of the U.S. Constitution. After the board of education affirmed the decision of the principal and superintendent, the student sued the school board, superintendent, and principal in a federal district court.

The student alleged a violation of the Equal Access Act which prohibits public secondary schools that receive federal funding and that maintain a "limited open forum" from denying "equal access" to students who wished to meet. The Act defines a limited open forum as being an allowance by a school to let noncurriculum related groups meet. The Act is designed to prohibit groups from being discriminated against on the basis of the content of their speech at the meetings. The district court ruled in favor of the school, holding that the other clubs at the school related to the school's curriculum and, thus, the school was not under the Equal Access Act because it did not have an open forum. The student appealed to the U.S. Court of Appeals, Eighth Circuit, which ruled in favor of the student. The court of appeals held that the other clubs at the high school were not curriculum-related clubs and thus were covered under the Equal Access Act. Further, it stated that the Equal Access Act did not violate the Establishment Clause. The school appealed to the U.S. Supreme Court, asserting that the Equal Access Act violated the Establishment Clause.

The Supreme Court stated that the other clubs did not relate to any of the school's curriculum. Thus, the school must provide a limited open forum to all students wishing to participate in groups. The Act provides that the school can limit activities that substantially interfere with the orderly conduct of the school. The Court also stated that the Act did not violate the Establishment Clause because the Act had a secular purpose and because it limited the role of teachers working with religious clubs. Thus, the Court affirmed the court of appeals' decision, holding that the school violated the Equal Access Act and that the Act did not violate the Establishment Clause. *Bd. of Educ. of Westside Com. Sch. v. Mergens*, 496 U.S. 226, 110 S.Ct. 2356, 110 L.Ed.2d 191 (1990).

The Supreme Court held that a school district could not prohibit a church from using its facilities for the purpose of airing secular views with a religious point of view (where the subject matter was permissible by law).

The New York legislature passed the New York Education Law (Act) authorizing local school boards to pass regulations which allowed school property to be used in certain specified ways. The Act did not expressly authorize use of school grounds for religious purposes. A local school board issued regulations allowing "social, civic, or recreational uses (Rule 10) or limited use by political organizations (Rule 8)." Pursuant to the Act and relevant state case law, Rule 7 provided that the school not be used for religious purposes.

An evangelical church sought permission to use the school facilities to show a six-part film series. The film-series featured a well known licensed psychologist. It discussed the psychologist's views "on the undermining influences of the media that could only be counterbalanced by returning to traditional Christian family values instilled at an early age." The district denied the church permission to use the school grounds because the film was church-related and therefore violated Rule 7. The church filed suit in a federal court alleging that the district's denial violated its rights to free speech and assembly under the First Amendment. It further alleged violations of the Free Exercise Clause and the Establishment Clause of the First Amendment, and the Equal Protection Clause of the Fourteenth Amendment. The district court determined that the denial was "viewpoint neutral" and held for the district. The U.S. Court of Appeals, Ninth Circuit, affirmed, holding that the school was a "limited public forum" and that the district could exclude certain groups provided that the exclusion was "reasonable and viewpoint neutral." The church appealed to the U.S. Supreme Court.

The main issue on appeal was whether the school district violated the Free Speech Clause of the First Amendment when it denied the church permission to show a film about "family and child related issues" from a religious perspective. The Court assumed without deciding that the school property was a limited, rather than a traditional, public forum and that the school was not open for "indiscriminate public

use for communicative purposes." However, even in a limited public
forum, government exclusion of a category of speech must be "reasonable and viewpoint neutral." The Court noted that viewpoints about
family issues were not proscribed by the district's regulations. Although the film addressed the subject from a religious perspective, the
subject matter itself was permissible under Rule 10. The Court determined that exclusion of the subject matter because of its religious
content would impermissibly "favor some viewpoints or ideas at the
expense of others." Therefore, the regulation discriminated on the basis
of viewpoint and the exclusion of this particular church from school
property was not "viewpoint neutral" even though the district excluded
all religious organizations.

Next, the Court determined that since the film was not to be shown
during school hours and was to be open to those outside the church, the
public would not perceive the district to be endorsing religion. Further,
pursuant to the three-part test articulated in *Lemon v. Kurtzman,* 403
U.S. 602, 91 S.Ct. 2105, 29 L.Ed.2d 745 (1971), permission by the
school district would not violate the Establishment Clause of the First
Amendment. Specifically, the film had a secular purpose, its primary
effect was not to advance religion and the showing of the film would not
"foster excessive state entanglement with religion." Thus, speech about
"family and child related issues" from a religious perspective could
permissibly be aired on public school grounds without violating the
Establishment Clause. The holding of the court of appeals was reversed.
Lamb's Chapel v. Center Moriches Union Free School District, 508
U.S. 384, 113 S.Ct. 2141, 124 L.Ed.2d 352 (1993).

**In *Rosenberger*, the Supreme Court held that the University of
Virginia could not withhold authorization for payments to a printer
on behalf of a Christian student organization. Because the university had opened a limited public forum by paying other third-party
contractors on behalf of student groups, it could not deny payment
to the printer on the grounds that the student organization's
viewpoint was religious.**

The University of Virginia collected a mandatory $14 student
activity fee from full-time students each semester. The fees supported
extracurricular activities that were related to the educational purposes
of the university. University-recognized student groups could apply for
funding by the activities fund, although not all groups requested funds.
University guidelines excluded religious groups from student funding
as well as activities that could jeopardize the university's tax exempt

status. A university-recognized student group published a Christian newspaper for which it sought $5,862 from the activities fund for printing costs. The student council denied funding because the group's activities were deemed religious under university guidelines.

After exhausting appeals within the university, group members filed a lawsuit in the U.S. District Court for the Western District of Virginia, claiming constitutional rights violations. The court granted summary judgment to the university, and its decision was affirmed by the U.S. Court of Appeals, Fourth Circuit. The students appealed to the U.S. Supreme Court. The Court observed that government entities must abstain from regulating speech on the basis of the speaker's opinion. Upon establishing a limited public forum, state entities must respect the forum by refraining from the exclusion of speech based upon content.

Because the university had opened a limited public forum by paying other third-party contractors on behalf of student groups, it could not deny the religious group's claim for funds on the basis of its viewpoint. Allowing the payment of the group's printing costs amounted to a policy of government neutrality for different viewpoints. The Court distinguished the student fee from a general tax and placed emphasis on the indirect nature of the benefit. The Court reversed the lower court decisions, ruling that access to public school facilities on a neutral basis does not violate the Establishment Clause of the First Amendment. *Rosenberger v. Rector and Visitors of Univ. of Virginia*, 515 U.S. 819, 115 S.Ct. 2510, 132 L.Ed.2d 700 (1995).

V. STUDENT DISCIPLINE

School districts and colleges have the power to control student behavior through the use of disciplinary suspensions and expulsions. This power, however, must be wielded so that the students affected are accorded their constitutional rights to due process. Failure to follow due process requirements can lead to reversals of the suspensions or expulsions, expunging of records or proceedings from student files, lawsuits seeking damages against school districts, and lawsuits against school board members individually. School districts and colleges have greater control, however, in the area of academic suspensions and expulsions, which are rarely disturbed by the courts, so long as they are based on legitimate academic reasons and state and local laws or rules. Many states specifically allow the use of reasonable physical force by school authorities to restrain unruly students, to correct unacceptable behavior and to maintain the order necessary to conduct an educational program. Some states, however, specifically prohibit corporal punishment. Where state law permits, courts generally uphold the reasonable application of punishment and have been reluctant to find that such punishment violates student due process rights.

The U.S. Supreme Court has ruled that under the Fourth Amendment to the U.S. Constitution, searches of students by school officials need not adhere to the strict standard of "probable cause" imposed upon law enforcement officers. Rather, the legality of searches will depend upon the "reasonableness" of the search in light of all the circumstances. There must be reasonable grounds to believe that the search will reveal a violation of school rules or produce evidence of unlawful activity. The states remain free to provide greater protection for students, as Louisiana and California have done.

In *Goss v. Lopez,* the U.S. Supreme Court affirmed the constitutional rights of suspended students to due process through notice and hearing.

Ohio law authorized public school principals to suspend students for misconduct for up to ten days without a hearing. Several students who had participated in widespread demonstrations in the school system were suspended. Their suspensions were handed down without the benefit of a hearing, as authorized by state law. The students brought a class action against the school officials, seeking a declaration that the Ohio law permitting suspensions without hearings was unconstitutional. The district court held: 1) that the students had been denied due process of law because of the nature of the suspensions, and 2) that the Ohio law was unconstitutional.

On appeal to the U.S. Supreme Court, the Court held that students facing temporary suspension from public schools have a property and liberty interest that qualifies for protection under the Due Process Clause. Having chosen to extend the right of an education to the students, a state may not withdraw that right on grounds of misconduct, absent fundamentally fair procedures to determine whether misconduct has occurred. Students faced with such potential losses of liberty must be given oral or written notice of the charges against them along with the opportunity at a hearing to present their version of what happened. Recognizing that circumstances often do not allow time for adequate procedures prior to suspension, the Court stated that, at the very least, proper notice and hearing should be given as soon after the suspension as is practicable. The Court also stated that if a student is threatened with suspension longer than ten days, more elaborate safeguards might be necessary. *Goss v. Lopez,* 419 U.S. 565, 95 S.Ct. 729, 42 L.Ed.2d 725 (1975).

Title 42 of the United States Code, § 1983, provides that every person who acts under the authority of statute, regulation, ordinance or custom of any state to deprive another person's rights under the Constitution or laws of the United States, shall be subject to liability for that action. The statute speaks absolutely, Supreme Court doctrine does not. In the following case, the Supreme Court decided that school officials would be immune from liability under § 1983 unless the officials reasonably knew that the action in question would violate the students' rights, or the action was done with malicious intent.

A group of Arkansas high school students "spiked" the soft drink punch being served at a school function. When their actions were uncovered several days later the students admitted their prank to a teacher and the principal. The principal suspended the students for a two-week period subject to the decision of the school board. The board met and conferred, and obtained additional information from sources other than the students involved. The board then expelled the students from school for the balance of the semester, a period of approximately three months.

The students brought a suit in a federal district court asking for damages. The district court ruled that the board had not acted with malice; hence, the board could not be held liable in damages. On appeal, the U.S. Court of Appeals overturned the district court decision, holding that "specific intent to harm ... was not a requirement for the recovery of damages," but that the students need only show the board did not, in light of the circumstances, act in good faith. The case went before the U.S. Supreme Court where it was ultimately remanded to the court of appeals to settle questions of evidence.

The question before the Supreme Court was the extent to which immunity from liability would be granted school administrators in matters arising from their official duties. The Supreme Court ruled that common law traditions and strong public policy extend a qualified good faith immunity from liability for damages under the Civil Rights Act to school board members. But absolute immunity would not be justified since there would be no remedy for students subjected to intentional or otherwise inexcusable deprivations. The Supreme Court stated that in the specific context of school discipline, a school board member is not immune from liability for damages under § 1983 of the Civil Rights Act if that member knew, or reasonably should have known, that the action the member took within the sphere of official responsibility would violate the constitutional rights of the student affected, or if the member took the action with the malicious intention to cause a deprivation of constitutional rights or other injury to the student. *Wood v. Strickland*, 420 U.S. 308, 95 S.Ct. 992, 43 L.Ed.2d 214 (1975).

Many states specifically allow the use of physical force by school authorities to restrain unruly students, correct unacceptable behavior, and maintain order. Some states, however, also specifically prohibit corporal punishment. Where state law permits, courts generally uphold the reasonable application of punishment and have been reluctant to find that such punishment violates student rights. In the following case, the Supreme Court held that corporal punishment in the public schools is not subject to the Eighth Amendment's prohibition of "cruel and unusual punishment." The Court also held that students were not entitled to a hearing before beatings were administered.

During the 1970-71 school year many of the 237 schools in Dade County, Florida, used corporal punishment as a means of maintaining discipline. This was permissible under Florida law and local school board regulations. Two students who had been subjected to the punishment sued the school district both for individual damages and injunctive relief in federal district court. The students claimed that the beatings violated the Eighth Amendment's prohibition of cruel and unusual punishment. One student had been beaten so severely that he missed eleven days of school. The other lost the use of his arm for a week. The district court dismissed the complaint. The U.S. Court of Appeals, Fifth Circuit, reversed, but upon rehearing, affirmed the district court's decision. The U.S. Supreme Court then granted review.

The Supreme Court held that the Eighth Amendment's Cruel and Unusual Punishment Clause did not apply to disciplinary corporal punishment in the public schools. The Court stated that the Eighth Amendment was intended to protect accused criminals, not students. The Court stated that the openness of the public school and its supervision by the community afford significant safeguards against the kind of abuses from which the Eighth Amendment protects convicted criminals. The Court also held that the Due Process Clause of the Fourteenth Amendment did not require notice and hearing prior to the imposition of corporal punishment. Imposing this burden would significantly intrude into the area of educational responsibility. *Ingraham v. Wright*, 430 U.S. 651, 97 S.Ct. 1401, 51 L.Ed.2d 711 (1977).

In *Carey,* the U.S. Supreme Court held that compensation for a denial of procedural due process should be only nominal damages. Absent a showing of actual injury caused by the denial of due process, the students were to recover only a single dollar, since constitutional rights have no value in and of themselves. See *Memphis Community School District v. Stachura,* Chapter Four, Section III, for a similar ruling involving a teacher's lawsuit for his suspension.

Two students in Chicago in separate schools and circumstances were each given 20-day suspensions for alleged violations of school rules. One student had been accused of smoking marijuana and the other of displaying symbols indicating gang membership. Both were suspended without an adjudicatory hearing. Both brought lawsuits against school officials under § 1983 of the Civil Rights Act of 1871 contending that they had been deprived of procedural due process in their suspensions. The U.S. Court of Appeals, Seventh Circuit, held that even if the suspensions were justified, the students would be entitled to substantial nonpunitive damages, without proof of actual injury simply because they had been denied procedural due process.

The Supreme Court reversed this decision and held that while procedural due process is an absolute right because of its importance to organized society, a denial of procedural due process should be actionable for nominal damages only, absent proof of actual injury. The recovery of substantial damages must be based on proof of actual injury. The Court rejected the argument that substantial damages should be recoverable for presumed injuries resulting from procedural due process deficiencies. Further, the Court rejected the students' claim that constitutional rights are of value in and of themselves and that recoveries for such presumed injuries would deter violations of constitutional rights. The Court held that if on remand the district court determined that the suspensions were justified, the students would nevertheless be entitled to recover nominal damages not to exceed one dollar for violations of their procedural due process rights. *Carey v. Piphus,* 435 U.S. 247, 98 S.Ct. 1042, 55 L.Ed.2d 252 (1978).

Unlike dismissals for disciplinary reasons, dismissals for academic reasons do not require the procedural rigors as set down in *Goss v. Lopez,* above. School officials have a broader discretion in dealing with academic expulsions and suspensions than in disciplinary matters.

The academic performance of students at the University of Missouri-Kansas City Medical School was assessed periodically by the Council of Evaluation, a faculty-student body with the power to recommend probation or dismissal subject to approval by a faculty committee and the Dean. Several faculty members expressed dissatisfaction with the performance of a medical student. As a result, the Council of Evaluation recommended that she be advanced to her final year on a probationary status. Faculty complaints continued, and the Council warned the student that absent "radical improvement," she would be dismissed. She was allowed to take a set of oral and practical examinations as an "appeal" from the Council's decision.

The student spent a substantial portion of time with seven practicing physicians who supervised the examinations. Two recommended that she be allowed to graduate. Two recommended that she be dropped immediately from the school. The remaining three recommended that she not be allowed to graduate in June and be continued on probation pending further reports of her progress. Subsequent reports regarding the student were negative and she was dropped from the program following the Council's recommendation. The student sued, alleging that she had not been accorded due process prior to her dismissal. The district court determined that the student had been afforded all due process rights. The U.S. Court of Appeals, Eighth Circuit, reversed.

On appeal to the U.S. Supreme Court, the Court held that the student had been given due process as guaranteed by the Fourteenth Amendment. The procedures leading to the student's dismissal, under which the student was fully informed of faculty dissatisfaction with her progress, and the consequent threat to the student's graduation and continued enrollment did not violate the Fourteenth Amendment. As stated in *Goss v. Lopez*, dismissals for academic reasons do not necessitate a hearing before the school's decision-making body. *Board of Curators v. Horowitz*, 435 U.S. 78, 98 S.Ct. 948, 55 L.Ed.2d 124 (1978).

In *Wood v. Strickland*, above, the U.S. Supreme Court held that "section 1983 of 42 U.S.C. does not extend the right to relitigate in federal court evidentiary questions arising in school disciplinary proceedings or the proper construction of school regulations." In this case, the Supreme Court ruled that federal courts may not construe school regulations differently from the school board's construction.

A tenth grade Arkansas student left school grounds, consumed alcohol and returned to school intoxicated. He was immediately suspended from school pending a board hearing at which he was expelled. School regulations provided for suspension or expulsion of any student for good cause, including use or possession of alcoholic beverages or drugs. A subsequent section mandated expulsion for students using or under the influence of drugs or controlled substances. His parents sued for injunctive relief which was granted by a federal district court and later upheld by the U.S. Court of Appeals, Eighth Circuit. The district court and the court of appeals held that the school board had acted under the regulation section mandating expulsion but held the expulsion violative of substantive due process since the student had not used drugs but only alcohol. For this reason the lower courts held the student had been unfairly suspended.

On appeal to the U.S. Supreme Court, however, the school board's decision was upheld. The Court ruled that it was not within the purview of the district court or the court of appeals to substitute their own view of the facts for that of the school board's. The school board clearly had the authority to suspend the student for consuming alcohol. It was not for the lower federal courts to determine that the board acted under other sections when the expulsion was made. *Board of Education of Rogers v. McCluskey*, 458 U.S. 966, 103 S.Ct. 3469, 73 L.Ed.2d 1273 (1982).

Schools and universities are generally given a great deal of latitude by courts in making academic decisions. Their choices, however, must have some rational basis and may not be arbitrary. Here, the Supreme Court upheld a university's decision to dismiss a student from an advanced academic program based on poor performance.

A student was enrolled in the University of Michigan's "Inteflex" program, which is a special six-year course of study leading to both an undergraduate and medical degree. The student struggled with the curriculum for six years, completing only four years' worth of study and barely achieving minimal competence. Because he was given a grade of "incomplete" in several important classes and was forced to delay taking his examinations, he was placed on an irregular program. Finally, he completed the four years of basic study necessary to take the NBME Part I, a test administered by the National Board of Medical Examiners which is a prerequisite to the final two years of study under the Inteflex program. Unfortunately, the student failed the exam, receiving the lowest score ever in the brief history of the Inteflex program.

The university's medical school executive board reviewed the student's academic career and decided to drop him from registration in the program, and further denied his request that he be allowed to retake NBME Part I. The executive board was not swayed by arguments that his failure on the exam was due to his mother's heart attack 18 months previously, the excessive amount of time he had spent on an essay contest which he had entered, and his breakup with his girlfriend. The student brought suit in federal court claiming breach of contract under state law and also alleging a violation of his due process rights under the U.S. Constitution.

At trial, the evidence showed that the university had established a practice of allowing students who had failed the NBME Part I to retake the test one, two, three, or even four times. The student here was the only person ever refused permission to retake the test. The district court ruled against him on the contract claim and further held that his dismissal was not violative of the Due Process Clause. The U.S. Court of Appeals, Sixth Circuit, reversed and held that the student had possessed a property interest in his continued participation in the Inteflex program, and that the university had arbitrarily deprived him of that property interest by singling him out as the only student ever denied permission to retake the NBME Part I.

The U.S. Supreme Court unanimously reversed the court of appeals' decision and reinstated the district court's ruling against the student. The Due Process Clause was not offended because the university's liberal retesting custom gave rise to no state law entitlement to retake NBME Part I. Furthermore, the university had based its decision to dismiss the student upon careful, clear and conscientious deliberation which took his entire academic career into account. The university had acted in good faith. The Supreme Court further observed that the discretion to determine, on academic grounds, who may be admitted to study is one of the "four essential freedoms" of a university. The Court thus held that the Due Process Clause was not violated by the student's dismissal. *Regents of the University of Michigan v. Ewing*, 474 U.S. 214, 106 S.Ct. 507, 88 L.Ed.2d 523 (1985).

The Fourth Amendment protects people from unreasonable governmental search and seizure. What is unreasonable, however, is dependent upon who is conducting the search and the context in which the search is being carried out. Police have to meet the *probable cause* standard in conducting their searches. In the following case, the Supreme Court held school officials to a lower standard than probable cause, ruling that a search by school officials

need only be reasonable at its inception and that its scope may not exceed that which is necessary under the circumstances.

A teacher at a New Jersey high school found two girls smoking in the lavatory in violation of school rules. She brought them to the assistant vice principal's office where one of the girls admitted to smoking in the lavatory. However, the other denied even being a smoker. The assistant vice principal then asked the latter girl to come to his private office where he opened her purse and found a pack of cigarettes. As he reached for them he noticed rolling papers and decided to thoroughly search the entire purse. He found marijuana, a pipe, empty plastic bags, a substantial number of one dollar bills and a list of "people who owe me money." He then turned her over to the police. A juvenile court hearing was held and the girl was adjudged delinquent. She appealed the juvenile court's determination, contending that her constitutional rights had been violated by the search of her purse. She argued that the evidence against her obtained in the search should have been excluded from the juvenile court proceeding.

The U.S. Supreme Court held that the search did not violate the Fourth Amendment prohibition against unreasonable search and seizure. The Court stated: "The legality of a search of a student should depend simply on the reasonableness, under all the circumstances, of the search." Two considerations are relevant in determining the reasonableness of a search. First, the search must be justified initially by reasonable suspicion. Second, the scope and conduct of the search must be reasonably related to the circumstances which gave rise to the search, and school officials must take into account the student's age, sex and the nature of the offense. The Court upheld the search of the student in this case because the initial search for cigarettes was supported by reasonable suspicion. The discovery of the rolling papers then justified the further searching of the purse since such papers are commonly used to roll marijuana cigarettes. The "reasonableness" standard was met by school officials in these circumstances and thus the evidence against the girl was properly obtained. *New Jersey v. T.L.O.*, 469 U.S. 325, 105 S.Ct. 733, 83 L.Ed.2d 720 (1985).

The Individuals with Disabilities Education Act (IDEA), originally enacted as the Education of the Handicapped Act (EHA), requires that prior written notice of any proposed change in placement of a child with a disability must be given to the parents of the child. If the parents wish to contest the change in placement, a hearing must be granted. The IDEA further requires that during

the pendency of such review proceedings, the child is to remain in the then current educational placement. Whether suspension or expulsion of students with disabilities from school constitutes a "change in placement" for purposes of the IDEA is an issue which has been presented before the court. The U.S. Supreme Court clarified the issue in *Honig v. Doe*. Indefinite suspensions violate the "stay put" provisions of the IDEA. Suspensions up to ten days do not constitute a change in placement. The Individuals with Disabilities Education Act Amendments of 1997 now allow schools to remove disruptive students from class for up to 55 days.

Two emotionally disturbed children in California were given five-day suspensions from school for misbehavior which included destroying school property and making sexual comments to other students. Pursuant to state law, the suspensions were continued indefinitely during the pendency of expulsion proceedings. The students sued the school district in U.S. district court contesting the extended suspensions on the ground that they violated the "stay put" provision of the IDEA which provides that a student must be kept in his or her "then current" educational placement during the pendency of proceedings which contemplate a change in placement. The district court issued an injunction preventing the expulsion of any disabled student for misbehavior which arises from the student's disability, and the school district appealed.

The U.S. Court of Appeals, Ninth Circuit, determined that the indefinite suspensions constituted a prohibited "change in placement" under the IDEA and that no "dangerousness" exception existed in the IDEA's "stay put" provision. It ruled that indefinite suspensions arising out of students' disabilities violated the IDEA. The court of appeals also ruled, however, that fixed suspensions of up to 30 school days did not constitute a "change in placement." It determined that a state must provide services directly to a disabled child when a local school district fails to do so. The California Superintendent of Public Instruction petitioned for a review by the U.S. Supreme Court on the issues of whether a dangerousness exception existed to the "stay put" provision and whether the state had to provide services directly when a local school district failed to do so.

The Supreme Court declared that the intended purpose of the "stay put" provision was to prevent schools from changing a child's educational placement over his or her parents' objection until all review proceedings were completed. While the IDEA provided for interim placements where parents and school officials were able to agree on one, no emergency exception for dangerous students was included. The Court concluded that it was "not at liberty to engraft onto the [IDEA] an exception Congress chose not to create." The Court went on to say that where a disabled student poses an immediate threat to the safety of others, school officials may temporarily suspend him or her for up to ten school days. The Court held that this authority insured: 1) that school officials can protect the safety of others by removing dangerous students, 2) that school officials can seek a review of the student's placement and try to persuade the student's parents to agree to an interim placement, and 3) that school officials can seek court rulings to exclude students whose parents "adamantly refuse to permit any change in placement."

School officials could seek such a court order without exhausting the IDEA's administrative remedies "only by showing that maintaining the child in his or her current placement is substantially likely to result in injury either to himself or herself, or to others." The Court therefore affirmed the court of appeals' decision that indefinite suspensions violated the "stay put" provision of the IDEA. It modified that court's decision on fixed suspensions by holding that suspensions of up to ten rather than up to 30 days did not constitute a change in placement. The Court also upheld the court of appeals' decision that states could be required to provide services directly to disabled students where a local school district fails to do so. *Honig v. Doe*, 484 U.S. 305, 108 S.Ct. 592, 98 L.Ed.2d 686 (1988).

In *U.S. v. Lopez*, below, the Supreme Court declared unconstitutional the Gun-Free School Zones Act, which made it a federal crime for any individual to knowingly possess a firearm in a school zone. The power of the Commerce Clause, although broad, did not allow Congress to enact a criminal law that did not substantially affect interstate commerce.

The Gun-Free School Zones Act of 1990, 18 U.S.C. § 922(q)(1)(A), makes it a federal crime for any individual to knowingly possess a firearm in a school zone. The act defines a school zone as an area within 1,000 feet of any public or private school ground. A twelfth grade Texas student came to school with a concealed .38 caliber handgun and five bullets and was apprehended by school authorities who were acting on an anonymous tip. He was initially charged with firearms possession on school grounds in violation of Texas law but the following day the state charges were dismissed when federal agents filed a complaint under the Gun-Free School Zones Act. A federal district court convicted the student of violating the act, and sentenced him to six months' imprisonment and two years of supervised release. The student appealed to the U.S. Court of Appeals, Fifth Circuit, which held the Gun-Free School Zones Act unconstitutional and reversed the conviction. The federal government appealed to the U.S. Supreme Court.

On appeal, the government argued that possession of a gun in a school zone could result in the commission of a violent crime which would affect the functioning of the national economy because of the high cost of violent crime. It also affected interstate commerce by discouraging individuals from traveling in areas perceived to be unsafe. The Court evaluated prior decisions under the Commerce Clause—Article I, § 8 of the U.S. Constitution—which upheld legislation where the regulated activity substantially affected interstate commerce. The Court observed that the statute was a criminal law that had nothing to do with commerce. Although the Commerce Clause gave broad regulatory powers to Congress, it did not give Congress the authority to regulate every aspect of local schools. The possession of a gun in a local school zone did not constitute economic activity. There was no evidence that the student or his gun had recently moved in interstate commerce. The Court affirmed the reversal of the conviction, declaring the act unconstitutional. *U.S. v. Lopez*, 514 U.S. 549, 115 S.Ct. 1624, 131 L.Ed.2d 626 (1995).

The Supreme Court examined the privacy expectations of student athletes in a drug testing case and found that they were not sufficiently high to bar a school district's right to conduct the testing as a means of addressing drug use by students who risked physical harm while playing sports. The Court stated that the invasion of privacy at issue was no worse than what was typically encountered in public restrooms.

An Oregon school district experienced an increase in drug-related student misconduct, including widespread rebelliousness, a doubling of disciplinary referrals, and at least one severe sports injury. School administrators identified interscholastic athletes as the ringleaders of an emerging drug culture in the district's high school. Following a public meeting, the school adopted a drug testing program under which any student wishing to play sports was required to sign a consent form. Parents were also required to give their consent. By signing the form, student athletes agreed to take a drug test at the beginning of the season, and submit to random testing thereafter. Testing took place before a same-sex monitor and students testing positive were allowed a second drug test.

In the event of a second positive test, the district imposed an automatic suspension from sports participation for two seasons unless the student agreed to a six-week assistance program with weekly urinalysis. A student seeking to play football in a district school refused to sign the consent form and with his family filed a lawsuit in the U.S. District Court for the District of Oregon, seeking a declaration that the program violated the Fourth Amendment to the U.S. Constitution and the Oregon Constitution. The district court's dismissal order was reversed by the U.S. Court of Appeals for the Ninth Circuit. The district appealed to the U.S. Supreme Court.

The Court stated that under its prior cases the reasonableness of a search under the Fourth Amendment required balancing the interests between the government and individual. Prior decisions of the Court indicated that students had a lesser expectation of privacy than the general populace, and that student-athletes had an even lower expectation of privacy in the locker room. The invasion of privacy in this case was no worse than what was typically encountered in public restrooms. Positive test results were disclosed to only a limited number of school employees. The insignificant invasion of student privacy was outweighed by the school district's important interest in addressing drug use by students who risked physical harm while playing sports. The Court vacated and remanded the decision of the court of appeals. *Vernonia School Dist. 47J v. Acton*, 515 U.S. 646, 115 S.Ct. 2386, 132 L.Ed.2d 564 (1995).

CHAPTER FOUR

Employment

I. EMPLOYEE SPEECH RIGHTS

A. Employment Termination and Speech Rights

The following case, *Pickering v. Board of Education*, is one of the Court's most important First Amendment decisions affecting the speech rights of public employees. In the 1968 decision, involving an Illinois teacher's lawsuit against his school district, the Court ruled that teachers are entitled to constitutional protection to communicate on matters of public concern unless there is proof that a communication was made in reckless disregard for the truth. Speech on matters of public importance could not form the basis for discharge.

An Illinois school district fired a high school teacher for sending a letter to the editor of the local newspaper. The letter criticized the board and district superintendent for their handling of school funding methods. Voters in the district voted down a tax rate increase to fund a bond issue for two new schools. The local teachers organization published an article in support of a second tax increase, as did the superintendent. District voters then rejected a second tax rate increase proposal. The teacher's letter came as a response to the superintendent and teacher organization articles and the second electoral defeat of the tax rate increase. The letter particularly criticized the board's handling of the bond issue and allocation of funding between school educational and athletic programs. The teacher also charged the superintendent with attempting to stifle opposing views on the subject.

The board then held a hearing at which it charged the teacher with publishing a defamatory letter. After deeming the teacher's statements to be false, the board fired the teacher. An Illinois court affirmed the board's action, finding substantial evidence that publication of the letter was detrimental to the district's interest. The Illinois Supreme Court affirmed the dismissal, ruling that the teacher was unprotected by the First Amendment because he had accepted a position that required him to refrain from commenting about school operations.

The U.S. Supreme Court reversed and remanded the case, finding no support for the state supreme court's view that public employment subjected the teacher to deprivation of his constitutional rights. The state interest in regulating employee speech was to be balanced with individual rights. The Court outlined a general analysis for evaluating public employee speech, ruling that employees are entitled to constitutional protection to comment on matters of public concern. The public interest in free speech and debate on matters of public concern was so great that it barred public officials from recovering damages for defamatory statements unless they were made with reckless disregard for their truth. Because there was no evidence presented that the letter damaged any board member's professional reputation, the teacher's comments were not detrimental to the school system, but only constituted a difference of opinion. Since there was no proof of reckless disregard for the truth by the teacher and the matter concerned the public interest, the board could not constitutionally terminate his employment. The Court reversed and remanded the state court decision. *Pickering v. Board of Education*, 391 U.S. 563, 88 S.Ct. 1731, 20 L.Ed.2d 811 (1968).

In 1968, the Court invalidated an Arkansas statute banning the teaching of Darwinian theory in state-supported schools. It reasoned that the statute had been passed in order to support a particular religious theory and was therefore impermissible government support of religion.

An Arkansas biology teacher was instructed by her administrator to use a new textbook which included a chapter based upon Darwinian theory, which teaches that man evolved from lower forms of life. However, the state of Arkansas had passed a statute which made it unlawful for any teacher in a state-supported school or university to teach or to use a textbook that teaches "that mankind ascended or descended from a lower order of animals." The teacher, being caught in a dilemma, filed suit in an Arkansas trial court to have the statute declared unconstitutional and to prevent the school district from firing her for violating the statute. The trial court held that the statute violated the teacher's speech rights under the First and Fourteenth Amendments. The Supreme Court of Arkansas then reversed, ruling that the statute was a legitimate exercise of a school district's discretion to establish curriculum. The U.S. Supreme Court granted certiorari.

The Court initially noted that the teacher was not being prosecuted under the Arkansas anti-evolution statute. It declined to decide whether the statute was too vague to satisfy due process requirements under the Fourteenth Amendment. Rather, the Court struck the statute down as an unconstitutional establishment of religion by the government in violation of the First Amendment's Establishment Clause, applicable to the states through the Fourteenth Amendment. The Court ruled that the First Amendment demands religious neutrality by government and required it to remain neutral between religion and atheism. The Court reasoned that the statute had been passed because particular religious unprotected by the First Amendment. The Court's previous decisions in *Pickering v. Board of Education* and *Mt. Healthy City Board of Education v. Doyle*, above, did not stand for the proposition that public employee expression in private was without constitutional protection. Those cases had involved public employees making public criticism of school policies. However, protection of speech was not solely dependent on the public character of the speech. The Court refused to rule that the First Amendment makes a distinction between private and public speech by public employees. The principal, by opening his door to the teacher, had not been an "unwilling recipient" of the teacher's views. The Court vacated the court of appeals' decision and remanded the case. *Givhan v. Western Line Consolidated School District*, 439 U.S. 410, 99 S.Ct. 693, 58 L.Ed.2d 619 (1978).

The Court used the balancing test it devised in *Pickering v. Bd. of Educ.*, above, in the following case, reaffirming the rule that public employee speech is protected when it affects matters of public concern, but is unprotected when it affects only a personal interest in employment.

An assistant district attorney in New Orleans had the responsibility of trying criminal cases. When the district attorney proposed to transfer the assistant to prosecute cases in a different section of the criminal court, she opposed the transfer. She then expressed her views on the matter to several of her superiors. Shortly thereafter, she prepared and distributed a questionnaire to other assistant district attorneys in the office concerning the office's transfer policy, morale, the level of confidence in superiors, and whether the employees felt pressured to work for political campaigns, among other things. The district attorney then fired her for refusing the transfer and for the act of insubordination in distributing the questionnaire. The assistant sued in federal court, alleging that she had been discharged in violation of her First Amendment rights. The district court agreed and she was reinstated with backpay and attorney's fees. The U.S. Court of Appeals, Fifth Circuit, affirmed and the U.S. Supreme Court granted review.

The Court stated that in order to determine a public employee's rights of free speech, the balancing test of *Pickering v. Bd. of Educ.*, above, must be utilized. The interests of the employee as a citizen in commenting upon matters of public concern must outweigh the interest of the state, as employer, in promoting efficiency in the workplace. The Court held that when a public employee speaks upon matters of only personal interest in employment, not as a citizen upon matters of public concern, a federal court is not an appropriate forum in which to review the wisdom of a personnel decision taken by a public agency in reaction to the employee's speech. Here, except for the assistant's question regarding pressure to work in political campaigns, the questions were not matters of public concern. The state also need not prove substantial disruption of the office in order to justify dismissal when the First Amendment right is limited. In this case, the district attorney's action was reasonable if he thought that the speech in question would disrupt the office, undermine his authority and destroy working relationships in the office. *Connick v. Myers,* 461 U.S. 138, 103 S.Ct. 1684, 75 L.Ed.2d 708 (1983).

In the following case, the Court explained that under *Connick v. Myers*, above, government action based on protected speech may violate the First Amendment even if the public employer believes the speech is unprotected.

A nurse at an Illinois public hospital allegedly gave a negative report about the obstetrics department to a cross-trainee. For example, she stated that the department was a bad place to work, that her supervisor was trying to find reasons to fire her, and that she had been wrongly blamed following a patient complaint. She also criticized her supervisors, saying that they were "ruining the hospital." The cross-trainee reported this conversation to the nurse's supervisor. After twice reviewing the record, the hospital discharged the nurse. The nurse filed suit in a U.S. district court alleging that the discharge was in response to her criticism of the hospital's cross-training and staffing policies in violation of her First Amendment rights. The district court held for the supervisor and the hospital. On appeal, the U.S. Court of Appeals for the Seventh Circuit reversed, holding that the employee had been dis-charged for engaging in protected speech. The supervisor and the hospital appealed to the U.S. Supreme Court.

The issue on appeal was whether the test set out in *Connick v. Myers*, above, should be applied to what the government employer reasonably thought was said, or to what the trier of fact ultimately determines was said. The Court noted that government action based on protected speech may violate the First Amendment even if the public employer honestly believes the speech is not protected. However, the Court expressly declined to adopt a specific test to determine when to adopt procedural safeguards for employee speech. Instead, the Court held that it must look to the facts as the employer reasonably found them to be. For example, it may be unreasonable for the employer to take adverse employment actions based on extremely weak evidence. Here, the court determined that the employee had sufficient evidence to create a material issue of disputed fact about the supervisor's actual motivation. The supervisor had previously reacted negatively to the employee's criticisms of the cross-training and staffing policies. On remand, if a jury determined that the employee was discharged for these reasons, the court would then have to determine whether the employee's criticisms were protected speech. The case was vacated and remanded for further proceedings. *Waters v. Churchill*, 511 U.S. 661, 114 S.Ct. 1878, 128 L.Ed.2d 686 (1994).

In *Board of County Commissioners, Wabaunsee County, Kansas v. Umbehr*, the Court utilized the balancing test it established in *Pickering*, above, in order to evaluate the government's interests against the First Amendment rights of a private contractor doing business with a public agency.

A Kansas trash hauler who had an at-will contract with a county to haul trash was an outspoken critic of the board of county commissioners. After the commissioners voted to terminate (or prevent the automatic renewal of) the contract, he sued two of the commissioners in a federal district court under 42 U.S.C. § 1983, alleging that they had terminated his contract in retaliation for his criticisms. The court held that the contract had been terminated in retaliation for the speech, but that the First Amendment did not prohibit the commissioners from considering the criticisms as a factor in deciding to terminate the contract. The U.S. Court of Appeals, Tenth Circuit, reversed, holding that "an independent contractor is protected under the First Amendment from retaliatory government action, just as an employee would be."

On further appeal, the U.S. Supreme Court held that the First Amendment protects independent contractors from the termination or prevention of automatic renewal of their at-will government contracts in retaliation for their exercise of freedom of speech. The Court utilized the *Pickering* balancing test to weigh the government's interests as a contractor against the trash hauler's First Amendment rights. Although government and individual rights are generally weaker in an independent contractor case than in an employment case, the fact that independent government contractors are similar in most relevant respects to government employees compels the conclusion that the same form of balancing analysis should apply to each. The Court affirmed the court of appeals' decision. *Board of County Commissioners, Wabaunsee*

County, Kansas v. Umbehr, 518 U.S. 668, 116 S.Ct. 2342, 135 L.Ed.2d 843 (1996).

B. Loyalty Oaths

The cases in this section trace the response of public employees to government policies which became common during the Cold War years, when many local governments required their employees to take loyalty oaths and disavow any Communist Party affiliation. In a 1950 case, the Court ruled that such restrictions on new public employees were permissible as an exercise of legislative standards on employee competency.

In 1941, the California legislature amended the city of Los Angeles charter to disqualify from public employment any public employee or official who had taught or advocated the violent overthrow of the government during the previous five years. In accordance with the charter, the city then passed an ordinance requiring all city officers and employees to take an oath swearing that they had not and would not become members of the Communist Party, nor advocate the violent overthrow of the government. The ordinance also required that employees execute affidavits swearing that they had never been Communist Party members, or if they had been, certifying the dates during which they were members.

After they were discharged for refusing to execute affidavits or refusing to take oaths, a group of civil service employees sued the city board in a California trial court for reinstatement and unpaid salaries. They attacked the ordinance, claiming that it violated Article I, § 10 of the Constitution, which prohibits states from passing bills of attainder and ex post facto laws. In addition, the group alleged that the ordinance deprived them of freedom of speech and assembly, and the right to petition the government for a redress of grievances. After a California appellate court denied the group's claims, the employees appealed to the U.S. Supreme Court.

The Court held first that the affidavit provision of the ordinance was valid because states have a legitimate interest in inquiring into employee backgrounds. This was because past conduct and loyalty may have a reasonable relationship to present and future trust. The Court then upheld the oath provision of the charter, stating that it was valid under the Constitution as a reasonable regulation to protect municipal service. The Court held that the ordinance was not an ex post facto law and rejected the group's argument that the ordinance was a bill of

statute did not satisfy this test. The Court reversed the state supreme
court's decision and struck down the statute. The Court distinguished its
decision in *Adler v. Board of Education*, above, on the basis that the law
there required knowledge of organizational purpose before the regulation applied. Because the employees did not have an opportunity to take
the oath after the statute was interpreted, knowledge was not a factor in
the Oklahoma statute. Association membership may be innocent and
the state could not infer intent by association. The consequences of
discharge for an employee who failed to take the oath were great and
long lasting. The Court refused to decide whether a right to public
employment exists. It held only that public employees affected by an
arbitrary or discriminatory statute enjoyed constitutional protection.
Wieman v. Updegraff, 344 U.S. 183, 73 S.Ct. 215, 97 L.Ed. 216 (1952).

**In 1955, as McCarthyism waned, the Court invalidated a New
York City charter provision which purported to deprive Communist Party members of their Fifth Amendment right against self-
incrimination.**

Section 903 of New York City's charter provided that any city
employee who used the Fifth Amendment's self-incrimination privilege to avoid answering a question relating to official conduct would
lose tenure and be ineligible for future city employment. An associate
professor of German at Brooklyn College was called before the U.S.
Senate Judiciary Committee's Internal Security Subcommittee to testify about subversive influences within the nation's educational system.
The professor testified that he was not a member of the Communist
party and was completely willing to answer questions about his political
affiliation from 1941 to the present date. However, he refused to answer
questions about his political beliefs during 1940 and 1941 on the
grounds that his answers might incriminate him. Allegations had
previously been made before another investigative committee that the
professor was a Communist party member in 1941. After the professor
testified before the Internal Security Subcommittee, the college suspended him even though he had taught there 27 years and was entitled
to tenure under New York state law. Three days later, his position was
vacated in accordance with § 903. If not for § 903, because he was
tenured, the professor would have been entitled to notice, hearing and
the opportunity to appeal an unfavorable decision, with discharge for
just cause being the only appropriate result.

The New York Court of Appeals had previously held that using the
self-incrimination privilege as a defense in tenure cases was tantamount

to resignation. Thus, the professor was not entitled to the usual procedural safeguard requirements. The professor filed suit in a New York
trial court, challenging the constitutionality of § 903. He argued that the
section violated the Privileges and Immunities Clause of the Fourteenth
Amendment since it effectively imposed a penalty on the exercise of a
federally guaranteed right in a federal proceeding. He also argued that
it violated his due process rights under the Fifth and Fourteenth
Amendment because the statute did not provide a reasonable basis for
his termination.

The Court ruled that the statute violated the Due Process Clause and
therefore did not consider the Privileges and Immunities Clause claim.
It distinguished *Garner v. Los Angeles Board*, above, from this case
because in *Garner*, due process in the form of notice and a hearing was
provided to the employee. Here, the teacher was dismissed without a
hearing. The Court also ruled that taking the self-incrimination privilege could not automatically be interpreted to mean that the teacher had
been a Communist Party member. The Court held that such an arbitrary
dismissal violated due process. *Slochower v. Board of Education*, 350
U.S. 551, 76 S.Ct. 637, 100 L.Ed. 692 (1955).

**The Court declared unconstitutional a New Hampshire inqui-
sition into the political affiliation and activities of an author who
had lectured before a state college. The state had no legitimate
interest in controlling political expression.**

In the early 1950's, the New Hampshire legislature conducted
investigations into subversive activities. The investigations were part of
a scheme to regulate Communist Party activities. Organizations which
were declared subversive were deemed illegal, and members were
made ineligible for public employment. Those already in government
and public positions were required to take loyalty oaths. As part of this
effort, the attorney general was appointed to investigate such activities
and became a *de facto* one-person legislative committee. The attorney
general was given broad powers to delegate authority and to subpoena
witnesses and documents.

An author was called to testify before the attorney general on two
occasions. On the first occasion, he was interrogated about his political
associations and activities. The author refused to answer several questions. The second time, the author was questioned about an article he
had written and about a lecture he had given at the University of New
Hampshire. Again, the author refused to answer, arguing that his speech
was protected by the First Amendment. The attorney general then
petitioned a New Hampshire trial court to compel the author to answer

his questions. After the author again refused to answer what the court called "pertinent questions," he was held in contempt of court and jailed. The New Hampshire Supreme Court affirmed. The author appealed to the U.S. Supreme Court.

The Court noted that although legislative investigations have broad powers which sometimes infringe upon individual constitutional rights, including free speech, incarceration of the author after he refused to answer questions about the lecture violated his First and Fourteenth Amendment Rights. Teachers and students must be free to inquire and hypothesize, especially in a university setting, or democracy will be crippled. Political expression rights are essential to freedom. The Court held that the state had no interest in infringing the constitutional rights of the author. It was effectively silencing a dissident minority interest, and had violated his free speech rights. The Court ruled the New Hampshire legislative inquiry and the authorizing statute unconstitutional. *Sweezy v. New Hampshire*, 354 U.S. 234, 77 S.Ct. 1203, 1 L.Ed.2d 1311 (1956).

In 1957, the Supreme Court upheld the constitutionality of a Pennsylvania teacher's termination. Because the district had based the teacher's termination on his failure to answer questions about his fitness to teach rather than alleged disloyalty, and had warned him that failure to answer the questions was grounds for termination, the termination met minimal Due Process Clause standards.

A teacher who had taught for 22 years in Philadelphia public schools refused to answer his superintendent's questions regarding his affiliation with Communist organizations. The superintendent had previously warned him that the questions were pertinent to his job as a teacher and that he could be dismissed if he refused to answer them. The city board of education held a hearing in which it found that the teacher's refusal to answer the superintendent's questions represented incompetency. The teacher was accordingly dismissed. The Pennsylvania state school superintendent sustained the board's dismissal decision. However, a Pennsylvania trial court reversed this decision and held that the board should have followed procedures outlined in Pennsylvania's Loyalty Act. The Loyalty Act provided for public employee discharge on grounds of subversive conduct or disloyalty. The Act also outlined specific procedures for discharge on those grounds. The Pennsylvania Supreme Court, Eastern District, upheld the dismissal. The U.S. Supreme Court granted certiorari.

Before the Court, the teacher contended that he had been denied property without due process of law, in violation of the Fourteenth Amendment. The Court upheld the dismissal and denied the teacher's claim. It held that although the teacher had the right to associate or believe in whatever he wanted, he also had obligations of cooperation and candor in answering the superintendent's questions. The school board had a right to inquire into the teacher's activities in order to determine whether he was fit to be a teacher. The teacher's discharge had been based upon his refusal to answer the questions rather than his lack of loyalty to the board's political philosophy. The teacher had legitimately been discharged in accordance with the school code and had not been denied his property right to tenure in violation of the Fourteenth Amendment. Finally, the Court rejected the teacher's claim that he had been denied due process because he had not been told that he would be dismissed if he did not answer the questions. The Court stated that the record showed otherwise. *Beilan v. Board of Education*, 357 U.S. 399, 78 S.Ct. 1317, 2 L.Ed.2d 1414 (1957).

The Court invalidated an Arkansas statute which required teachers in state supported schools to file annual affidavits listing every organization to which the teacher belonged in the previous five years. The statute interfered with the teachers' speech and association rights and went beyond the state's legitimate interest in the fitness of its teachers.

The Arkansas legislature established a statute which required every teacher employed by a state supported school or college to file an annual affidavit listing every organization to which he or she had belonged in the past five years. Arkansas had no real tenure system and teachers were not considered within the civil service system. Teachers were hired on a year-to-year basis, but were automatically renewed if the teacher was not notified within ten days after the end of the school year. A teacher who had worked for an Arkansas school system for 25 years (and a member of the NAACP) was told he would have to file such an affidavit before the start of the next school year. After he failed to do so, his contract for the next year was not renewed.

The teacher then filed a class action lawsuit against the school district in a federal district court. The court found that the teacher was not a member of the Communist Party, nor of any organization advocating the violent overthrow of the government. It upheld the statute, finding that the information requested by the school district was relevant. The Supreme Court of Arkansas had previously upheld the statute's constitutionality in a case brought in the state court system by other teachers. The U.S. Supreme Court agreed to hear both cases and consolidated them for a hearing.

Both groups challenging the act argued that it deprived teachers of their rights to personal, associational and academic liberty as protected by the Fourteenth Amendment's Due Process Clause. The Court noted that the state certainly had a right to investigate teachers, since education of youth was a vital public interest. It stated that the requirement of the affidavit was reasonably related to the state's interest. However, the Court held that requiring teachers to name all their associations was an interference of teacher speech and association rights. The Court ruled that because fundamental rights were involved, governmental screening of teachers was required to be narrowly tailored to the state's ends. Because the statute went beyond what was necessary to meet the state's inquiry into the fitness of its teachers, the Court ruled it unconstitutional. *Shelton v. Tucker*, 364 U.S. 479, 81 S.Ct. 247, 5 L.Ed.2d 231 (1960).

In 1961, the Court struck down a Florida loyalty oath statute because it was impermissibly vague. The statute failed to adequately advise employees of the standard of conduct to which they were to be held.

Florida law required each state employee to submit a written oath, certifying that he or she had never lent counsel, advised, aided or supported the Communist party. A failure to submit such an oath resulted in the employee's immediate termination. A teacher who had taught in the same Florida school district for nine years was dismissed when he refused to sign the oath. The teacher sought a declaration that the statute was unconstitutional and an injunction to prevent its enforcement. He argued that the statute was an ex post facto law and a bill of attainder. A Florida trial court refused to grant an injunction, and the Florida Supreme Court affirmed this decision.

After determining that the case was based on federal law and was properly a matter in which it had jurisdiction, the U.S. Supreme Court struck the statute down as a violation of the Fourteenth Amendment's Due Process Clause. The statute was too vague to pass constitutional standards. It compelled state employees to take the oath or face immediate dismissal. Because the statute lacked objective standards, no employee could truthfully take the oath. Statutes which made persons of average intelligence guess at their possible meanings and applications violated the Due Process Clause because they did not constitute true rules or standards. The Court reversed the Florida court decisions, ruling for the teacher. *Cramp v. Board of Public Instruction of Orange County*, 368 U.S. 278, 82 S.Ct. 275, 7 L.Ed.2d 285 (1961).

A Washington statute attempted to prohibit persons identified as subversives from employment as public school teachers. The Court noted the absence of clearly defined standards within the act and struck it down as unconstitutionally vague.

Faculty members at the University of Washington brought a class action suit to declare two state statutes unconstitutional. One statute required all state employees to take loyalty oaths, and the other required all teachers to take an oath as a condition of employment. Both oaths dealt with employee loyalty to the Federal Constitution and to the government. The public employee statute applied to all public employees and defined a "subversive person" as one who conspired to overthrow the government. The Communist Party was also named as a subversive organization. Persons designated as subversives or Communist Party members were ineligible for public employment. The university board of regents sent a memorandum to all its instructors, requiring them to take the oath. A federal district court held that the public employee act was constitutional. It abstained from ruling on the teachers' act pending consideration by the state courts. The teachers appealed to the U.S. Supreme Court.

Before the Court, the teachers argued that the statutes were vague and overbroad, and violated the Fourteenth Amendment's Due Process Clause. The Court reversed the appeals court decision, holding that both statutes were too unspecific to provide sufficient notice of what conduct was prohibited. This constituted a denial of the teachers' due process rights. The university could not require its teachers to take an oath which applied to some vague behavior in the future, especially since there were First Amendment speech and association claims at stake. Finally, the court of appeals should have decided the constitutionality of the teachers' act to avoid piecemeal legislation and to avoid possible inhibition of First Amendment rights. *Baggett v. Bullitt*, 377 U.S. 360, 84 S.Ct. 1316, 12 L.Ed.2d 377 (1963).

In accordance with its decision in *Baggett v. Bullitt*, above, the Court invalidated an Arizona statute containing a loyalty oath. The statute attempted to outlaw some political groups. The Court ruled

that unless the group showed some specific intent to carry out an illegal purpose, the government could not punish its members.

An Arizona teacher who was a Quaker refused to take an oath required of all public employees under Arizona law. The oath swore that the employee would support both the Arizona state and the Federal constitution as well as state laws. The legislation also stated that anyone who took the oath and supported the Communist party or the violent overthrow of government would be discharged from employment and charged with perjury. The teacher sued for declaratory relief in the Arizona courts, having decided she could not take the oath in good conscience because she did not know what it meant. The case eventually reached the Arizona Supreme Court, which upheld the constitutionality of the oath and potential sanctions under the statute. The U.S. Supreme Court vacated the court's decision and remanded the case for reconsideration in light of its then-recent decision in *Baggett v. Bullitt*, above. On reconsideration, the Arizona Supreme Court again upheld the oath, distinguishing the case from *Baggett*. The U.S. Supreme Court granted the teacher's petition for review.

The Court began by noting that political groups may have both legal and illegal aims and that there should not be a blanket prohibition on all groups that might have both legal and illegal goals. Such a prohibition would threaten legitimate political expression and association. The Court held that mere association with a group cannot be prohibited without a showing of "specific intent" to carry out the group's illegal purpose. The Court held that the Arizona statute was constitutionally deficient because it was not confined to those employees with a "specific intent" to do something illegal. The statute infringed upon employee association rights by not punishing specific behavior that yielded a clear and present danger to government. The statute was struck down as unconstitutional. *Elfbrandt v. Russell*, 384 U.S. 11, 86 S.Ct. 1238, 16 L.Ed.2d 321 (1965).

In 1967, the Court overruled its *Adler v. Board of Education* decision, holding that New York statutory prohibitions on treasonable and seditious speech by public employees were unconstitutionally vague. The statute might have allowed dismissal of employees who believed in such doctrine, without actually advocating it.

A group of faculty members were employed by the privately owned University of Buffalo in New York. They continued their employment when the university merged into a state operated university. Because they became public employees, the faculty members were required to comply with a state plan that disqualified subversive persons from public employment. Four professors refused to sign a certificate that they were not Communists and that if they ever had been, they had notified the state university's president. One instructor was dismissed immediately for refusing to sign the certificate. Two more continued to teach until their contracts ran out. Another employee who worked in the library refused to answer under oath whether he had ever been a Communist party member and was dismissed. The group sought injunctive and declaratory relief in a federal district court. The district court held that the state requirements were constitutional. The U.S. Supreme Court agreed to hear the case.

The Court first recounted its decision in *Adler v. Board of Education*, above, in which it upheld the constitutionality of the Feinberg law. The Court then examined the statute which allowed the removal of public school teachers for "treasonable or seditious" utterances or acts. The Court held that such words were too vague to allow teachers to know the difference between seditious and nonseditious utterances or acts. In addition, another section of the statute allowed dismissal of any person who "by word of mouth or writing willfully and deliberately advocates, advises or teaches the doctrine" of the violent overthrow of government. The Court struck it down as too vague and sweeping, stating that it might allow dismissal of an employee who merely believes in such doctrine, without actually advocating it. Because of such vague provisions, teachers would not know exactly what is prohibited and would stay away from all utterances or acts that might constitute treachery or sedition. Thus, teachers' speech and association rights would be inhibited. Although the state has a legitimate interest in screening teachers, it must do so only in a manner that does not stifle fundamental personal rights.

The Court expressed the nation's deep commitment to academic freedom and the free flow of ideas. States may only legislate within a narrow specificity directly related to their interests. Finally, the Court struck down New York's scheme as unconstitutionally vague. The Court went on to attack the *Adler* premise, that public employment may be conditioned upon the surrender of constitutional rights. In rejecting this premise, the Court struck down the scheme's provision that proscribed mere membership in a communist organization as grounds for dismissal without any showing of specific intent to further an organization's aims. Such a provision is unconstitutionally overbroad and thus infringes on individual rights. The Court reversed the district court's decision. *Keyishian v. Board of Regents*, 385 U.S. 589, 87 S.Ct. 675, 17 L.Ed.2d 629 (1967).

The Court ruled in a 1967 Maryland case involving a loyalty oath that the line between permissible and impermissible conduct must be clearly drawn.

A teacher was offered a position with the University of Maryland. However, he refused to take a loyalty oath required by the university for its employees. The oath required the employee to swear that he was not engaged in any attempt to overthrow the government by force or violence. It was authored by the state attorney general and approved by the university board of regents under a state statute which authorized state agencies to establish procedures to determine whether a prospective employee was a subversive person under the act. The act defined a subversive person as someone who attempted or advocated the overthrow, destruction or alteration of the government by revolution, force or violence, or someone who was a member of such an organization. The teacher filed suit in a federal district court, challenging the oath's constitutionality. The district court dismissed the teacher's challenge. The U.S. Supreme Court granted certiorari.

The Court first decided that the oath's constitutionality had to be considered in conjunction with the state statute allowing the university board of regents to establish the oath. In addition, speech rights were implicated because the First Amendment protects controversial as well as conventional dialogue. The Court held that the authorizing statute was too vague and overbroad. It falsely assumed that someone belonging to a subversive group also supported the violent overthrow of the government. The statute also put continuous surveillance on teachers by imposing a perjury threat. Such a concept was hostile to academic freedom, limiting the free flow of ideas in places of learning. The Court ruled that the line between permissible and impermissible conduct must be clearly drawn. Because the statute failed to clearly define prohibited behavior, the Court reversed the district court's decision. *Whitehill v. Elkins*, 389 U.S. 54, 88 S.Ct. 184, 19 L.Ed.2d 228 (1967).

In 1970, the Supreme Court ruled unconstitutional part of a Florida statute which required public employees to state under oath that they did not believe in the violent overthrow of the government. This violated the Due Process Clause rights of the employees.

Florida law required all public employees to swear to a loyalty oath as a condition of employment. Employees were required to swear that they were not members of the Communist party, nor any other organization that believes in the violent overthrow of the government. Employees were also required to swear that they did not believe in the violent overthrow of the government. A woman who had been hired as a substitute teacher was dismissed for refusing to sign the loyalty oath. A federal district court declared that the portion of the statute requiring the oath disavowing Communist Party affiliation was unconstitutional. However, it upheld the statements pertaining to supporting the Constitution. The teacher appealed to the U.S. Supreme Court, challenging the constitutionality of the last part of the oath.

The Court held that the section of the oath requiring employees to pledge support to the Constitution and the government was no different from that required of all state and federal officers. Therefore, it passed constitutional scrutiny. However, the oath requiring employees to state that they did not believe in the violent overthrow of the government was unconstitutional, since it denied employee due process rights under the Fourteenth Amendment. *Connell v. Higginbotham*, 403 U.S. 207, 91 S.Ct. 1772, 29 L.Ed.2d 418 (1970).

II. EMPLOYMENT DISCRIMINATION

A. Race and National Origin Discrimination

Title VII of the 1964 Civil Rights Act of 1964, 42 U.S.C. § 2000e *et seq.*, is the federal government's primary antidiscrimination law, prohibiting covered employers from taking adverse employment action on the basis of race, color, sex, national origin and religion. Most of the race and sex discrimination cases in this Chapter include Title VII claims. In *Griggs v. Duke Power Co.*, below, the Court held that Title VII forbids not only practices adopted with a discriminatory motive, but also those that have a discriminatory effect.

In *Griggs,* a group of African-American employees sued a North Carolina power plant under Title VII, challenging their employer's requirement that they either possess a high school diploma or pass an intelligence test as a condition of employment or prerequisite to any job transfer at the plant. Section 703 of the Act authorized the use of an ability test, so long as it was not intended or used to discriminate. The district court held that the employer's prior policy of racial discrimination had ended, and the U.S. Court of Appeals, Fourth Circuit, upheld that determination. The employees appealed to the U.S. Supreme Court.

The Supreme Court held that Title VII requires the elimination of artificial, arbitrary, and unnecessary barriers to employment that discriminate on the basis of race. If a practice excludes minorities and cannot be shown to be related to job performance, it is prohibited, even if the employer lacked discriminatory intent. Title VII does not preclude the use of testing or measuring procedures so long as they are demonstrably a reasonable measure of job performance. In this case, the procedures were not related to job performance. Therefore, they violated Title VII. The Court reversed the lower court decisions. *Griggs v. Duke Power Co.,* 401 U.S. 424, 91 S.Ct. 849, 28 L.Ed.2d 158 (1971).

In the landmark case of *McDonnell Douglas Corp. v. Green*, below, the Court adopted an evidentiary framework to accommodate the lack of direct evidence that is characteristic of discrimination cases. Under this framework, the complaining party in a Title VII case has the initial burden of establishing a *prima facie* case of discrimination, which is satisfied when the party shows that she belongs to a protected class, has applied for a job that the employer was trying to fill, but was rejected despite being qualified for the position. The complaining party must also show that the employer continues to seek applicants with her qualifications. The burden then shifts to the employer to prove a legitimate business reason for its decision. The burden then reverts to the complaining party to demonstrate that the employer's stated reason for the adverse decision is a pretext. The complaining party retains the ultimate burden of persuasion throughout the proceeding.

In *McDonnell Douglas Corp. v. Green*, an African-American civil rights activist engaged in disruptive and illegal activity against his former employer as part of his protest that his discharge, and the employer's general hiring practices, were racially motivated. Soon after, the employer advertised for qualified personnel, but rejected the activist's reemployment application on the grounds of his illegal conduct. The activist filed a complaint with the Equal Employment Opportunity Commission (EEOC), claiming a Title VII violation. The EEOC found that there was reasonable cause to believe that the discharge violated § 704(a) of Title VII, which forbids discrimination against applicants or employees for protesting against discriminatory employment conditions. The activist eventually sued the employer in a federal district court, which held that his activity was not protected by § 703(a). The court dismissed the § 703 claim because the EEOC had made no finding with respect to that section. The court of appeals affirmed, and stated that § 703(a)(1), which prohibits discrimination in any employment decision, could also be used to make a viable claim. The employer sought review from the U.S. Supreme Court.

The Supreme Court held that a reasonable cause finding by the EEOC is not necessary in order for a party to raise a § 703(a)(1) claim at trial. It further held that in a private complaint under Title VII (other than a class action) the complaining party has the burden of establishing a *prima facie* case, which can be satisfied by showing that he belongs to a protected class, has applied for and is qualified for a job the employer is trying to fill, was rejected, and the employer continues to seek applicants with the complainant's qualifications. Even though the employee had done this, the employer carried its burden in showing that it had a reason for rejecting the applicant. The Court remanded the case, but allowed the activist an opportunity to show that the employer's reason for refusal was simply a pretext for a racially discriminatory decision. *McDonnell Douglas Corp. v. Green*, 411 U.S. 792, 93 S.Ct. 1817, 36 L.Ed.2d 668 (1973).

In the following 1977 employment discrimination case, the Court stated that under Title VII, employers accused of employment discrimination are entitled to meet the complaining parties' evidence with their own evidence to rebut an inference of discrimination.

A suburban St. Louis, Missouri, school district had a racial composition of only 1.8 percent black teachers, compared to an area-wide rate of 15.4 percent. School principals in the suburban district had almost unlimited discretion in their hiring policies. The district's attendance rate was only two percent black compared to 50 percent black students in the nearby St. Louis city school district. The U.S. government sued the suburban school district on the theory that the district had a pattern or practice of racially discriminatory hiring practices. The government based its case on statistical disparities, subjective hiring practices and evidence from 55 unsuccessful black teaching applicants.

The court ruled that there was no pattern or practice of discrimination in the district's hiring practices. It noted that the district had never operated a racially segregated dual school system, and that the small percentage of black employees corresponded with the small number of black students in the district. On appeal, the U.S. Court of Appeals, Eighth Circuit, reversed the district court's decision ruling that teacher-student ratios were irrelevant and that the correct comparison was between the district's black employment rate and that of the local labor market. The district petitioned to the U.S. Supreme Court, which granted certiorari.

The Court held that employment statistics were relevant in establishing a pattern or practice of race discrimination under Title VII. However, the court of appeals had erroneously substituted its judgment for that of the district court when it found that the government successfully proved its case. The court of appeals should have permitted the district to meet the government's evidence with its own evidence in rebuttal to contradict the evidence of employment discrimination. Title VII was inapplicable to public employers until March 24, 1972, and employers who used nondiscriminatory policies after that date were not in violation of the act despite prior transgressions. The district had hired progressively more black teachers in years after 1972, making necessary a remand to the district court for further findings consistent with the Court's opinion. *Hazelwood School District v. U.S.*, 433 U.S. 299, 97 S.Ct. 2736, 53 L.Ed.2d 768 (1977).

The government interest in ensuring public school teaching standards must be rationally related to the method used to advance the interest under the Fourteenth Amendment's Equal Protection Clause. The Court upheld a New York law which prohibited aliens from obtaining teacher certification, since it bore a rational relationship to the government's interest in inculcating students with civic values.

A New York law prohibited any person who was not a citizen of the United States from gaining certification as a public school teacher unless that person manifested an intention to apply for citizenship. Unless a teacher obtained certification, the teacher could not work in public schools in New York. The state Commissioner of Education was authorized to create exemptions from this prohibition, and had done so on several occasions. A citizen of Great Britain who had resided in the U.S. since 1965 and was married to a U.S. citizen sought certification and was denied. A Finnish citizen also applied and was rejected. Both applicants sued the commissioner in a federal district court, seeking to enjoin enforcement of the statute. The complaining parties argued that it violated the Equal Protection Clause of the Fourteenth Amendment. A federal district court held that the statute violated the Equal Protection Clause, and the Supreme Court granted review.

The Court held that the law did not violate the Equal Protection Clause. The state needed to show some rational relationship between excluding the aliens and a governmental interest. The Court stated that the New York statute bore a rational relationship to the state's interest in furthering its educational goals, especially with respect to having an obligation to promote civic virtues and understanding. The Court reversed and remanded the district court's decision. *Ambach v. Norwick*, 441 U.S. 68, 99 S.Ct. 1589, 60 L.Ed.2d 49 (1979).

In a 1980 employment case brought under Title VII, the Court concluded that the statute of limitations began to run on the date the teacher was denied tenure, rather than on his final employment date.

A black Liberian teacher taught at a state-supported Delaware college which was attended predominantly by blacks. The faculty committee on tenure recommended that he not be given tenure, and the college faculty senate and board of trustees adhered to this recommendation. The teacher then filed a grievance with the board's grievance committee, which took the case under advisement. The college offered him a one-year "terminal contract" in accordance with state policy. After the teacher had signed the terminal contract without objection, the grievance committee denied his grievance. The teacher then attempted to file a complaint with the Equal Employment Opportunity Commission (EEOC). However, he was notified that he would first have to exhaust state administrative remedies if he wanted to file a claim under Title VII of the 1964 Civil Rights Act. After the appropriate state agency waived its jurisdiction, the EEOC issued a right-to-sue letter.

The teacher then filed a lawsuit in a federal district court, alleging that the college had discriminated against him on the basis of his national origin in violation of Title VII and 42 U.S.C. § 1981. The district court dismissed the teacher's claims as untimely because the Title VII complaint had not been filed with the EEOC within 180 days and the § 1981 claim had not been filed in federal court within three years. The U.S. Court of Appeals, Third Circuit, reversed, holding that the limitations on Title VII and § 1981 did not begin to run until the teacher's terminal contract expired. It reasoned that a terminated employee should not have to file suit until termination had actually occurred. The U.S. Supreme Court granted certiorari.

The Court reversed the court of appeals' decision and reinstituted the district court's finding that both the Title VII and § 1981 claims were untimely. It held that statutes of limitations exist to ensure that plaintiffs promptly assert their rights and to protect employers from the burden of defending stale actions. The teacher's complaint did not state that the college discriminated against him on the basis of national origin, it simply concentrated on the college's denial of tenure. The teacher had failed to make out a *prima facie* case of employment discrimination under Title VII, because he had stated no continuing violation of his civil rights. The Court noted that, in fact, the teacher had received essentially the same treatment accorded to other teachers who were denied tenure. It was insufficient for the teacher to allege that his termination "gives present effect to the past illegal act and therefore perpetuates the consequences of forbidden discrimination." The statute of limitations began to run when the teacher was denied tenure, specifically, on the date when the college had offered him a terminal contract. As the district court was correct in that holding, the Court upheld its decision. *Delaware State College v. Ricks*, 449 U.S. 250, 101 S.Ct. 498, 66 L.Ed.2d 431 (1980).

In a 1986 memorandum decision, the Court compelled a private college to disclose employment records in an administrative proceeding before the Equal Employment Opportunity Commission (EEOC). The EEOC enforces Title VII and other antidiscrimination laws.

The U.S. Supreme Court refused to intervene in *EEOC v. Franklin & Marshall College*, 775 F.2d 110 (3d Cir.1985). The case arose when a professor, who had been employed at a private school in Pennsylvania for three years, was denied tenure. The school's professional standards committee, composed of the dean and five faculty members, recommended that tenure not be granted to the professor. The committee's recommendation was reaffirmed by the college's grievance committee. The professor then filed a complaint with the EEOC, alleging discrimination based on his French national origin. The EEOC issued a subpoena for the committee's records. Although the EEOC offered to accept the records with names deleted, the school refused to disclose them. The EEOC then filed suit in federal district court to compel the college to comply with the subpoena.

The district court ordered disclosure of the records and the college appealed. Before the court of appeals, the college argued that "the quality of a college and ... academic freedom, which has a constitutional dimension, is inextricably intertwined with a confidential peer review process." The court of appeals held that although the disclosure might burden the tenure process or invade the privacy of other professors, the records had to be disclosed because they were "relevant" to the EEOC's case. The records were ordered disclosed to the EEOC. The college appealed to the U.S. Supreme Court, but its petition for review was denied. *Franklin & Marshall College v. EEOC*, 476 U.S. 1163, 106 S.Ct. 2288, 90 L.Ed.2d 729 (1986).

The Court ruled in 1986 that a state administrative proceeding on a Title VII discrimination claim filed in a state court could be appealed to the federal court system when the state administrative proceeding remained unreviewed by state courts.

The University of Tennessee Agricultural Extension Service discharged a black employee, allegedly for inadequate work and misconduct on the job. The employee requested a hearing under the state Uniform Administrative Procedures Act to contest his termination. Before his administrative hearing took place the employee also filed a claim in a U.S. district court under federal civil rights laws, alleging that his dismissal had been racially motivated. The district court entered a temporary restraining order halting the state administrative hearing, but it later allowed the hearing to go forward. The hearing officer determined that the dismissal had not been racially motivated. The university moved to dismiss the employee's federal court lawsuit because it had already been resolved in the administrative hearing. The district court agreed and dismissed the case, holding that it would not afford the employee a chance to relitigate the same case in federal court.

The U.S. Court of Appeals, Sixth Circuit, reversed the decision and allowed the case to remain in federal court. The university appealed the decision to the U.S. Supreme Court, which held that the case should be heard by the district court. The Court ruled that a state administrative proceeding on a Title VII claim not reviewed by a higher state board could be heard in federal court. Since the decision made at the employee's administrative hearing was not reviewed by the state courts, it had no preclusive effect. The employee had the right to introduce his claim anew. *University of Tennessee v. Elliot*, 478 U.S. 788, 106 S.Ct. 3220, 92 L.Ed.2d 635 (1986).

In the following case, the Court clarified the standard it had announced in earlier Title VII cases, under which the complaining party first establishes a *prima facie* case of discrimination, giving rise to a presumption of unlawful discrimination that requires the employer to prove that adverse employment action was justified by legitimate, nondiscriminatory reasons.

A Missouri halfway house employed an African-American correctional officer. After being demoted and ultimately discharged, the officer sued the employer in a federal district court, alleging that these

manifest racial imbalance. The Court reversed the court of appeals' decision and upheld the plan. *United Steelworkers, Etc. v. Weber*, 443 U.S. 193, 99 S.Ct. 2721, 61 L.Ed.2d 480 (1979).

The Supreme Court invalidated an affirmative action plan approved by a Michigan school board and teachers' association which enhanced minority teacher rights in the event of a layoff. The plan would have permitted layoffs of more senior whites in an attempt to preserve the racial balance of the teaching force.

A Michigan local education board attempted to implement a collective bargaining agreement provision which impaired the seniority rights of certain white teachers in favor of less senior minority teachers in the event of a layoff. A group of white teachers sued the board in a federal district court under the Equal Protection Clause and Title VII, as well as state law. The court ruled that the importance of providing minority teachers as role models for minority students as a remedy for past societal discrimination justified the layoff provision. The U.S. Court of Appeals, Sixth Circuit, affirmed the decision and the white teachers appealed to the Supreme Court. The Court held that the board had discriminated against the white teachers in violation of the Equal Protection Clause. A total of six different opinions were filed in the case as the justices failed to agree on an appropriate standard of review for government affirmative action programs.

The majority opinion rejected the school board's argument that race-based layoffs were necessary to remedy the effects of societal discrimination. Clear and convincing evidence must be presented to prove that the government entity in question had engaged in past racial discrimination. The Court rejected the role model justification for retaining minority teachers, because it would allow race-based layoffs long after they were needed to cure the ills of past discrimination. "Carried to its logical extreme, the idea that black students are better off with black teachers could lead to the very system the Court rejected in *Brown v. Board of Education. . . .*"

The Court held that even if the school board had sufficient justification for engaging in remedial or benign racial discrimination, a layoff of white teachers was too drastic and intrusive a remedy. While hiring goals and promotion policies favorable to minorities were acceptable under the Equal Protection Clause, the actual layoff based on racial criteria was unconstitutional. "Denial of future employment is not as intrusive as loss of an existing job." The blanket rejection of race-based layoffs in the majority opinion was tempered by the observation of

Justice O'Connor who wrote in a separate opinion that the race-based layoffs might be constitutionally acceptable if narrowly tailored to reflect the percentage of qualified minority teachers in the school district's area labor pool. However, the layoffs were geared to the number of minority students, and therefore, were impermissible. The lower court rulings were reversed. *Wygant v. Jackson Board of Education*, 476 U.S. 267, 106 S.Ct. 1842, 90 L.Ed.2d 260 (1986).

In 1987, the Supreme Court held that an affirmative action plan which took sex into account as one factor in the hiring decision was valid. The plan was not a quota system, and it presented a case-by-case approach. Further, the Court reaffirmed its decision in *United Steelworkers v. Weber,* above, that an employer seeking to implement an affirmative action plan need not point to its own prior discriminatory practices, but need only identify a conspicuous imbalance in traditionally segregated job categories.

A California county transportation agency voluntarily adopted an affirmative action plan. The plan allowed the agency to consider, as one factor, the sex of an applicant in making promotions. The long term goal of the plan was to achieve a workforce whose composition reflected the proportion of women and minorities in the area labor force. When a road dispatcher position opened up, the agency promoted one of the qualified female applicants. A male employee who was passed over sued the agency in a federal district court. The court found that the woman had been selected because of her sex and invalidated the agency's plan. The court of appeals reversed this decision, and the man further appealed the case to the U.S. Supreme Court.

The Supreme Court held that the agency had appropriately taken the woman's sex into account as one factor in promoting her. It found that the agency plan was flexible and presented a case-by-case approach to gradually improving the representation of women and minorities in the agency. Thus, the plan was fully consistent with Title VII. Even though the male candidate had shown a *prima facie* case of discrimination on the part of the agency, the agency had shown a nondiscriminatory rationale for its decision, namely the affirmative action plan. Further, the Court noted that an employer need not identify its own prior discriminatory practices to justify its adoption of such a plan. It need only show a conspicuous imbalance in traditionally segregated areas of employment. Since the plan had taken into account distinctions in qualifications to provide guidance, the agency had not merely engaged in blind hiring by the numbers. The Court affirmed the court of appeals' decision and upheld the affirmative action plan. *Johnson v. Transportation Agency, Santa Clara County,* 480 U.S. 616, 107 S.Ct. 1442, 94 L.Ed.2d 615 (1987).

In *City of Richmond v. J.A. Croson Co.*, below, the Court held that an affirmative action plan must be justified by a compelling governmental interest, which can be shown by evidence of past discrimination by the entity which maintains the plan. According to the Court, it is not enough to assert in only general terms that past discrimination has occurred.

The city of Richmond, Virginia adopted a plan requiring prime contractors awarded city construction contracts to subcontract at least 30 percent of the dollar amount of each contract to one or more minority business enterprises (MBEs). These were defined as businesses from anywhere in the country which were owned and controlled (at least 51 percent) by black, Spanish-speaking, Asian, Indian, Eskimo, or Aleut citizens. The plan purported to be remedial in nature, but no direct evidence was presented at the hearing prior to its adoption that the city had discriminated on the basis of race in letting contracts. After the sole bidder on a city contract was denied a waiver of the MBE requirement and lost its contract, it sued the city under 42 U.S.C. § 1983, alleging that the plan was unconstitutional under the Fourteenth Amendment's Equal Protection Clause. The federal court upheld the plan and the U.S. Court of Appeals, Fourth Circuit, affirmed. The U.S. Supreme Court vacated and remanded the case for further consideration in light of *Wygant v. Jackson Board of Educ.*, above. On remand, the court of appeals held that the plan violated the Constitution. The case again came before the Supreme Court.

The Court held that the city had failed to demonstrate a compelling governmental interest through evidence of past discrimination in the city's construction industry. It is not enough to generally assert that past discrimination has occurred. Next, the Court held that the plan was not narrowly tailored to remedy the effects of prior discrimination since it allowed minority entrepreneurs from anywhere in the country to obtain a preference over other citizens based solely on race. The lower court decision was affirmed. *City of Richmond v. J.A. Croson Co.,* 488 U.S. 469, 109 S.Ct. 706, 102 L.Ed.2d 854 (1989).

An affirmative action decree may have a later restrictive effect upon the rights of individuals who were not participants in the

original litigation, who may then reopen the case and attempt to join it, as shown in the following case.

In 1974, the NAACP and seven black persons entered into consent decrees with an Alabama city and a county personnel board. The decrees stated that the city and board had practiced discriminatory employment practices in violation of Title VII and other civil rights statutes. They mandated an extensive remedial plan, including annual hiring and promotional goals for black firefighters. A federal district court approved the decrees, which were then challenged by the city firefighters' labor organization in a reverse discrimination lawsuit. The court ruled against the firefighters' association and its decision was affirmed by the U.S. Court of Appeals, Eleventh Circuit.

A second group of white firefighters then sued the city and board in a federal district court, claiming that they had been denied promotions in favor of less qualified blacks. The district court dismissed their lawsuit, ruling that the city was required to promote blacks under the consent decree. The firefighters appealed to the Eleventh Circuit Court of Appeals, which ruled in favor of the firefighters. It found that they had not participated in the consent decrees and were bringing independent racial discrimination claims. The court rejected the doctrine of impermissible collateral attack, which had been used by other U.S. circuit courts to immunize parties participating in consent decrees from reverse discrimination complaints by nonparties. The U.S. Supreme Court agreed to hear the appeal of both the city and a group of intervening black firefighters.

The Supreme Court noted that nonparties are not bound by judgments and decrees among parties to a lawsuit. Moreover, Rule 19(a) of the Federal Rules of Civil Procedure required mandatory joinder where parties to the lawsuit had inconsistent obligations to persons claiming an interest in the action. Litigants are presumed to know the nature and scope of their litigation, and they should bear the burden of bringing in additional parties when required. The Court rejected the argument that this burden would discourage civil rights litigation because of the perceived difficulty in identifying numerous adverse claimants. This difficulty was an effect of the broad remedial relief that resulted from consent decrees in racial discrimination cases. Parties seeking the aid of courts to change existing employment policies and employers were best able to bear the burden of identifying potentially affected third parties. The Supreme Court affirmed the court of appeals' decision. *Martin v. Wilks,* 490 U.S. 755, 109 S.Ct. 2180, 104 L.Ed.2d 835 (1989).

In the following case, the Supreme Court reaffirmed the application of strict scrutiny to all racial classifications for federal, state and local governments. Moreover, the Court narrowed affirmative action program requirements to ensure a sufficiently detailed examination.

The Federal Lands Highway Division, part of the U.S. Department of Transportation, awarded a highway construction contract to a Colorado contractor. The contractor received additional compensation for hiring a subcontractor controlled by "socially and economically disadvantaged individuals." The highway division construed the relevant federal statute as containing a presumption that African-American, Hispanic, Asian-Pacific, Subcontinent Asian, Native American, and female individuals were socially and economically disadvantaged. The contractor rejected the low bidder on the subcontract, because it was not controlled by disadvantaged persons. The subcontractor filed suit in a federal district court, claiming that the race-based presumption violated its right to equal protection. The district court granted the U.S. government's motion for summary judgment, and the U.S. Court of Appeals, Tenth Circuit, affirmed. The subcontractor appealed to the U.S. Supreme Court.

The Supreme Court reversed the Tenth Circuit decision, ruling that the standard of review for federal, state and local governments should be strict scrutiny. Affirming the principles laid out in *City of Richmond v. J.A. Croson Co.,* above, the Court held that the Fifth and Fourteenth Amendments require that all racial classifications be narrowly tailored to further a compelling government interest. The Court rejected the government's plea for a less rigorous standard, ruling that only strict scrutiny would submit racial classifications to a sufficiently detailed examination. It noted that heightened scrutiny would "smoke out illegitimate uses of race by assuring that the legislative body is pursuing a goal important enough to warrant use of a highly suspect tool." The Court reversed and remanded the case to determine whether the use of the subcontractor compensation clauses could be properly described as compelling. *Adarand Constructors, Inc. v. Pena*, 515 U.S. 200, 115 S.Ct. 2097, 132 L.Ed.2d 158 (1995).

C. Sex Discrimination

In 1974, three teachers challenged school district rules which required them to take mandatory unpaid leaves of absence at specified times during and after childbirth. The Supreme Court

held that the mandatory cut-off dates were arbitrary and bore no rational relationship to the state interest in continuity of instruction. Because the rules created an irrebuttable presumption of physical incompetency by pregnant teachers even where contrary medical evidence was present, the rules violated the Due Process Clause of the Constitution.

Two public school teachers in Ohio and one in Virginia brought lawsuits challenging maternity leave rules maintained by their employers. The Cleveland, Ohio, school board rule required a pregnant teacher to take unpaid maternity leave five months before the expected childbirth. The teacher could return to work at the next regular school semester following the date when her child attained the age of three months. The Chesterfield County, Virginia, school board rule required teachers to take leaves of absence four months before the anticipated childbirth with reemployment guaranteed no later than the first day of the school year following the date they were declared re-eligible. Both rules required a physician's written statement prior to re-employment. The teachers challenged the constitutionality of the mandatory leave of absence rules in separate federal actions that were later consolidated on appeal.

The United States Supreme Court held that the rules of both school boards regarding leave of absence at mandatory and fixed time periods violated the Due Process Clause of the Fourteenth Amendment. The Court said that the arguments advanced by the school districts in defense of their rules, such as continuity of classroom instruction, physical inability of teachers to teach and health of the teacher and unborn child contained arbitrary irrebuttable presumptions. The arbitrary fourth or fifth month maternity leave rules bore no rational relationship to the state interest in continuity in the classroom, and could work against continuity by requiring that leaves be taken in mid-semester even when the teacher could have finished the semester.

The Court then held that the return to work provisions of the rules were valid with respect to physical examination before returning to work and the dates of reemployment. However, the Court struck down the Cleveland, Ohio, board's rule requiring teachers to wait for reemployment until the child was three months old. The Court found the rule in violation of due process because the irrebuttable presumptions contained in the rule bore no rational relationship to any legitimate school interest. *Cleveland Board of Education v. LaFleur*, 414 U.S. 632, 94 S.Ct. 791, 39 L.Ed.2d 52 (1974).

In 1983, the Supreme Court held that differential treatment of pregnant employees is gender-based discrimination because only women can become pregnant. However, in an earlier case, the Court held that a school district could deny a pregnant teacher the benefit of her accumulated sick leave pay for the period in which she wasn't working.

When a California school teacher became pregnant, her school district threatened to require her to stop working on a date earlier than she and her doctor believed necessary, and threatened to deny her the benefit of accumulated sick leave pay while she was not working. The teacher subsequently filed a sex discrimination charge with the Equal Employment Opportunity Commission, and then sued the school district under Title VII. A federal district court ruled in her favor, finding that the district's maternity leave policy violated Title VII. The U.S. Court of Appeals, Ninth Circuit, affirmed the district court's decision. However, on further appeal to the U.S. Supreme Court, the judgment was vacated and the case remanded under *General Electric Co. v. Gilbert,* 429 U.S. 125, 97 S.Ct. 401, 50 L.Ed.2d 343 (1976), in which the Court held that the failure of a disability benefits plan to cover pregnancy-related disabilities did not amount to a Title VII violation, absent any indication that the exclusion of pregnancy disability benefits was a pretext for discriminating against women. *Richmond Unified School District v. Berg,* 434 U.S. 158, 98 S.Ct. 623, 54 L.Ed.2d 375 (1977).

The Supreme Court held that two New York City agencies could be found liable for damages for maintaining an official policy under which pregnant employees were compelled to take unpaid leaves of absence. Because of the case's significance in the development of 42 U.S.C. § 1983 case law, it is more fully summarized in section III of this chapter, below.

A group of female employees of New York City's Department of Social Services and Board of Education sued the department and its commissioner, the board and its chancellor and the city and mayor for constitutional rights violations under 42 U.S.C. § 1983. They complained that the department and board maintained official policies of compelling pregnant employees to take unpaid leaves of absence before such leaves were required for medical reasons. A federal district court ruled that the group's petition was moot because the city had since changed its policy, but also held that requiring pregnant employees to take a leave of absence was unconstitutional. It denied an award of back wages to the complaining parties because this would run afoul of the sovereign immunity principle embodied in the Eleventh Amendment and common law. The U.S. Supreme Court reversed the district court's decision, holding that nothing in the legislative history of § 1983 precluded municipal liability. Both agencies had violated the employees' constitutional rights. *Monell v. Department of Social Services*, 436 U.S. 658, 98 S.Ct. 2018, 56 L.Ed.2d 611 (1978).

In an employment discrimination lawsuit filed under Title VII, the aggrieved party bears the burden of proving that the employer's refusal to hire is a pretext for unlawful discrimination.

In an employment discrimination case against a state college, a federal district court ruled that the college had discriminated against a professor on the basis of sex. The U.S. Court of Appeals, Fifth Circuit, affirmed the decision, ruling that Title VII of the 1964 Civil Rights Act, 42 U.S.C. § 2000e *et seq.*, required the college to prove absence of discriminatory motive. In a per curiam opinion, the U.S. Supreme Court held that this burden was too great. It ruled that in an employment discrimination case, the employer need only "articulate some legitimate, nondiscriminatory reason for the employee's rejection." In other words, the employee has the burden of proving that the reason for the employee's rejection was a mere pretext. The Court vacated the court of appeals' decision and remanded the case for reconsideration under the lesser standard. *Trustees of Keene State College v. Sweeney*, 439 U.S. 24, 99 S.Ct. 295, 58 L.Ed.2d 216 (1978).

A Title VII wage discrimination claim does not limit available remedies under the Equal Pay Act. Title VII bars sex-based wage discrimination but permits differentials if they are justifiable under the Equal Pay Act.

Female guards at an Oregon county jail were paid substantially less than male guards at the same facility. The county eliminated the female section of the jail, transferred its prisoners to a neighboring county and terminated the employment of the female guards. The terminated guards sued the county in a federal district court under Title VII of the 1964 Civil Rights Act, 42 U.S.C. § 2000e *et seq.,* seeking back wages and alleging that they had been unlawfully paid unequal wages for substantially similar work as that performed by the male guards. The court held that the male guards supervised over ten times as many prisoners and did less clerical work than their female counterparts. It ruled that the females were not entitled to equal pay because they did not perform substantially similar work, and that the pay inequity was not attributable to sex discrimination. The court held that because the females had not met the standard of the 1963 Equal Pay Act, 29 U.S.C. § 206(d), no Title VII action was possible. The female employees appealed to the U.S. Court of Appeals, Ninth Circuit, which reversed, holding that alleged sex discrimination victims were entitled to Title VII protection. The county appealed to the U.S. Supreme Court.

The Court first noted that the case did not involve a comparable worth analysis, but was simply a sex discrimination case. It stated that the court of appeals had correctly ruled that Title VII wage discrimination claims could be brought in this situation, and that the female guards were not limited to remedies under the Equal Pay Act. Title VII by its terms barred sex-based wage discrimination but permitted differentials if they could be justified under the Equal Pay Act. This included seniority, merit, quantity or quality of work or other bona fide factors. Title VII claims for sex-based wage discrimination were thus permissible. In this case, the county had evaluated the female guards' job worth at 95 percent of the male guards, yet had paid them only 70 percent as much. The court of appeals had correctly ruled that this presented a viable Title VII complaint for sex discrimination. *County of Washington v. Gunther*, 452 U.S. 161, 101 S.Ct. 2242, 68 L.Ed.2d 751 (1981).

Title IX of the 1972 Education Amendments, 20 U.S.C. § 1681 *et seq.*, prohibits gender discrimination in education programs and activities which receive federal financial assistance. Sanctions for noncompliance include termination of funding for specific future grants. In 1982, the Supreme Court ruled that Title IX's nondiscrimination requirements applied not only to students and academic policies, but to employment as well.

In 1975, the U.S. Department of Education issued regulations prohibiting gender-based employment discrimination in all federally-funded education programs. The regulations pertained to many employment practices including job classification and pregnancy leave. A tenured Connecticut public school teacher took a one-year maternity leave. The school, which received Title IX funds, refused to rehire the teacher and she filed an administrative appeal, resulting in an education department request to investigate school district employment practices. The district refused the request for an investigation and sued the U.S. government in a federal district court, which granted an injunction against enforcing the nondiscrimination regulations.

The court ruled that Title IX's nondiscrimination mandate applied only to discrimination practices against students and not to teachers and employment practices. The district court also rejected another Title IX complaint by a Connecticut public school guidance counselor who claimed that her school district gave her discriminatory work assignments and failed to renew her contract on the basis of her sex. The U.S. Court of Appeals, Second Circuit, consolidated the two cases and reversed the district court decisions. The U.S. Supreme Court agreed to review the case.

The Supreme Court found no reason to limit Title IX to discrimination complaints by students alone. Section 901(a) of the statute broadly stated that "No person in the United States shall, on the basis of sex, be excluded from participation in, be denied the benefits of, or be subjected to discrimination under any education program or activity receiving Federal financial assistance. . . ." An extensive review of the statute's legislative history revealed evidence that employment practices were within the scope of Title IX. The Court affirmed the appeals court's decision, although it rejected the court's attempt to expand potential funding termination beyond the particular program which was found to be in noncompliance. The Court remanded the case with instructions to apply the act to the cases, permitting funding termination on a program-specific basis only, if the records justified a finding of gender-based discrimination in a federally-funded program. *North Haven Board of Education v. Bell*, 456 U.S. 512, 102 S.Ct. 1912, 72 L.Ed.2d 299 (1982).

In 1978, Congress amended Title VII by enacting the Pregnancy Discrimination Act to prohibit discrimination on the basis of pregnancy. In the following case, the Court held that an employer health plan which provided reduced benefits for certain employees violated the act.

Following the enactment of the Pregnancy Discrimination Act, an employer amended its health insurance plan to provide its female employees with hospitalization benefits for pregnancy-related conditions to the same extent as for other medical conditions. However, the plan provided less extensive pregnancy benefits for spouses of male employees. The employer then filed an action in a Virginia federal district court challenging the Equal Employment Opportunity

Commission's guidelines which indicated that its health insurance plan was unlawful. The EEOC joined the action, asserting that the plan was discriminatory. The district court ruled for the employer, but the U.S. Court of Appeals reversed. The case then came before the U.S. Supreme Court.

The Supreme Court stated that pregnancy limitations for spouses of male employees discriminated against the men who worked for the employer. The plan provided less protection to married male employees than it did to married female employees. The Pregnancy Discrimination Act provided that it is discriminatory to exclude pregnancy coverage from an otherwise inclusive benefits plan. The act not only overturned the holding of *General Electric Co. v. Gilbert*, 429 U.S. 125, 97 S.Ct. 401, 50 L.Ed.2d 343 (1976), which held that it was lawful to exclude disabilities caused by pregnancy from a disability plan which provided general coverage; it also rejected that Court's reasoning that differential treatment of pregnancy is not gender-based discrimination even though only women can become pregnant. The Court affirmed the court of appeals' decision for the EEOC. *Newport News Shipbuilding and Dry Dock Co. v. EEOC,* 462 U.S. 669, 103 S.Ct. 2622, 77 L.Ed.2d 89 (1983).

In *Meritor Savings Bank, FSB v. Vinson*, below, the Court held that sexual harassment is a form of sex discrimination that is protected by Title VII. It reasoned that sexual harassment can create a hostile work environment.

A woman worked for a bank in various capacities over a four-year period. Her supervisor allegedly harassed her during this period, demanding sexual favors, and forcibly raping her on several occasions. When the employee took an indefinite sick leave, the bank discharged her. She then brought suit against the bank, claiming that she had been subjected to sexual harassment in violation of Title VII. On conflicting trial testimony, a federal district court ruled for the bank, finding that the bank did not have notice of any harassment, and that its policies forbade such behavior. The U.S. Court of Appeals reversed, and appeal was taken to the U.S. Supreme Court.

The Supreme Court first noted that sexual harassment is clearly a form of sex discrimination prohibited by Title VII. It then stated that while absence of notice of harassment will not necessarily shield an employer from liability, employers are not always liable automatically for sexual harassment by their supervisory employees. The Court determined that Congress intended agency principles to apply to some extent. The Court also held that it was not improper to admit into evidence the complainant's "sexually provocative speech and dress." Even though voluntariness in the sense of consent is not a defense to a sexual harassment claim, such information bears on the issue of whether the complainant has found particular sexual advances unwelcome. The Court affirmed the court of appeals' holding, and remanded the case. *Meritor Savings Bank, FSB v. Vinson*, 477 U.S. 57, 106 S.Ct. 2399, 91 L.Ed.2d 49 (1986).

In an action based upon a state civil rights enforcement agency's jurisdiction over a private school, the Supreme Court ruled that federal courts should permit the state agency proceedings to run their course.

An Ohio private school refused to renew the contract of a teacher after it discovered that she was pregnant, due to its belief that a mother should stay home with her young children. The teacher contacted an attorney and threatened the school with a lawsuit. The school rescinded its nonrenewal decision, but then terminated her employment because she had circumvented the school's internal grievance procedure. This, the school claimed, violated the "biblical chain of command." After the termination, the teacher filed a sex discrimination complaint with the Ohio Civil Rights Commission (OCRC). When the OCRC began its investigation of the complaint, the school sued in federal district court to prevent any action by the OCRC. The school based its arguments on the First Amendment's guarantee of freedom of religion. The district court dismissed the complaint, but the U.S. Court of Appeals, Sixth Circuit, reversed the decision. The court of appeals agreed that the OCRC investigation would impermissibly interfere with the practice of the school's religious beliefs.

On appeal to the U.S. Supreme Court, the district court's ruling was reinstated. The federal courts should be reluctant to interfere with a state administrative or judicial proceeding until the proceeding is completed. Further, the Supreme Court was unwilling to find that merely because an administrative body had jurisdiction over a religious school the school's First Amendment rights would be violated. The OCRC was allowed to go forward with its investigation. *Ohio Civil Rights Commission v. Dayton Christian Schools*, 477 U.S. 619, 106 S.Ct. 2718, 91 L.Ed.2d 512 (1986).

In certain cases, an employer may be motivated to discharge an employee for more than one reason. In the following case, the Supreme Court held that if a dual motive for the action exists, and

one is discriminatory, the employer must demonstrate that it would have made the same decision absent the impermissible motive of discrimination. **The Civil Rights Act of 1991 changes the result reached in this case by prohibiting only certain injunctive relief, such as reinstatement.**

A woman worked for a nationwide accounting firm as a senior manager and was proposed as a candidate for partnership. She was refused admission as a partner and sued the firm in a federal district court under Title VII, charging that the firm had discriminated against her on the basis of sex in its partnership decisions. The district court found that the firm had discriminated against the manager, but held that it could avoid equitable relief if it could prove by clear and convincing evidence that it would have made the same decision in the absence of a discriminatory motive. The U.S. Court of Appeals, District of Columbia Circuit, affirmed, and noted that the firm could avoid all liability if it showed that it would have made the same decision without the discrimination (again, by clear and convincing evidence). The case came before the U.S. Supreme Court.

The Supreme Court held that under Title VII, the employer could avoid liability if it showed by a mere preponderance of the evidence that it would have made the same decision even if it had not taken the manager's gender into account. This preserved the employer's freedom of choice. The Court then reversed and remanded the case for a determination of whether the same decision would have been made absent the discrimination. *Price Waterhouse v. Hopkins*, 490 U.S. 228, 109 S.Ct. 1775, 104 L.Ed.2d 268 (1989).

[Note: Under the Civil Rights Act of 1991, if it is shown that discrimination is a contributing factor in the employment decision, then (assuming that the employer can show that it would have made the same decision absent the discrimination) courts will be prohibited from ordering certain injunctive relief—like reinstatement. However, money damages may still be available.]

Discrimination on the basis of sex violates Title VII unless the employer is able to establish a legitimate business reason for its policies. The employer in the following case attempted to justify a discriminatory policy based upon the risk to female reproductive health. The Court held that if a class of employees wishes to be exposed to risks that another class is encountering, the employer cannot prevent those employees from so exposing themselves.

A company manufactured batteries, the primary ingredient of which was lead. As a result, in 1982, the company began a policy of excluding pregnant women and women capable of bearing children from jobs involving lead exposure. In 1984, a group of affected employees initiated a class action against the company, challenging its fetal protection policy as sex discrimination that violated Title VII. A federal district court granted summary judgment to the company, finding that it had established a business necessity defense. The U.S. Court of Appeals, Seventh Circuit, affirmed, and the employees petitioned the U.S. Supreme Court for review.

The Court noted that there was a clear bias in the company's policy, allowing fertile men but not women the choice of risking their reproductive health. Thus, there was clear sex discrimination involved. Even though there was no malevolent motive involved, the policy could not be termed "neutral." Accordingly, the only way for the company to justify the discrimination was by establishing that gender was a bona fide occupational qualification (BFOQ). The Court then stated that the company could not show a valid BFOQ. Decisions about the welfare of future children must be left to parents rather than their employers.

The Court next looked to the issue of tort liability and found that it was unlikely that a person could bring a negligence action against the company at a later date for prenatal injuries. Since the company complied with the lead standard developed by the Occupational Safety and Health Administration and issued warnings to its female employees about the dangers of lead exposure, it was not negligent and it would be difficult for a court to find liability against the company. The Court therefore reversed the judgment and struck down the company's fetal protection policy. *International Union, UAW v. Johnson Controls*, 499 U.S. 187, 111 S.Ct. 1196, 113 L.Ed.2d 158 (1991).

Title VII prohibits employment discrimination by employers that have 15 or more employees during 20 or more calendar weeks in the current or preceding calendar year. For purposes of determining when an employer "has" an employee, the Court held that an employer has an employee if an employment relationship exists between the parties.

An employee of an Illinois educational materials company filed a sex discrimination complaint against her employer with the EEOC, asserting that she should have received a promotion. The employer then fired her. The EEOC filed a federal district court action on behalf of the employee against the employer for unlawful retaliation under Title VII. The employer moved to dismiss the case, stating that it did not have 15 employees during 20 weeks in the past two years and did not come within the coverage of the act. The court agreed with the employer, and the U.S. Court of Appeals, Seventh Circuit, affirmed. The U.S. Supreme Court agreed to review the case.

On appeal, the employer argued that an employer "has" an employee for Title VII purposes only when it is actually compensating an individual on a particular working day. The EEOC argued that the appropriate test for when an employer has an employee is whether the parties have an employment relationship on the day in question. This test was already used by the EEOC in age discrimination regulations and the U.S. Department of Labor in Family and Medical Leave Act regulations. The Court agreed with the EEOC that an employer has an employee if an employment relationship exists between the parties. Applying this test, the employer had employment relationships with 15 or more employees for 38 weeks of the calendar year in question and was an employer within the meaning of Title VII. The Court reversed and remanded the case. *Walters v. Metropolitan Educational Enterprises, Inc.*, 519 U.S. 202, 117 S.Ct. 660, 136 L.Ed.2d 644 (1997).

In 1998, the Supreme Court extended Title VII protections to same-sex harassment cases. The Court found that Title VII does not bar a sex discrimination claim when the complaining party and alleged perpetrator are of the same sex.

A Louisiana offshore service employed a roustabout to work on oil platforms in the Gulf of Mexico. He claimed that he was forcibly subjected to sex-related humiliating actions, assault and threats of rape by coworkers, including two employees with supervisory authority. When he complained to the employer's safety compliance clerk, the clerk did nothing and stated that he had also been subjected to abuse by the coworkers. Eventually, the roustabout quit and sued the employer in the U.S. District Court for the Eastern District of Louisiana, alleging sex discrimination in violation of Title VII of the Civil Rights Act of 1964. The court granted summary judgment to the employer, holding that the roustabout had no viable cause of action under Title VII since the harassment was caused by same-sex coworkers. The U.S. Court of Appeals, Fifth Circuit, affirmed the judgment and the roustabout appealed to the U.S. Supreme Court.

The Court stated that sex discrimination in the form of same-sex harassment that is so objectively offensive that it alters the conditions of employment is actionable under Title VII. The Court found no language in Title VII that bars a sex discrimination claim when the complaining party and alleged perpetrators are of the same sex, and it rejected the employer's assertion that allowing the claim would transform Title VII into a general code of workplace civility. The Court noted that not all verbal or physical harassment in the workplace is prohibited by Title VII, since it does not cover conduct that is not severe or pervasive enough to create an objectively hostile or abusive work environment. The Court reversed the lower court decisions and remanded the case. *Oncale v. Sundowner Offshore Services, Inc.*, 523 U.S. 75, 118 S.Ct. 998, 140 L.Ed.2d 201 (1998).

In *Burlington Industries, Inc. v. Ellerth*, the Supreme Court held that an employer may be held vicariously liable for a supervisor's actions under Title VII when the supervisor harasses a subordinate, even in the absence of tangible employment action against the subordinate. The decision established a defense for employers where the subordinate fails to abide by the employer's reporting procedures under a sexual harassment policy.

An Illinois employee alleged that she was subjected to constant sexual harassment from a supervisor who had the authority to hire and promote, subject to higher approval, but who was not considered a policymaker. The employee refused all of the supervisor's advances, but suffered no tangible retaliation and was even promoted once. Despite her knowledge of the employer's sexual harassment policy, she never complained to upper level management about the supervisor's behavior. The employee resigned and sued the employer in a federal district court alleging sexual harassment and constructive discharge in violation of Title VII of the Civil Rights Act of 1964. The district court granted the employer's motion for summary judgment and the U.S. Court of Appeals, Seventh Circuit, reversed. The U.S. Supreme Court granted review.

The Supreme Court held that Title VII imposes vicarious liability on an employer for actionable discrimination caused by a supervisor with authority over an employee. When a supervisor discriminates in the terms and conditions of a subordinate's employment, his actions draw upon his authority over the subordinate. However, in cases where there is no tangible employment action taken against the employee, the employer may assert a two-pronged affirmative defense. First, the employer must prove that it exercised reasonable care to prevent and promptly correct any sexual harassment. Second, it must prove that the employee unreasonably failed to avail herself of any employer remedies or failed to avoid harm otherwise. However, the affirmative defense is unavailable to the employer when the supervisor's harassment culminates in a tangible employment act such as discharge or demotion. The Court remanded the case for further consideration. *Burlington Industries, Inc. v. Ellerth*, 524 U.S. 742, 118 S.Ct. 2257, 141 L.Ed.2d 633 (1998).

In a companion case decided on the same day as *Ellerth*, the Supreme Court found a Florida city vicariously liable for maintaining a hostile work environment because of ongoing harassment of an employee by her supervisors.

A Florida city lifeguard had two male supervisors who controlled all aspects of her job, including work assignments and discipline. She was subjected to severe and pervasive unwelcome touching, sexual comments, and other offensive behavior from the two supervisors. Although the city had a policy against sexual harassment, it failed to disseminate the policy to the lifeguard's department. Also, the policy did not assure that any harassing supervisors could be bypassed in registering complaints. The employee did not report this harassment to higher management from whom she was completely isolated. She eventually resigned and sued the city in a federal district court alleging sexual harassment in violation of Title VII of the Civil Rights Act of 1964 and 42 U.S.C. § 1983. The district court found the city liable for the harassment. The U.S. Court of Appeals, Eleventh Circuit, reversed. Using the same reasoning as it did in *Ellerth,* the Supreme Court found the city vicariously liable for the hostile environment created by the supervisors. The Court reversed and remanded the case for reinstatement of the district court decision. *Faragher v. City of Boca Raton*, 524 U.S. 775, 118 S.Ct. 2275, 141 L.Ed.2d 451 (1998).

D. Other Employment Discrimination Cases

When teachers select an exclusive bargaining representative, they impliedly surrender some of their personal choice, including some forms of religious accommodation. This follows from the premise that the state has a strong interest in hearing only one voice in collective bargaining matters.

A Connecticut high school teacher belonged to a church which required its members to refrain from secular employment during designated holy days. This practice caused the teacher to miss approximately six school days each year for religious purposes. The teacher worked under terms of a bargaining agreement between the school board and his teachers' union which allowed only three days of leave for religious observation. The agreement also allowed leave for "necessary personal business" which could not be used for religious purposes. The teacher took either unauthorized leave for the extra three religious days he required, scheduled hospital visits on church holidays, or worked on those holidays. He repeatedly asked for permission to use three days of his "necessary personal business" leave for religious purposes. He also offered to pay for a substitute teacher if the school board would pay him for the extra days that he missed. These alternatives were turned down by the school board. When all administrative alternatives were exhausted, he filed a lawsuit alleging that the board's "necessary personal business" leave policy was discriminatory on the basis of religion. A federal district court dismissed the case and the teacher appealed to the U.S. Court of Appeals, Second Circuit, which held the board was bound to accept one of the teacher's proposed solutions unless it caused an undue hardship for the board.

The U.S. Supreme Court modified the appellate court's decision. It held that the school district was not required to accept the teacher's proposals even if acceptance would not result in "undue hardship." The board was only bound to offer a fair and reasonable accommodation of the teacher's religious needs. The bargaining agreement policy of allowing three days off for religious purposes was found to be reasonable. Because none of the lower courts had decided whether this policy had been administered fairly the case was remanded for a determination of that question. *Ansonia Board of Education v. Philbrook*, 479 U.S. 60, 107 S.Ct. 367, 93 L.Ed.2d 305 (1986).

In 1987, the Supreme Court decided that a Florida teacher with tuberculosis should have an opportunity to demonstrate to a federal district court that she was entitled to Rehabilitation Act protection, since she alleged that she was otherwise qualified to hold her job and that she could be reasonably accommodated.

The U.S. Supreme Court ruled that tuberculosis is a disability under § 504 of the Rehabilitation Act. Federal statutes define an individual with a disability as "any person who (i) has a physical or mental impairment which substantially limits one or more of such person's major life activities, (ii) has a record of such impairment or (iii) is regarded as having such an impairment." It defines "physical impairment" as disorders affecting, among other things, the respiratory system and defines "major life activities" as "functions such as caring for one's self . . . and working." The case involved a Florida elementary school teacher who was discharged because of the continued recurrence of tuberculosis. The teacher sued the school board under § 504 but a U.S. district court dismissed her claims. However, the U.S. Court of Appeals, Eleventh Circuit, reversed the district court's decision and held that persons with contagious diseases fall within § 504's coverage. The school board appealed to the U.S. Supreme Court.

The Supreme Court ruled that tuberculosis was a disability under § 504 because it affected the respiratory system and affected the teacher's ability to work. The school board contended that in defining an individual with a disability under § 504, the contagious effects of a disease can be distinguished from the disease's physical effects. However, the Court reasoned that the teacher's contagion and her physical impairment both resulted from tuberculosis. It would be unfair to allow an employer to distinguish between a disease's potential effect on others and its effect on the afflicted employee in order to justify discriminatory treatment. Allowing discrimination based on the contagious effects of a physical impairment would be inconsistent with the underlying purpose of § 504. That purpose is to ensure that persons with disabilities are not denied jobs because of prejudice or ignorance. It noted that society's myths and fears about disability and disease are as handicapping as the physical limitations that result from physical impairment, and concluded that contagion cannot remove a person from § 504 coverage. The Supreme Court remanded the case to the district court to determine whether the teacher was "otherwise qualified" for her job and whether the school board could reasonably accommodate her as an employee. *School Board of Nassau County v. Arline*, 480 U.S. 273, 107 S.Ct. 1123, 94 L.Ed.2d 307 (1987).

Title VII employment restrictions do not apply to religious educational institutions. In a 1987 decision, the Court ruled that religious schools were free from Title VII's scope even when the job involved did not affect a program of religious instruction.

In a decision affecting private religious educational institutions, the U.S. Supreme Court ruled that such institutions may discriminate on the basis of religion in hiring for nonreligious jobs involving nonprofit activities. The case involved a man who worked at a Mormon church-operated gymnasium for 16 years. After being discharged for failing to meet several church-related requirements for employment, he sued the church in a federal district court, alleging religious discrimination in violation of Title VII. The church moved for dismissal claiming that § 702 of Title VII exempted it from liability. The man claimed that if § 702 allowed religious employers to discriminate on religious grounds in hiring for nonreligious jobs, then Title VII would be in violation of the Establishment Clause of the First Amendment. The district court ruled for the man, and the church appealed directly to the U.S. Supreme Court.

The question before the Court was whether applying § 702 to the secular nonprofit activities of religious organizations violated the Establishment Clause. Section 702 provides that Title VII "shall not apply ... to a religious corporation, association [or] educational institution ... with respect to the employment of individuals of a particular religion to perform work connected with the carrying on by such [an organization] of its activities." In ruling for the church, the Supreme Court applied the three-part test set out in *Lemon v. Kurtzman*, see Chapter Two, above. *Lemon* requires first that a law serve a secular legislative purpose. Section 702 meets this test, said the Court, since it is a permissible legislative purpose to alleviate significant governmental interference with the ability of religious organizations to define and carry out their missions. The second test required that § 702 have a primary effect that neither advances nor inhibits religion. Section 702 meets that requirement since a law is not unconstitutional simply because it *allows* churches to advance religion, stated the Court. Section 702 does not violate the third part of the *Lemon* test because it does not impermissibly entangle church and state. The Supreme Court reversed the district court's decision and upheld the right of nonprofit religious employers to impose religious conditions for employment in nonreligious positions involving nonprofit activities. *Corporation of the Presiding Bishop of the Church of Jesus Christ of Latter-Day Saints v. Amos*, 483 U.S. 327, 107 S.Ct. 2862, 97 L.Ed.2d 273 (1987).

The U.S. Supreme Court issued a ruling affecting the right of a former private university employee to have his case returned to state court rather than dismissed at the federal court level.

A private university employee sued the university in a Pennsylvania trial court, claiming that the school had violated the federal Age Discrimination in Employment Act (ADEA). He also brought state law claims for wrongful discharge, breach of contract and other violations. The employee was allowed to remove the case from state court to a federal district court because the alleged violation of the ADEA gave federal court jurisdiction over the entire lawsuit. The employee then discovered that he had failed to file a timely age discrimination charge with a federal or state agency. He requested that the federal claim be deleted and that the case be remanded to the Pennsylvania trial court in which it was filed. The U.S. district court granted this request. The university then requested that the U.S. Court of Appeals, Third Circuit, order the U.S. district court not to remand the case to the state court. The court of appeals denied the request and the university asked the U.S. Supreme Court to review that decision.

The Supreme Court noted that when a case is removed from state to federal court because it contains a federal claim, the federal court has jurisdiction over the entire case, including claims arising under state law. The federal and state law claims must arise from the same "operative facts." In cases where the federal claim is dropped from the lawsuit after removal, a federal court has discretion to dismiss the case and let the plaintiff start over again in state court. The question in this case, however, was whether the federal court has discretion to remand the case to the state court, thereby preserving state law claims that would otherwise be lost if state statutes of limitation have run before the plaintiff can start again in state court. The Supreme Court concluded that federal courts had discretion to remand a case which had been removed from state court back to state court if such action would best accommodate the values of economy, convenience, fairness and comity. The Court ruled that the employee's case could be remanded to the Pennsylvania trial court in which it was filed. *Carnegie-Mellon University v. Cohill*, 484 U.S. 343, 108 S.Ct. 614, 98 L.Ed.2d 720 (1988).

For over a decade, legal experts predicted that under *School Board of Nassau County v. Arline*, above, the U.S. Supreme Court would find HIV-positive individuals entitled to the protection of federal antidiscrimination laws. These predictions proved accurate when, in 1998, the Court held that an HIV-positive person was entitled to consideration as an individual with a disability under the Americans with Disabilities Act (ADA), which applies legal standards developed under the Rehabilitation Act.

The case involved an HIV-positive patient who disclosed her condition to her dentist. He refused to fill her cavity in his office, but offered to perform the work in a hospital if the patient would pay for the use of the hospital's facilities. The patient refused and sued the dentist in a Maine federal district court, alleging that the dentist discriminated against her in violation of § 302 of the ADA [42 U.S.C. § 12182]. The court granted the patient summary judgment. The U.S. Court of Appeals, First Circuit, affirmed, holding that although she was asymptomatic, she was disabled. It also found that treating her in the dental office did not pose a direct threat to the health or safety of others so as to justify refusing to provide such treatment.

The U.S. Supreme Court granted review and held that HIV infection must be regarded as a physical impairment because HIV has an immediate, constant and detrimental effect on the blood and lymph systems in each stage of the infection, whether symptomatic or not. Since reproduction is no less important than working, learning, or other activities cited in the federal regulations, it is a major life activity. Although conception and childbirth are not impossible for an HIV-positive person, they are dangerous to the public health and amount to a substantial limitation. The patient was thus an individual with a disability under the ADA. However, the Court did not decide whether HIV infection was a *per se* disability under the ADA. The Court affirmed the lower court's ruling, but remanded the case for consideration of whether the patient's HIV infection posed a significant threat to the health and safety of others so as to justify the dentist's refusal to treat her in his office. *Bragdon v. Abbott,* 524 U.S. 624, 118 S.Ct. 2196, 141 L.Ed.2d 540 (1998).

In two ADA disability cases decided during the 1998-99 term, the Supreme Court concluded that the question of whether an impairment rises to the level of "substantially limiting" should be made with reference to the mitigating measures employed. This holding contradicts established EEOC guidelines.

In the first case, twin sisters with uncorrected vision of 20/200 or worse but corrected vision of 20/20 or better were denied jobs as global airline pilots with a commercial airline because their uncorrected vision did not meet the airline's minimum uncorrected vision standard. The sisters filed an ADA claim against the airline, which was dismissed by a federal district court. On appeal, the U.S. Court of Appeals, Tenth Circuit affirmed.

The Supreme Court agreed with the lower court decisions, finding the sisters had not demonstrated they were disabled under the ADA. The Court stated that mitigating measures had to be taken into account when evaluating whether an individual was disabled, and that, because glasses or contacts corrected the sisters' vision to 20/20 or better, they were not substantially limited in a major life activity, as required by the ADA. The sisters were also not regarded as disabled, as there was no evidence that the airline perceived them to be substantially limited in a major life activity. *Sutton v. United Airlines, Inc.,* 119 S.Ct. 2139, ___ L.Ed.2d ___ (1999).

In the second case, the Supreme Court concluded that a mechanic with high blood pressure who was fired from his job was not disabled under the ADA. Because the mechanic was able to control his high blood pressure with medication, he was not substantially limited in a major life activity. The court did not address the issue of whether the mechanic would be considered disabled while taking his medication. The mechanic was also not regarded as disabled. At most, the employer regarded the mechanic as unable to perform the job of mechanic because it believed his high blood pressure exceeded the U.S. Department of Transportation's requirements for drivers of commercial motor vehicles. *Murphy v. United Parcel Service, Inc,* 119 S.Ct. 2133, ___ L.Ed.2d ___ (1999).

III. CLAIMS FILED UNDER 42 U.S.C. § 1983

One of the Reconstruction Era Civil Rights Acts, 42 U.S.C. § 1983, is a federal civil rights statute which creates a legal cause of action against state actors for violations of rights protected by the U.S. Constitution or laws. Any action brought under the section must refer to an underlying federal right that has been allegedly violated by a state official who acts "under color of state law." The following decision changed the nature of litigation involving school districts, because the Supreme Court held that districts could be held liable for monetary damages under § 1983 to the extent that they denied individuals their civil rights under an official practice or policy.

A group of female employees of New York City's Department of Social Services and Board of Education sued the department and its commissioner, the board and its chancellor and the city and mayor under 42 U.S.C. § 1983. They complained that the department and board had an official policy of compelling pregnant employees to take unpaid leaves of absence before such leaves were required for medical reasons. A federal district court ruled that the group's petition was moot because the city had since changed its policy. The new policy stated that no pregnant employee would be forced to take a leave unless she was medically unable to perform her job. The district court held that requiring pregnant employees to take a leave of absence was unconstitutional. However, the court denied a backpay award to the complaining parties because any damages would have had to come from the city.

This ran afoul of the sovereign immunity principle embodied in the Eleventh Amendment and common law. When the aggrieved employees appealed to the U.S. Supreme Court, it agreed to hear the case.

The Court reversed the district court's decision, reversing a previous case that held that municipalities are immune from liability in lawsuits brought under 42 U.S.C. § 1983. The Court had previously interpreted Congress' rejection of the "Sherman Amendment" to the Civil Rights Act of 1871, which later became § 1983, as a rejection of liability for municipalities. The Court determined that nothing in the legislative history of § 1983 precluded municipal liability. The Court applied § 1983 to the local school district as though it were a municipality. It held that municipalities cannot be held liable under the theory of *respondeat superior*; in other words, municipalities are not automatically liable for the acts of their employees. Claims against school districts must show that district employees acted under some official policy which caused them to violate individual constitutional rights. The Court reversed the district court's decision, finding that the employees' constitutional rights had been violated as a direct result of the department's official policy. *Monell v. Department of Social Services*, 436 U.S. 658, 98 S.Ct. 2018, 56 L.Ed.2d 611 (1978).

Section 1983 contains no statute of limitations. Courts must look to local law for an appropriate limit on actions. In a 1981 case, the Court agreed with a federal district court that a one-year statute of limitations on lawsuits found in local law was to be strictly construed.

Nontenured administrators in the Puerto Rico Department of Education were given termination letters before June 18, 1977. However, the terminations were not to take place until a month or more later. Exactly one year and one day after the termination letters were delivered, one of the administrators filed suit under 42 U.S.C. § 1983, which allows a person to sue in federal court for constitutional and statutory rights violations caused by those acting under color of state law. A federal district court dismissed the suit, stating that the suit was barred by a local one-year statute of limitations. The U.S. Supreme Court agreed, interpreting its prior decision in *Delaware State College v. Ricks*, above, to mean that the statute of limitations begins to run when the employee has been terminated, rather than the date that his employment actually ends. *Ricks* established that the focus should be on the discriminatory act and not when the consequences occur. In this case, the employees had been provided with appropriate notice when they were terminated. This did not extend the statute of limitations and the claim was barred. *Chardon v. Fernandez*, 454 U.S. 6, 102 S.Ct. 28, 70 L.Ed.2d 6 (1981).

In a 1982 case involving a Florida university secretary's § 1983 lawsuit, the Court stated that there was no purpose in requiring § 1983 plaintiffs to exhaust their state administrative remedies. This was because § 1983 had been enacted in the Reconstruction Era as a response to Congressional perceptions that individual civil rights would be abused by state officials.

A white female secretary worked for a Florida university. She alleged that during her employment there, she had been passed over for employment promotions, even though she was qualified for the positions. She sued the university in a federal district court under 42 U.S.C. § 1983, alleging gender and race discrimination. The secretary also claimed that the university actively sought to hire minorities and separated applicant files according to race and gender. A panel of the U.S. Court of Appeals, Fifth Circuit, dismissed the secretary's complaint for failure to exhaust her state administrative remedies.

The court then agreed to hear the case *en banc* to determine whether the employee should be required to exhaust her state administrative remedies before she was entitled to file a § 1983 claim in the federal court system. Although the U.S. Supreme Court had on several occasions rejected the argument that a § 1983 action should be dismissed where the plaintiff had not exhausted administrative remedies, the court of appeals held that adequate and appropriate state administrative remedies must be exhausted before a plaintiff could bring a § 1983 action in federal court. The U.S. Supreme Court agreed to hear the case.

The Court considered its rationale in prior decisions, when it considered the policy of exhausting administrative remedies. Administrative remedy exhaustion ensures that the parties attempt a settlement before proceeding to federal court. The Court examined Congress' intent in not specifically requiring exhaustion of state administrative remedies in § 1983 actions. Congress assigned to the federal courts the primary role of securing individual constitutional rights in the years after the Civil War. Section 1983 was passed during the Reconstruction Era in response to state-sanctioned constitutional violations of blacks after the ratification of the Fourteenth Amendment. To now require plaintiffs to go through state administrative processes contradicted this purpose. Congress had intended that § 1983 plaintiffs be able to choose the federal district courts as the forum for civil rights lawsuits. The Court rejected the policy reasons adopted by the court of appeals for requiring state administrative remedy exhaustion. It stated that reducing federal court case loads and using state agency expertise in these cases did not outweigh the purposes of § 1983. *Patsy v. Board of Regents*, 457 U.S. 496, 102 S.Ct. 2557, 73 L.Ed.2d 172 (1982).

In *Rendell-Baker v. Kohn*, the Court stated the following test for attributing state action to private employers for the purposes of liability under 42 U.S.C. § 1983: Is the alleged civil rights violation "fairly attributable" to the state?

The Fourteenth Amendment prohibits state action which deprives any person within that state's jurisdiction from rights, privileges or immunities secured by the U.S. Constitution. When a privately operated school in Massachusetts fired a teacher for speaking out against school policy, she sued the school under 42 U.S.C. § 1983 on the grounds that the state, acting through the school, had abridged her First Amendment right to free speech. As evidence of the control the state had over the private school she contended that the school issued diplomas approved by the local school districts whose special students this private school contracted to teach, that the private school received 99 percent of its funding from state sources, and that her position on the staff had been created and funded by a state agency. The case was consolidated with that of other teachers and a vocational counselor at the school who were also fired. A federal district court held that the employees were properly dismissed. There was no evidence of government control over school personnel actions. The Supreme Court granted review.

The Court noted that unlike Title VII claims and complaints filed under the National Labor Relations Act, § 1983 claims required an affirmative showing by the complaining parties that they had suffered some constitutional infringement at the hands of a state actor, or by one acting under color of state law. According to the Court, state action was present only when the alleged violation of federal rights was fairly attributable to the state, which required a showing of coercion by the state. Even though all of the employees' evidence of state control and funding was true, these factors in themselves were insufficient to show that the state had created an agency with the private school which made the school's actions its own. Absent a showing of actual control by the state, any deprivation of constitutional rights claimed by the employees were matters between them and another private party. Such complaints between private parties are not within the scope of § 1983. The Court affirmed the district court decision for the school. *Rendell-Baker v. Kohn*, 457 U.S. 830, 102 S.Ct. 2764, 73 L.Ed.2d 418 (1982).

In 1984, the Court considered *Migra v. Warren City School Board*, another § 1983 case which differed significantly in its procedural posture from the *Patsy* case, above. In *Migra*, the Court stated that the judicial doctrine of *res judicata*, or claim preclusion, barred the filing of a new § 1983 lawsuit when the complaining party had already filed a lawsuit based on the same facts in state court proceedings.

An Ohio woman worked under successive contracts as a supervisor of elementary schools. The district offered her a new contract for an upcoming school year, but later revoked the offer and decided not to renew the contract. The supervisor sued the school district in an Ohio trial court for breach of contract and wrongful interference with her employment contract with the school board. The trial court held for the supervisor on the basis of these state law complaints, and ordered her reinstated with compensatory damages. The supervisor then filed a new lawsuit in a federal district court under 42 U.S.C. § 1983, alleging that the school district had refused to renew her contract in retaliation for her creation of a desegregation plan and a social studies curriculum which she had proposed. She claimed that the district had violated her rights to free speech, due process and equal protection under the U.S. Constitution. She sought injunctive relief as well as compensatory and punitive damages. The district court dismissed her claim and the U.S. Court of Appeals affirmed the decision.

The supervisor appealed to the U.S. Supreme Court which affirmed the lower court decisions, holding that it "is now settled that a federal court must give to a state court judgment the same preclusive effect that would be given that judgment under the law of the state in which the judgment was rendered." Because the supervisor had not raised her § 1983 claim at the same time she brought her state law claims, she could not now bring a lawsuit based upon the same set of acts under a new theory. The underlying purpose of § 1983 was to create a federal forum for constitutional and civil rights violations. This purpose was not undermined by giving deference to a state court decision based upon state laws. The Court dismissed the supervisor's § 1983 lawsuit. *Migra v. Warren City School District*, 465 U.S. 75, 104 S.Ct. 892, 79 L.Ed.2d 56 (1984).

Section 1983 claimants who prevail in federal court proceedings are entitled to attorney fees under 42 U.S.C. § 1988. However, claimants are not entitled to fees for counsel in administrative

hearings, such as the school board's termination hearings in the following case.

A black elementary school teacher was fired by a Tennessee school board in 1974, following complaints by white parents that he had administered corporal punishment to their children. He retained an attorney to help fight what he felt was a racially motivated dismissal. After four years of administrative proceedings the board finally decided not to rehire him. He then sued the board in a federal court under § 1983 of the Civil Rights Act, alleging racial discrimination. The court ordered the teacher reinstated and awarded him $15,400 in damages. The teacher then filed a motion with the court to collect the cost of his attorney's fees from the board. He sought to collect $21,165, based on an hourly rate of $120. This included the time his attorney spent in representing him before the school board in administrative hearings. The district court awarded the teacher only $9,734 and the U.S. Court of Appeals, Sixth Circuit, affirmed. The case was appealed to the U.S. Supreme Court.

The Supreme Court upheld the lower court decisions and ordered the board to pay the attorney's fees for the teacher's federal court proceedings but not the costs of the administrative proceedings before the board. Because the lawsuit had been filed under § 1983 of the Civil Rights Act, the teacher was entitled to attorney's fees only for court proceedings. The Court stated that if the teacher had filed suit under Title VII of the Civil Rights Act he would have received attorney's fees for all stages of the proceedings, including his numerous appearances before the school board. *Webb v. Board of Education of Dyer County*, 471 U.S. 234, 105 S.Ct. 1923, 85 L.Ed.2d 233 (1985).

Section 1983 contains no statute of limitations, and courts must apply the applicable statute from the jurisdiction in which the alleged civil rights violation occurs. In a 1985 Pennsylvania case, the Court ruled that the limitation period should be based on the state's six-year personal injury statute, rather than a six-month limitation on claims brought against government employees.

A woman sued a Pennsylvania school district for failing to promote her to an administrative position for three consecutive years. She brought the claim in a federal district court under 42 U.S.C. § 1983, alleging that she was being discriminated against on the basis of gender. The last incident of discrimination she alleged occurred over six months before she began her lawsuit. A state law set a six-month limitations period for lawsuits brought against government officials for alleged acts or omissions resulting from the execution of official duties. The district court dismissed her claim because it was not brought within the six-month limitations period.

The U.S. Court of Appeals, Third Circuit, reversed the district court's decision. It ruled that the application of the six-month limitation would undermine the purposes of § 1983 in providing a remedy for constitutional violations. The U.S. Supreme Court granted certiorari. It vacated the court of appeals' decision and held that § 1983 claims should be characterized as a personal injury for the purpose of determining which state statute of limitations should apply. The Court remanded the case to the district court. *Springfield Township School District v. Knoll*, 471 U.S. 288, 105 S.Ct. 2065, 85 L.Ed.2d 275 (1985).

In 1986, the Court held that § 1983 damages were not permissible where the alleged injury was based only on abstract constitutional rights. Section 1983 damages are available only to compensate for injuries caused by a deprivation of a well-defined constitutional right.

A Michigan public school teacher taught seventh grade courses in life science using a textbook approved by his school board. The course included a six-week section on human growth and sexuality. After instructing his students to obtain signed parental permission slips, the teacher showed two films on human reproduction and sexual development. The films were obtained from the county health department and had been shown in previous school years without incident. The films were shown with boys and girls in separate rooms, the boys viewing "From Boy to Man" and the girls viewing "From Girl to Woman." When rumors spread that the films were explicit, some parents appeared at a school board meeting, demanding that the teacher be fired. Some parents demanded that he be tarred and feathered. The board suspended the teacher without pay. He then filed a § 1983 lawsuit against the school district in a federal district court, claiming that the suspension constituted a violation of his constitutional rights. The court awarded the teacher a final judgment of almost $300,000 in compensatory and punitive damages. The U.S. Court of Appeals, Sixth Circuit, affirmed and the school district appealed to the U.S. Supreme Court.

The Supreme Court held that the trial court had erroneously instructed the jury to attempt to place a dollar value on abstract constitutional rights, rather than to focus on a provable injury. According to the Court, an award of money damages under § 1983 is possible as compensation to a person for actual injuries as the result of a recognized Constitutional violation, such as a due process violation. The deprivation of a right without corresponding actual injury was insufficient to justify a § 1983 damage award. The Court reversed the lower court decisions and remanded the case to the district court. *Memphis Community School District v. Stachura*, 477 U.S. 299, 106 S.Ct. 2537, 91 L.Ed.2d 249 (1986).

Another part of the Reconstruction Era Civil Rights Act is 42 U.S.C. § 1981. Section 1981 states that "[a]ll persons... shall have the same right to make and enforce contracts... as is enjoyed by white citizens. . . ." In 1987, the Court ruled that although originally intended to vindicate the rights of former slaves, § 1981 extended to persons of Arab ancestry and others besides American blacks.

A private college in Pennsylvania denied tenure to a professor it had employed under a one-year nonrenewable contract. The professor was a Muslim who was born in Iraq but was a U.S. citizen. He claimed that the college had refused to grant tenure on the basis of his national origin and religion in violation of state and federal civil rights laws, including § 1981. The professor sued the college in a federal district court, which dismissed many of the claims because they were too late to meet local statutes of limitations.

The court also dismissed the § 1981 claim, ruling that the act did not extend to the professor. It ruled that § 1981, which forbids racial discrimination in the making and enforcement of any contract, does not reach claims of discrimination based on Arab ancestry. The court stated that Arabs were Caucasians, and that since § 1981 was not enacted to protect whites, an Arab professor could not rely upon the statute. The professor appealed to the U.S. Court of Appeals, Third Circuit. The appeals court affirmed the district court's decision that the professor's Title VII claim was untimely, but reversed its decision regarding the § 1981 claim. The College appealed to the U.S. Supreme Court, which agreed to review only the § 1981 portion of the professor's claim.

In affirming the court of appeals' decision, the Supreme Court noted that although § 1981 does not use the word "race," the Court has construed the statute to forbid all racial discrimination in the making of private as well as public contracts. It observed that persons who might be thought of as Caucasian today were not thought to be of the same race at the time § 1981 became law. The Court cited several dictionary and encyclopedic sources to support its decision that for the purposes of §

1981, Arabs, Englishmen, Germans and certain other ethnic groups are not to be considered a single race.

Based on the history of § 1981 the Court reasoned that Congress "intended to protect from discrimination identifiable classes of persons who are subjected to intentional discrimination solely because of their ancestry or ethnic characteristics." If the professor could prove that he was subjected to intentional discrimination because he was an Arab, rather than solely because of his place of origin or his religion, the lawsuit could proceed under § 1981. The court of appeals' decision in favor of the professor was affirmed and the case was remanded for trial. *St. Francis College v. Al-Khazraji*, 481 U.S. 604, 107 S.Ct. 2022, 97 L.Ed.2d 749 (1987).

The NCAA has been held not to be a state actor by the Supreme Court. In a 1988 Nevada case, the Court concluded that the NCAA did not have the power to discipline a school's coach, and thus could not be liable for sanctions imposed against him.

Following a lengthy investigation of allegedly improper recruiting practices by the University of Nevada, Las Vegas (UNLV), the NCAA found 38 violations, including ten by the school's head basketball coach. The NCAA proposed a number of sanctions and threatened to impose more if the coach was not suspended. UNLV decided to suspend the coach. Facing an enormous pay cut, the coach sued the NCAA under 42 U.S.C. § 1983 for violating his due process rights. The Nevada Supreme Court held that the NCAA's conduct constituted state action for constitutional purposes. It upheld a Nevada trial court's dismissal of the suspension and award of attorney's fees. The NCAA appealed to the U.S. Supreme Court.

The Supreme Court held that the NCAA's participation in the events which led to the suspension did not constitute state action within the meaning of § 1983. The NCAA was not a state actor on the theory that it misused the power it possessed under state law. UNLV's decision to suspend the coach in compliance with the NCAA's rules and recommendations did not turn the NCAA's conduct into state action. This was because UNLV retained the power to withdraw from the NCAA and establish its own standards. The NCAA could not directly discipline the coach, but could threaten to impose additional sanctions against the school. It was the school's decision and not the NCAA's decision to suspend the coach. *NCAA v. Tarkanian*, 488 U.S. 179, 109 S.Ct. 454, 102 L.Ed.2d 469 (1988).

If a party has prevailed on any significant issue in a claim under 42 U.S.C. § 1983, he or she will be entitled to attorney's fees under 42 U.S.C. § 1988 at least to the extent of the fees expended in litigating that issue.

A Texas school district prohibited teachers from discussing employee organizations during the school day. The district denied employee organizations access to school facilities during school hours and prohibited them from using school mail and internal communications systems. The district's regulation permitted employee organizations to recruit or meet with teachers on school premises before or after the school day "upon request and approval by the school principal." The state and local teachers' associations and several of their members and employees sued the district in a federal district court under 42 U.S.C. § 1983, alleging that the district's policy violated their First and Fourteenth Amendment rights. The court dismissed most of the claims. On appeal, the U.S. Court of Appeals, Fifth Circuit, granted the associations' summary judgment motion on their claim that the prohibition of teacher-to-teacher discussions during the school day and use of internal mail and bulletin board facilities was unconstitutional.

After the U.S. Supreme Court summarily affirmed the court of appeals' judgment, the associations filed for an award of attorney's fees under 42 U.S.C. § 1988. The district court held that the associations were not "prevailing parties" within the meaning of § 1988 and thus were ineligible for any fee award. The court of appeals affirmed, ruling that the associations had not prevailed on the central issue in the litigation. The associations then appealed to the U.S. Supreme Court. The Supreme Court stated that a party did not need to prevail on the "central issue" in a case in order to be afforded "prevailing party" status for purposes of attorney's fees. The party need only succeed on "any significant issue" that materially alters the legal relationship between the parties. Since the associations prevailed on some of the relief they sought, they had established the basis for an award of attorney's fees. *Texas State Teachers Ass'n v. Garland Indep. School Dist.*, 489 U.S. 782, 109 S.Ct. 1486, 103 L.Ed.2d 866 (1989).

The Supreme Court has stated that a municipality cannot be held liable for its employees' violations of 42 U.S.C. § 1981 under a theory of vicarious liability. A person discriminated against by a state actor must bring an action against the actor under 42 U.S.C. § 1983.

A white male was employed by the Dallas Independent School District (DISD) as a teacher, athletic director and head football coach at a predominantly black high school. After numerous problems with the school's principal over school policies, the principal recommended that the teacher be relieved of his duties as athletic director and coach. The district's superintendent reassigned the teacher to a teaching position in another school where he had no coaching duties. The teacher sued the school district and the principal, claiming that they had discriminated against him on the basis of race in violation of 42 U.S.C. §§ 1981 and 1983. A federal district court held in the teacher's favor.

The U.S. Court of Appeals, Fifth Circuit, reversed in part and remanded, finding that the district court's jury instructions did not make clear that the school district's liability could only be based on the actions of the principal or superintendent if those officials had been delegated policy-making authority or had acted according to a well settled custom or official policy. Even if the superintendent could be considered a policy-maker for purposes of transferring personnel, the jury did not find that the superintendent's decision to transfer the teacher had been either improperly motivated or consciously indifferent to the principal's improper motivations. The court of appeals also rejected the district court's conclusion that the district's § 1981 liability for the principal's actions could be predicated on a vicarious liability theory or that municipalities could be liable for their employees' acts. The Court noted that Congress did not intend that municipalities be subject to vicarious liability under § 1983. The teacher then appealed to the U.S. Supreme Court.

The Supreme Court stated that a municipality may not be held liable for its employees' violations of § 1981 under a vicarious liability theory. The express "action at law" provided by § 1983 for the deprivation of rights secured by the Constitution and laws of the United States is the exclusive federal remedy for the violation of rights guaranteed by § 1981 when the claim is pressed against a state actor. The Supreme Court affirmed part of the court of appeals' decision and remanded the case in order to determine if the superintendent possessed policy-making authority in the area of employee transfer, and if so, whether a new trial was required to determine the DISD's responsibility for the principal's actions in light of this determination. *Jett v. Dallas Indep. School Dist.*, 491 U.S. 701, 109 S.Ct. 2702, 105 L.Ed.2d 598 (1989).

IV. TENURE AND DUE PROCESS

In 1937, the U.S. Supreme Court rejected the Indiana Supreme Court's position that teacher tenure could be created and later repealed by the legislature in the form of amendments to a state statute. Tenure constitutes a property right and repeal of a portion of the state tenure act violated the Contract Clause, Article I, § 10 of the Federal Constitution.

The Indiana legislature passed the Teachers' Tenure Law. The statute stated that teachers having contracts for five years would become permanently tenured. A school district could only cancel tenured teacher contracts after first providing the teacher with notice and a hearing, and only on the grounds of incompetence, insubordination, neglect of duty, immorality, justifiable decrease in the number of teaching positions, or other good cause. An Indiana township public school teacher entered into a contract with her school district and taught continuously for ten years. Her employment contract contained a clause which stated that it complied with tenure law provisions, and that the statute governed contractual terms.

The teacher's school district notified her that her teaching contract would be terminated for cause. Meanwhile, the state legislature repealed the part of the tenure law concerning teachers in township schools. A hearing was held and the county superintendent upheld the termination. The teacher filed a lawsuit in an Indiana trial court. At trial, the teacher argued that termination of her contract constituted a breach by the school district. The trial court affirmed her termination, ruling that the tenure law had been repealed as it applied to teachers in township schools. The teacher appealed to the Indiana Supreme Court, which affirmed the trial court's decision. It added that the repeal of the tenure law in township schools did not deprive the teacher of any vested property right, nor did it impair a contract under the Constitution. The U.S. Supreme Court granted a writ of certiorari.

The Supreme Court rejected the Indiana court's decision that a property right could be created by the legislature and later repealed. Although the Court acknowledged state powers to formulate and set employment policies, it also ruled that legislation contained provisions that individuals might act upon, thus creating a contract between the individual and the state. Therefore, a repeal of that legislation might violate Article I, Section 10 of the U.S. Constitution, which prohibits states from impairing contracts.

Giving deference to the Indiana Supreme Court's articulation that school policy was not to bind schools for more than one year, the Court examined whether a contract had been created between the teacher and the school by the teachers' tenure law. It concluded that the teacher had a valid contract by virtue of the tenure law and that its repeal interfered with that contract in violation of the Constitution. The state had a history of extending contracts to teachers and upholding their contractual rights. The tenure law clearly indicated that the annual agreements were to be contracts. Repeal by the legislature would have to be for a legitimate state end and the means adopted would have to be reasonably adapted to that end. The school district failed to show that the legislature had repealed the law based on this test. The case was remanded. *Indiana ex rel. Anderson v. Brand*, 303 U.S. 95, 58 S.Ct. 443, 82 L.Ed. 685 (1937).

Two 1972 Supreme Court cases of enduring importance help to define the concept of due process in public employment. In *Perry v. Sindermann* and *Board of Regents v. Roth*, below, the Court held that liberty and property rights are *created* by contract or state law, and *protected* by the Constitution. Tenured teachers enjoy property interests in continued employment under state tenure laws. However, untenured teachers have no more than "a unilateral expectation" of reemployment.

The Wisconsin state university system hired an assistant professor under a one-year contract. As the year drew to a close, the university notified the teacher that his contract would not be renewed. The notice conformed to university rules, which did not require any reason for nonretention or any hearing for the teacher. Wisconsin tenure law required teachers to have four years of service before becoming "permanent" employees. The teacher sued the state college board in a federal district court, alleging that he was being terminated for making critical statements about university administrators. The teacher also claimed that the failure of university officials to give any reason for nonretention violated his procedural due process rights. The court held for the teacher on his due process claim and the U.S. Court of Appeals, Seventh Circuit, affirmed this decision. The U.S. Supreme Court agreed to hear the university board's petition.

In dismissing the teacher's due process claims, the Supreme Court stated that no liberty interest was implicated because in declining to rehire the teacher, the university had not made any charge against him such as incompetence or immorality. Such a charge would have made it difficult for the teacher to gain employment elsewhere and thus would have deprived him of liberty. As no reason was given for the nonrenewal of his contract, the teacher's liberty interest in future employment was not impaired and he was not entitled to a hearing on these grounds.

The Court declared that because the teacher had not acquired tenure he possessed no property interest in continued employment at the university. The teacher had a property interest in employment during the term of his one-year contract, but upon expiration the interest ceased to exist. The Court stated: "To have a property interest in a benefit, a person clearly must have more than an abstract need or desire for it. He must have more than a unilateral expectation of it. He must, instead, have a legitimate claim of entitlement to it." Because the teacher's contract secured no interest in reemployment for the following year, he had no property interest in reemployment. The Court reversed the lower court decisions and remanded the case. *Board of Regents v. Roth*, 408 U.S. 564, 92 S.Ct. 2701, 33 L.Ed.2d 548 (1972).

A fair and impartial hearing, conducted in accordance with procedural safeguards, must be given to a dismissed teacher if there is a property or a liberty interest involved or if the dismissal involves a stigma upon the character of the teacher. Such hearings are part of the minimal due process requirements accorded to a dismissed teacher.

The *Sindermann* case involved a teacher employed at a Texas university for four years under a series of one-year contracts. When he was not rehired for a fifth year he brought suit contending that due process required a dismissal hearing. The Supreme Court held that "a person's interest in a benefit is a 'property' interest for due process purposes if there are such rules and mutually explicit understandings that support his claim of entitlement to the benefit that he may invoke at a hearing. "Because the teacher had been employed at the university for four years, the Court felt that he may have acquired a protectable property interest in continued employment. The case was remanded to the trial court to determine whether there was an unwritten "common law" of tenure at the university. If so, the teacher would be entitled to a dismissal hearing. *Perry v. Sindermann*, 408 U.S. 593, 92 S.Ct. 2694, 33 L.Ed.2d 570 (1972).

In a case appealed to the United States Supreme Court, the nonrenewal of a tenured teacher's contract because of her failure to earn continuing education credits was held constitutionally

allowable and not a deprivation of her substantive due process and equal protection rights.

A tenured Oklahoma teacher failed to earn required continuing education credits. This violated her school district's policy, and she forfeited salary increases to which she would have been otherwise entitled. The state legislature then mandated salary raises for teachers regardless of compliance with continuing education requirements. The district threatened to terminate the teacher's employment unless she fulfilled the continuing education requirements. When she refused, the district refused to renew her contract. She sued the district in a federal district court, which dismissed her case. However, the U.S. Court of Appeals, Tenth Circuit, reversed the district court's decision, and the district appealed to the U.S. Supreme Court.

Regarding the Due Process Clause aspect of the teacher's claim the Court said that the district's rule was endowed with a presumption of legislative validity and the teacher failed to rebut that presumption. The desire of the district to provide well qualified teachers was not arbitrary—especially when it made every effort to give this specific teacher a chance to meet the requirements. The rule was reasonable and the teacher's interest in continued employment did not outweigh the compelling state interest in public education. Nor was there a deprivation of equal protection since all teachers were obligated to obtain the same credits. The sanction of contract nonrenewal was rationally related to the district's objective of enforcing the continuing education obligation of its teachers. The Court reversed the court of appeals' decision, finding the district sanctions constitutional on both Due Process and Equal Protection Clause grounds. *Harrah Independent School District v. Martin*, 440 U.S. 194, 99 S.Ct. 1062, 59 L.Ed.2d 248 (1979).

The Due Process Clause of the Fourteenth Amendment protects individuals from state interference with rights to life, liberty and property by requiring minimal procedural protections. The level of protection depends upon the state law which creates the property right. Public employees are vested by state law with the right to notice and a hearing at some point in the termination process. Under an Ohio statute, employees were limited to notice and an informal hearing in termination matters, but had no full administrative hearing rights until after the termination. The Court upheld the statute under the Due Process Clause.

Ohio law protected all civil service employees from dismissal except for "misfeasance, malfeasance, or nonfeasance in office." Employees who were terminated for cause were entitled to an order of removal stating the reasons for termination. Unfavorable orders could be appealed to a state administrative board whose determinations were subject to state court review. A security guard hired by a school board stated on his job application that he had never been convicted of a felony. Upon discovering that he had in fact been convicted of grand larceny, the school board dismissed him for dishonesty in filling out the job application. He was not afforded an opportunity to respond to the dishonesty charge or to challenge the dismissal until nine months later. In the second case, a school bus mechanic was fired because he had failed an eye examination. The mechanic appealed his dismissal after the fact because he had not been afforded a pretermination hearing. A federal district court rejected both of the employees' claims and they appealed to the U.S. Court of Appeals, Sixth Circuit, which reversed the district court's decisions. The U.S. Supreme Court consolidated the appeals by the school districts.

The Supreme Court held that the employees possessed a property right in their employment and were entitled to a pretermination opportunity to respond to the dismissal charges against them. The pretermination hearing, stated the Court, need not resolve the propriety of the discharge, but should be a check against mistaken decisions— essentially a determination of whether there are reasonable grounds to believe that the charges against the employee are true and support the proposed action. The Supreme Court upheld that portion of the lower court decisions which found that the delay in the guard's administrative proceedings did not constitute a separate constitutional violation. The Due Process Clause requires a hearing "at a meaningful time," and here the delay stemmed in part from the thoroughness of the procedures afforded the guard. On the matter of the right to a pretermination hearing, however, both cases were remanded for further proceedings consistent with the Court's decision. *Cleveland Board of Education v. Loudermill*, 470 U.S. 532, 105 S.Ct. 1487, 84 L.Ed.2d 494 (1985).

The Supreme Court held that a university police officer who had been arrested on felony drug charges could be suspended without pay prior to a hearing. Due process did not require that the officer receive notice and a hearing prior to the university's action.

A police officer employed by a Pennsylvania state university was arrested in a drug raid and charged with several felony counts related to marijuana possession and distribution. State police notified the university of the arrest and charges, and the university's human resources director immediately suspended the officer without pay pursuant to a state executive order requiring such action where a state employee is formally charged with a felony. Although the criminal charges were dismissed, university officials demoted the officer because of admissions he had made to the state police. The university did not inform the officer that it had obtained his confession from police records and he was thus unable to fully respond to damaging statements in the police reports. He filed a federal district court action against university officials for failing to provide him with notice and an opportunity to be heard before his suspension without pay. The court granted summary judgment to the officials, but the U.S. Court of Appeals, Third Circuit, reversed and remanded the case.

The U.S. Supreme Court agreed to review the case, and stated that the court of appeals had improperly held that a suspended public employee must always receive a paid suspension under *Cleveland Bd. of Educ. v. Loudermill*, above. The Court held that the university did not violate due process by refusing to pay a suspended employee charged with a felony pending a hearing. It accepted the officials' argument that the Pennsylvania executive order made any presuspension hearing useless, since the filing of charges established an independent basis for believing that the officer had committed a felony. The Court noted that the officer here faced only a temporary suspension without pay, and not employment termination, as was the case in *Loudermill*. The Court reversed and remanded the court of appeals' judgment for consideration of the officer's arguments concerning a postsuspension hearing. *Gilbert v. Homar*, 520 U.S. 924, 117 S.Ct. 1807, 138 L.Ed.2d 120 (1997).

V. LABOR RELATIONS

Non-union members of represented bargaining units have contested the collection of agency fees by labor unions on grounds that they may not be compelled to fund non-bargaining uses. The Court has held that this impairs their constitutional speech rights. School boards derive their authority from state laws, and are generally authorized to make employment decisions including hiring, firing and negotiating employment contracts. The fact that school boards must negotiate with collective bargaining representatives as adversaries in contract negotiations does not deprive school boards of their status as impartial decisionmakers in employment matters.

Without a showing of actual bias, school boards are presumed to be impartial when they conduct employment termination hearings.

Wisconsin education law prohibited strikes by teachers. Under state law, school boards had sole authority to make hiring and firing decisions and were required to negotiate employment terms and conditions with authorized collective bargaining representatives. When contract negotiations between teachers and their local school board became protracted, the teachers called a strike. The board attempted to end the strike, noting it was in direct violation of state law. When the teachers refused to return to work, the board held disciplinary hearings and fired the striking teachers. The teachers appealed to the Wisconsin courts, arguing that the school board was not an impartial decisionmaker and that their discharges had violated their due process rights. The Wisconsin Supreme Court ruled that due process under the Fourteenth Amendment required that the teachers' conduct and the board's response to that conduct be evaluated by an impartial decisionmaker and that the board itself was not sufficiently impartial to make the decision to discharge the teachers. The board appealed this decision to the Supreme Court of the United States.

The Supreme Court reversed the Wisconsin Supreme Court decision and held that there was no evidence that the board had been unable to make an impartial decision to discharge these teachers. The fact that the board was involved in negotiations with the teachers did not support a claim of bias. The board was the only body vested with statutory authority to employ and dismiss teachers, and its participation in contract negotiations with the teachers was required by law. This involvement prior to the decision to discharge the teachers was not a sufficient showing of bias to disqualify the board as a decisionmaker under the Due Process Clause of the Fourteenth Amendment. *Hortonville Joint School District No. 1 v. Hortonville Education Association*, 426 U.S. 482, 96 S.Ct. 2308, 49 L.Ed.2d 1 (1976).

In a 1976 case, the Supreme Court rejected a decision by the Wisconsin Supreme Court which would have severely curtailed the rights of teachers to speak publicly about collective bargaining issues. However, union representatives did not have a monopoly on speaking about collective bargaining issues.

The Madison Board of Education and an employee labor union conducted collective bargaining negotiations. One of the proposals submitted by the union called for the approval of a "fair share" clause, which would require all teachers to pay a fee for collective bargaining expenses, regardless of whether the teachers were union members. The school board resisted this provision and another that required binding arbitration for teacher dismissals. The negotiations came to a standstill. Two Wisconsin teachers, who were bargaining unit members but not union members, mailed letters of opposition to the "fair share" proposal to other teachers. Almost 200 teachers responded, most expressing opposition to the proposal. The two teachers created a petition calling for a one-year delay in the fair share implementation. At the next public school board meeting, the union president spoke and presented a petition signed by 1,300 teachers requesting the expedient resolution of the negotiations. One of the teachers who supported the fair share petition also spoke and presented the petition. He stated that because teachers were confused about the fair share proposal, it should be delayed.

The board acquiesced to all union demands, except for the fair share proposal. The union then approved the agreement. A month later, the union filed a complaint with the Wisconsin Employment Relations Committee (WERC), claiming that the board had engaged in unfair labor practices by allowing the teacher opposed to the fair share arrangement to speak at the board meeting. The union alleged that allowing the teacher to speak constituted negotiations with someone other than the union's exclusive collective-bargaining representative, in violation of Wisconsin labor law. The WERC concluded that the board was in violation of state law and ordered it not to allow nonunion representatives to speak at future board meetings on collective bargaining issues.

A Wisconsin trial court affirmed the action, granting an injunction against future board appearances by the nonunion teacher. The Wisconsin Supreme Court also affirmed the decision, ruling that individual speech rights could be regulated in this case because the speech represented a "clear and present danger" to labor-management relations. The nonunion teacher's speech amounted to negotiation and would undermine exclusive bargaining as guaranteed by state law. The U.S. Supreme Court agreed to hear the case.

The Court reversed the Wisconsin Supreme Court's decision, ruling that the teacher's speech did not present a "clear and present danger" which justified infringement of individual First Amendment speech rights. The Court re-examined the trial court's conclusion that the teacher's statement constituted negotiation. It held that the teacher was only making a position statement, and was not seeking to negotiate or enter into an agreement with the board. The speech did not change the fact that union representatives were the exclusive bargaining entities. The meeting was open to the public and the teacher had made his presentation as a concerned citizen. He was not required to relinquish his free speech rights because he was a teacher. To allow only union representatives to exercise their speech rights would amount to a monopoly. The ban on future appearances by teachers before the board would effectively ban all citizens' rights to petition their government. The Court struck down the injunction. *Madison School District v. Wisconsin Employment Relations Commission*, 429 U.S. 167, 97 S.Ct. 421, 50 L.Ed.2d 376 (1976).

In 1977, the Court ruled that the First Amendment prohibited states from compelling teachers to pay union dues or agency fees where their labor unions used the fees for purposes that were unrelated to collective bargaining.

Michigan authorized local government employees to select collective bargaining representatives. When labor unions and government employees agreed, "agency shops" were instituted so that, as a condition of employment, all bargaining unit employees were required to pay either union dues or an equivalent agency fee. Detroit teachers elected a labor association to become its exclusive collective bargaining representative, and instituted an agency shop agreement. All bargaining unit employees were to pay either union dues or the agency fee within 60 days of employment. Failure to pay this amount resulted in employment termination. Teachers were not otherwise required to participate in union activities. A group of teachers filed a class action lawsuit in a Michigan trial court, stating that they would not pay dues for agency fees because of their opposition to collective bargaining in the public sector. They specifically disapproved of the union's political and social activities, which they claimed were unrelated to the collective bargaining process.

The teachers argued that the agency shop agreement violated state law and the First and Fourteenth Amendments to the U.S. Constitution. The court dismissed the lawsuit for failure to state a claim upon which relief could be granted. The Michigan Court of Appeals consolidated the case with the complaint of another group of Michigan teachers. At about the same time, the Michigan legislature expressly authorized the agency shops by amending the state Public Employment Relations Act. The court of appeals then held that the amendment applied retroactively to the teachers, who then argued that retroactive application violated the federal Constitution. When the Michigan Supreme Court refused to review the case, the U.S. Supreme Court accepted jurisdiction on the federal constitutional complaints.

The Court drew on its earlier private sector decisions concerning labor relations and noted that compelled support of collective bargaining representatives implicated teacher First Amendment rights to free speech and association and religious freedom where individual teachers objected to union policies. However, some constitutional infringement on free speech, association and religious exercise was justified in the interest of peaceful labor relations. As long as the union acted to promote the cause of its membership, individual members were not free to withdraw their financial support. The interest in preserving peaceful labor relations was just as strong in the public sector as in the private sector, and the Court upheld the act. Public employees had no greater rights than private sector employees in avoiding compelled union contributions.

The Court agreed with the teachers that compelled agency fees should not be used to support political views and candidates which were unrelated to collective bargaining issues. Because the state court had dismissed the case without a trial, the teachers had not received the opportunity to make specific allegations that their contributions were being used to support activities with which they disagreed. There was no evidentiary record and the Court vacated and remanded the case. If the teachers could prove a First Amendment violation, they would be entitled to an injunction prohibiting the spending of their contributions for ideological causes to which they were opposed, or a pro rata refund of fees being used for such purposes. *Abood v. Detroit Board of Education*, 431 U.S. 209, 97 S.Ct. 1782, 52 L.Ed.2d 261 (1977).

In a 1979 case, the Court held that the National Labor Relations Board had no jurisdiction over religiously-affiliated schools because of potential infringement of school rights under the Religion Clauses of the Constitution.

The National Labor Relations Act (NLRA) (29 U.S.C. § 141 *et seq.*) established the National Labor Relations Board (NLRB), which governs unionization and collective bargaining matters in all aspects of the private sector, including private education. The courts have ruled that "pervasively religious" schools may be able to avoid any obligation under the NLRA to bargain with employees. This exception to the NLRA's coverage is based upon First Amendment religious freedom considerations. When the NLRB authorized labor associations to serve as certified collective bargaining representatives for Catholic high schools in Chicago, the Catholic Bishop refused to recognize the associations. The Bishop claimed that any intervention by the NLRB violated the church's right to freely exercise religion under the Constitution's Religion Clauses. The NLRB argued that the parochial school curriculum included secular instruction and accused the Bishop of unfair labor practices in violation of the NLRA. The case reached the U.S. Supreme Court.

The Court said that the religion clauses of the U.S. Constitution, which require religious organizations to finance their educational systems without governmental aid, also free the religious organizations of the obviously inhibiting effect and impact of unionization of their teachers. The Court agreed with the Bishop's contention that the very threshold act of certification of the union by the NLRB would necessarily alter and infringe upon the religious character of parochial schools. This would mean that the Bishop would no longer be the sole repository of authority as required by church law. Instead he would have to share some decisionmaking with the union. This, said the court, violated the Religion Clauses of the U.S. Constitution. *NLRB v. Catholic Bishop of Chicago*, 440 U.S. 490, 99 S.Ct. 1313, 59 L.Ed.2d 533 (1979).

In another private education case, the Court found a different ground for finding the NLRA inapplicable to a private university. Unlike *NLRB v. Catholic Bishop of Chicago*, above, in which the Court based its opinion on constitutional grounds, the Court used language from the NLRA itself. Because the university's faculty members had considerable managerial responsibilities, the Court deemed them to be outside the scope of the NLRA.

In *NLRB v. Yeshiva Univ.,* the U.S. Supreme Court held that in certain circumstances, faculty members at private educational institutions could be considered managerial employees. Yeshiva's faculty association had petitioned the NLRB seeking certification as bargaining agent for all faculty members. The NLRB granted certification but the university refused to bargain. After the U.S. Court of Appeals declined to enforce the NLRB's order that the university bargain with the labor union, the NLRB appealed to the U.S. Supreme Court, which upheld the appeals court decision. The Supreme Court's ruling was based on its conclusion that Yeshiva's faculty were managerial employees. It stated:

The controlling consideration in this case is that the faculty of Yeshiva University exercise authority which in any other context unquestionably would be managerial. Their authority in academic matters is absolute. They decide what courses will be offered, when they will be scheduled, and to whom they will be taught. They debate and determine teaching methods, grading policies, and matriculation standards. They effectively decide which students will be admitted, retained, and graduated. On occasion their views have determined the size of the student body, the tuition to be charged, and the location of a school. When one considers the function of a university, it is difficult to imagine decisions more managerial than these. To the extent the industrial analogy applies, the faculty determines within each school the product to be produced, the terms upon which it will be offered, and the customers who will be served.

The Court noted that its decision applied only to schools that were "like Yeshiva" and not to schools where the faculty exercised less control. Schools where faculty members do not exercise binding managerial discretion do not fall within the scope of the managerial employee exclusion. *NLRB v. Yeshiva University*, 444 U.S. 672, 100 S.Ct. 856, 63 L.Ed.2d 115 (1980).

In a 1983 case, the Court ruled that a school district's exclusive collective bargaining representative was entitled to use the school district's internal mail system and teacher mailboxes. A rival union which had lost the certification election had no right to use the mail system because the system was not a "public forum" for First Amendment purposes. The policy was also upheld on Equal Protection Clause grounds because the district could legitimately draw distinctions relating to special use of its property.

The Supreme Court of the United States upheld a collective bargaining agreement between an Indiana school board and the local teacher union which provided that the teacher union, to the exclusion of a rival union which was not certified by election, had access to the school district's internal mail and delivery system. The rival union challenged the denial of access to the mail system on grounds that the restriction violated its free speech rights under the First Amendment and the Equal Protection Clause of the Fourteenth Amendment. The Supreme Court, reversing a U.S. Court of Appeals decision, held that since the interschool mail system was not a public forum generally available for use by the public, access to it could be reasonably restricted without violating either free speech or equal protection rights. The court noted the special responsibilities of the exclusive bargaining representative and the fact that other channels of communication remained available to the rival union.

The school district had a legitimate interest in preserving the school mail facilities for their intended purpose, which was to enable the teachers' exclusive bargaining representative to perform its obligations. The noncertified union had no official responsibilities with the district and was not entitled to similar rights. The different treatment of labor organizations was constitutionally permissible because the school district had a strong interest in peaceful labor relations. As the district policy satisfied the Equal Protection Clause of the Fourteenth Amendment, the Court ruled for the school board and certified union. *Perry Education Association v. Perry Local Educators' Association*, 460 U.S. 37, 103 S.Ct. 948, 74 L.Ed.2d 794 (1983).

In 1984, the Court reaffirmed the view that an exclusive bargaining representative which is duly elected by school employees should have the sole voice in discussing employment-related matters with the employer.

The Minnesota Public Employment Labor Relations Act authorized state employees to use collective bargaining to determine employment terms and conditions with their employers. Under the statute, public employers were required to bargain only with the exclusive bargaining representative of public employees. The statute granted professional employees, such as college faculty members, the right to "meet and confer" with their employers on matters outside the scope of the collective bargaining agreement but required the employer to meet only the elected bargaining representative. Faculty members who were not union members objected to the "meet and confer" provision, saying that rights of professional employees within the bargaining unit who were not members of the exclusive representative and who might disagree with its views, were violated by their inability under the statute to express their views.

Non-union Minnesota community college faculty members brought suit against the Minnesota State Board for Community Colleges alleging that the statute violated their First Amendment rights of free speech and their equal protection rights. They claimed that they were denied an opportunity to participate in employer policy making. A federal district court agreed with the faculty members, granting an injunction against enforcement of the statute. The college board appealed to the U.S. Supreme Court.

The Supreme Court held that the "meet and confer" provision did not violate the faculty members' constitutional rights. There was no constitutional right, either as members of the public, as state employees, or as college instructors, to force public employers to listen to the non-union members' views. The fact that an academic setting was involved did not give them any special constitutional right to a voice in the employer's policymaking decisions. Further, the state had a legitimate interest in ensuring that its public employer heard one, and only one, voice presenting the majority view of its professional employees on employment related policy questions. The statute did not restrain non-union employees from free speech. Although the presence of a collective bargaining representative in the meet and confer process amplified the union's voice in the policy-making process, the union presence did not impair any employee constitutional rights. It was rational for the state to give the exclusive bargaining representative a unique role in employment policy matters as it helped ensure the state's legitimate interest in hearing a majority-view voice. The Supreme Court reversed the district court's decision. *Minnesota State Board for Community Colleges v. Knight*, 465 U.S. 271, 104 S.Ct. 1058, 79 L.Ed.2d 299 (1984).

When a school board and a teachers' union make an agency shop agreement which allows union dues to be deducted from the paychecks of nonunion teachers, the union must provide for a reasonably prompt decision by an impartial decision maker as to whether the deductions are being used properly. This requirement was imposed by the U.S. Supreme Court in instances where a school board compels nonmember employees to support their collective bargaining representative.

Although the Supreme Court held in *Abood v. Detroit Board of Education*, above, that nonunion teachers could be compelled to pay a "service fee" to the union to help defray the cost of contract administration and grievance handling, the court prohibited the use of such funds by the union for political or ideological activities not germane to the union's duties as collective bargaining agent. This prohibition was designed to prevent any infringement of nonmember teachers' speech rights in being forced to fund political causes with which they might disagree.

The Supreme Court found that the Chicago Teachers Union had not adequately protected the free speech rights of nonunion teachers. In 1982, the Chicago school board and the teachers' union agreed to deduct "proportionate share payments" from the paychecks of any nonunion employee. The deduction was fixed at 95 percent of the dues for union members, and no explanation was given as to how that figure was reached. This method of deduction was held to violate First Amendment freedom of speech protections. To guard against the possibility of nonunion teachers' service fee payments being used for political purposes that were disagreeable to the nonmembers, the Court ruled that the union must adequately account for and explain the deduction. In case of challenge there must be an opportunity for a reasonably prompt decision by an impartial decisionmaker to determine whether any part of the service fee deduction has gone to fund political causes. Any amount which was reasonably in dispute must be held in an escrow account during pendency of the challenge. *Chicago Teachers Union v. Hudson*, 475 U.S. 292, 106 S.Ct. 1066, 89 L.Ed.2d 232 (1986).

According to the following case, school districts do not have the authority to refuse to negotiate matters with represented employees if the subject matter of the negotiations falls within "conditions of employment."

A union's collective-bargaining agent who represented the employees of two schools owned and operated by the U.S. Army, submitted proposals asking for mileage reimbursement, paid leave, and salary increases on behalf of the schools' employees. The schools refused to negotiate, stating that under Title VII of the Civil Service Reform Act of 1978 they were not required to negotiate these matters. The union filed a complaint with the Federal Labor Relations Authority (FLRA) which held that the union's proposals were negotiable. The schools appealed to the U.S. Court of Appeals, Eleventh Circuit, which upheld the FLRA's decision. The schools then appealed to the U.S. Supreme Court.

Title VII of the Civil Service Reform Act defines conditions of employment as matters "affecting working conditions" but excludes matters relating to prohibited political activities, classification of positions, and those specifically provided for by federal statute. The Court determined that the union's proposals were "conditions of employment." The Supreme Court, affirming the appellate court's decision, held that the schools were required to negotiate salary increases and fringe benefits. *Fort Stewart Schools v. Federal Labor Relations Authority*, 495 U.S. 641, 110 S.Ct. 2043, 109 L.Ed.2d 659 (1990).

In *Lehnert v. Ferris Faculty Ass'n*, below, the Court held that in order to justify agency fees, the activities for which the fees are collected must be germane to collective bargaining activity, be justified by the government's interest in labor peace and the avoidance of free riders, and present only an insignificant burden upon employee speech.

A union that represented the faculty at a Michigan college entered into an agency-shop arrangement with the college, requiring non-union bargaining unit employees to pay a service fee equivalent to a union member's dues. Employees who objected to particular uses of their service fee by the unions brought a 42 U.S.C. § 1983 action against the union in a federal district court, claiming that using the fees for purposes other than negotiating and administering the collective bargaining agreement violated their First and Fourteenth Amendment rights. The court held that certain expenses were chargeable to the dissenting employees, the U.S. Court of Appeals affirmed, and the U.S. Supreme Court granted certiorari.

The Court first noted that chargeable activities must be "germane" to collective bargaining activity and be justified by the policy interest of avoiding "free riders" who benefit from union efforts without paying for union services. It then stated that the local union could charge the objecting employees for their pro rata share of costs associated with chargeable activities of its state and national affiliates, even if those activities did not directly benefit the local bargaining unit. The local could even charge the dissenters for expenses incident to preparation for a strike which would be illegal under Michigan law. However, lobbying activities and public relations efforts were not chargeable to the objecting employees. The Court affirmed in part and reversed in part the lower courts' decisions and remanded the case. *Lehnert v. Ferris Faculty Ass'n*, 500 U.S. 507, 111 S.Ct. 1950, 114 L.Ed.2d 572 (1991).

Ohio public university regents can set standards for faculty instructional workloads for the purpose of emphasizing undergraduate instruction, according to a 1999 Supreme Court decision.

The Ohio legislature passed a statute requiring state universities to adopt faculty workload policies and made them an inappropriate subject for collective bargaining. The law was enacted to address the decline in the amount of time faculty spent teaching, as opposed to time spent on research. Any university policy prevailed over the contrary provisions of collective bargaining agreements. One university adopted a workload policy pursuant to the law and notified the collective bargaining agent that it would not bargain over the policy. As a result, the professors' union filed a state court action, seeking an order that the statute violated public employee equal protection rights. The Supreme Court of Ohio struck down the statute, finding the collective bargaining exemption was not rationally related to the state's interest of encouraging public university professors to spend less time researching at the expense of undergraduate teaching. The U.S. Supreme Court accepted the university's appeal.

According to the Supreme Court, the state supreme court had not applied the correct standard of review under the Equal Protection Clause. In equal protection clause cases that do not involve fundamental rights or suspect classifications, there need only be a rational relationship between disparity of treatment and some legitimate government purpose. In this case, the disputed statute met the rational relationship standard. Ohio could reasonably conclude that the policy would be undercut if it were subjected to collective bargaining. The state legislature could properly determine that collective bargaining would interfere with the legitimate goal of achieving uniformity in faculty workloads. The Ohio Supreme Court decision was reversed and remanded. *Central State Univ. v. American Ass'n of Univ. Professors, Central State Univ. Chapter,* 119 S.Ct. 1162, 143 L.Ed.2d 227 (1999).

CHAPTER FIVE

School District Operations

I. SCHOOL DISTRICT BUDGET AND FINANCE

A. Federal Financial Assistance

The Court ruled that the government may withdraw Emergency School Aid to compel state compliance with desegregation efforts.

The purpose of the federal Emergency School Aid Act (ESAA) is to provide federal financial assistance to eliminate the effects of both *de jure* and *de facto* segregation. The Act contains provisions making an educational agency ineligible if it has practices resulting in disproportionate numbers of minority groups in instructional positions. The New York City Board of Education's applications for federal assistance were denied by the Department of Health, Education and Welfare (HEW) based upon statistical evidence resulting from a compliance investigation which showed a pattern of racially disproportionate assignments of minority teachers in the school system relative to the number of minority students involved. After rejection, the Board appealed to a federal district court claiming these disparities were the result of state law, provisions of collective bargaining agreements, licensing requirements for particular teaching positions, a bilingual instructions consent decree, and demographic changes in student population.

The district court concluded that HEW should have considered these proffered justifications for the statistical disparities, and remanded the case to HEW for further consideration. On remand, HEW determined that such justifications did not adequately rebut the *prima facie* evidence of discrimination established by the statistics. The district court upheld HEW's findings and the U.S. Court of Appeals,

Second Circuit, affirmed the decision, rejecting the Board's contention that HEW was required to establish that the statistical disparities resulted from purposeful or intentional discrimination in the constitutional sense.

On appeal, the U.S. Supreme Court upheld the court of appeals' decision. According to the Court, discriminatory impact is the standard by which ineligibility under the ESAA is to be measured, irrespective of whether the discrimination relates to demotion, dismissal, hiring, promotion or assignment. Legislative history and congressional intent point to a disparate impact test. To treat as ineligible only an applicant with a past or a conscious present intent to perpetuate racial isolation would defeat the stated objective of ending *de facto* as well as *de jure* segregation. The Court also noted that a *prima facie* case of discriminatory impact may be made by a proper statistical study. The burden of rebutting such a statistical case is on the petitioning board. *Board of Education v. Harris*, 444 U.S. 130, 100 S.Ct. 363, 62 L.Ed.2d 275 (1979).

The Tax Injunction Act states that where a taxpayer has "a plain, speedy and efficient remedy" available in state court for the alleged overpayment of taxes, federal district courts cannot enjoin the collection of any state tax.

The Federal Unemployment Tax Act established a cooperative federal-state scheme to provide benefits to unemployed workers. It exempts from mandatory state coverage employees of organizations "operated primarily for religious purposes and which [are . . .] principally supported by a church." A number of California churches and religious schools (including schools unaffiliated with any church) sued the Secretary of Labor, among others, in federal court to stop the secretary from conditioning his approval of the state's unemployment program on its coverage of their employees, and to enjoin the state from collecting unemployment taxes. The district court enjoined the collection of unemployment taxes, and appeal was taken to the U.S. Supreme Court.

The Court determined that it did not need to reach the question of whether the state and federal statutes violated the Establishment Clause and the Free Exercise Clause because the Tax Injunction Act deprived the district court of jurisdiction to hear the challenges. That act provides that district courts cannot enjoin the collection of any state tax where "a plain, speedy and efficient remedy" may be had in state court. Since the schools and churches had such a remedy available, the Court refused to consider their First Amendment claims. The Court vacated and remanded the case. *California v. Grace Brethren Church,* 457 U.S. 393, 102 S.Ct. 2498, 73 L.Ed.2d 93 (1982).

In 1982, the Court held that a gross receipts tax imposed by the state of New Mexico on the construction of new school facilities for a Navajo school board was preempted by federal law.

A Navajo school board obtained bids from non-Indian construction companies so that new school facilities could be built. The bids included the state of New Mexico's gross receipts tax as a cost of construction. During construction, the school board and the winning contractor sued in state court to obtain a refund of the gross receipts tax. The court ruled in favor of the state, and the court of appeals affirmed. Eventually, the case reached the U.S. Supreme Court, which held that the state-imposed gross receipts tax was preempted by federal law. Federal regulation of construction and financing of Indian educational institutions is both comprehensive and pervasive, noted the Court. The burden imposed by the state tax impeded the federal interest in promoting the quality and quantity of educational opportunities for Indians. Accordingly, the lower court decisions were reversed. *Ramah Navajo School Board v. Bureau of Revenue of New Mexico,* 458 U.S. 832, 102 S.Ct. 3394, 73 L.Ed.2d 1174 (1982).

The U.S. Supreme Court reaffirmed its previous ruling in the *Harris* case, above, that the Secretary of Education has the authority to demand a refund of misused funds granted to states under Title I of the Elementary and Secondary Education Act of 1965 (ESEA). Title I provides funding for local education agencies to prepare economically underprivileged children for school. Recipient states must provide assurances to the Secretary of Education that local educational agencies will spend the funds only on qualifying programs.

After federal auditors determined that the states of New Jersey and Pennsylvania had misapplied funds, the Secretary of Education ordered those states to refund to the federal government the amount of the misapplied funds. Both states appealed to the U.S. Court of Appeals, Third Circuit, arguing that, as originally enacted, the ESEA did not expressly authorize the secretary to demand a refund of misspent Title I funds. This authority was later conferred by the Education Amendments of 1978. Accordingly, it was argued that the secretary exceeded his statutory authority in ordering the refunds since the audits in both instances were for a period ending in 1973. The court of appeals held that the secretary did not have the authority to issue the orders.

The Supreme Court reversed the court of appeals' decision, holding that the ESEA, as originally enacted, gave the federal government a right to demand repayment once liability was established. The 1978 amendments were designed merely to clarify the Education Department's legal authority and responsibility to audit recipient states' programs and to specify the procedures to be used in the collection of any debts. *Bell v. New Jersey & Pennsylvania*, 461 U.S. 773, 103 S.Ct. 2187, 76 L.Ed.2d 312 (1983).

Under the Payment in Lieu of Taxes Act, federal funds may be used by the local government which receives them "for any governmental purpose." In the following case, the Court held that a school district could not force a local government to abide by a state law which required a set distribution amount to the school district. The Supremacy Clause of the U.S. Constitution mandated that the federal law preempt the state law.

The Payment in Lieu of Taxes Act compensates local governments for the loss of tax revenues resulting from the tax-immune status of federal lands (like wilderness areas) and for the cost of providing services related to these lands. This federal law provides that local governments may use the payments received by the federal government "for any governmental purpose." A South Dakota statute required local governments to distribute federal payments in lieu of taxes in the same way they distributed general tax revenues. One county allocated 60% of its general revenues to its school districts, but it refused to distribute the federal payments it received in accordance with state law. The school district sued to compel payment, but the state trial court held that the state law conflicted with federal law, and was thus preempted by it. The South Dakota Supreme Court reversed, and appeal was taken to the U.S. Supreme Court, which ruled that the state law was invalid under the Supremacy Clause. School districts were already fully funded by local revenues, and the receipt of the federal money would result in a windfall, not serving the intended federal purpose of compensating local governments for extraordinary or additional expenditures associated with federal lands. *Lawrence County v. Lead-Deadwood School Dist. No 40-1*, 469 U.S. 256, 105 S.Ct. 695, 83 L.Ed.2d 635 (1985).

The Court has established strict guidelines regarding the recovery of Title I funds. In the following two cases, it held that neither

struck down a voting scheme allowing the votes in some counties to have more weight than those in other counties. The Court held that the defect in that case was based on group characteristics such as geographical location. Such characteristics bore no relation to the group's interest in the present case. In other words, the "losing" votes were discarded simply because of geographical location. The Court recognized that the requirement discarded majority rule, giving disproportionate power to minority voters. However, simple ratification by the majority is not always sufficient. Important issues such as bonding, which puts future generations into debt, may require more than majority approval and this should be left to state discretion. As long as such provisions do not discriminate against an identifiable class, they do not violate the Equal Protection Clause. *Gordon v. Lance*, 403 U.S. 1, 91 S.Ct. 1889, 29 L.Ed.2d 273 (1971).

The following school tax case demonstrates the general rule that federal courts will abstain from a case if a state case which would decide the issue is pending in state court. The doctrine of abstention is based on comity, or respect and deference given to state matters. States must generally be given an opportunity to solve the problem or decide the issues on their own. Thus, states are sometimes allowed to strike down taxing systems before they get to federal court.

Florida passed a law known as the "Millage Rollback Law" in 1968 in order to finance the state's public schools. The law provided that a local school district, in order to be eligible for state money, must limit ad valorem taxes for school purposes to not more than ten mills of assessed valuation. A group of taxpayers filed a class action suit against enforcement of the tax, alleging that the tax's effect was invidious discrimination in violation of the Fourteenth Amendment's Equal Protection Clause. The group claimed that children in property-poor counties would receive less money than those in richer counties. A federal district court found that the rollback tax was unconstitutional and enjoined the state from withholding state funds from school districts not in compliance with the ad valorem tax. The U.S. Supreme Court agreed to hear the case.

The Court vacated the district court's decision and remanded the case. It ruled that the federal court should have abstained from considering the case because a case had been filed in state court challenging the rollback tax on state constitutional grounds. The Court stated that the district court should have waited until the state case had been decided because the tax could have been struck down on state constitutional grounds and thus, there would no longer be a need for the district court to hear the case. *Askew v. Hargrave*, 401 U.S. 476, 91 S.Ct. 856, 28 L.Ed.2d 196 (1971).

The Court has upheld individual constitutional rights, but has provided no guarantee that the individual will have full access to exercise those rights when they depend upon funding. An example of this is in the following case, where the Court upheld Texas' property tax system for funding schools.

The U.S. Supreme Court reversed a federal district court ruling which held the Texas school-financing system unconstitutional. In reversing the lower court decision, the Supreme Court took note of the apparent discrepancies created by such a system in which ad valorem taxes differ greatly from one district to another. In spite of the discrepancies, however, the Supreme Court made the following determinations: the Texas system does not work to the disadvantage of any group or class of citizens since the disadvantages occur only between districts regardless of the relative wealth of any family within the district. Hence, "poor" citizens throughout the system were not disadvantaged as a class.

The Texas system did not interfere with a "fundamental" right, since education, while undeniably of the highest importance, is not recognized by the Supreme Court as within those rights guaranteed by the Constitution. The school-financing system bore a rational relationship to a legitimate state purpose—education. While the same basic education is assured all children by virtue of the funding of all schools through the Texas Minimum Foundation School Program, the Texas system allowed and encouraged participation and control of each school at the local level. The Supreme Court therefore held the Texas school-financing system constitutional. *San Antonio School District v. Rodriguez*, 411 U.S. 1, 93 S.Ct. 1278, 36 L.Ed.2d 16 (1973).

Statutes may require employers under school district contracts to hire a quota of minorities. Such programs are often challenged, and federal courts are confronted with the task of determining how states can deal with racial discrimination. Challenges must be decided first on the basis of state law, if possible.

California passed a statute that required school districts to award any contracts for work involving more than $12,000 to the lowest "responsible" bidder. The Oakland school board provided that for projects over $100,000, "responsible" contractors are those that use minority-owned businesses for at least 25 percent of the amount of the entire bid. Contractors who had submitted the lowest bid, but who were disqualified as not "responsible," sued in a federal district court for damages. They also challenged the constitutionality of the statute as an affirmative action plan and claimed that it violated state law. The district court held that the scheme was constitutional. The U.S. Court of Appeals, Ninth Circuit, affirmed the district court's decision. In addition, the court of appeals declined to decide whether the scheme violated state law. It did, however, acknowledge that under one of its previous decisions, the plan might be violative of state law. It categorized the claim as "sensitive" and noted that the state courts should decide it.

The U.S. Supreme Court granted certiorari and vacated the court of appeals' decision. It held that the district court had abused its discretion in not deciding the state-law claim. If the plan had been invalid under state law, there would have been no need for the court of appeals to decide the federal constitutionality of the law. The case was remanded to the district court. *Schmidt v. Oakland Unified School District*, 457 U.S. 594, 102 S.Ct. 2612, 73 L.Ed.2d 245 (1982).

The Supreme Court held that certain school districts in Mississippi could sue in federal court to challenge the state's unequal distribution with respect to funding. The suit was not barred by the Eleventh Amendment because the alleged violations by the state were ongoing.

The federal government issued school land grants to Mississippi in the early 19th Century, but the grants did not apply to land held by the Chickasaw Indian Nation. Later, the Indians ceded this land to the United States, but none of the territory was reserved for public schools. Congress then gave certain lands to the state for the use of schools. However, the state sold the lands and invested the proceeds in loans to railroads which were destroyed in the Civil War. As a result, the northern 23 counties in the state were treated differently than the rest of the counties with respect to funding. Certain local school officials and students thus brought a lawsuit challenging Mississippi's distribution of public school land funds. The U.S. district court dismissed the suit on Eleventh Amendment grounds (which disallows certain lawsuits brought by citizens against a state in *federal* court). The U.S. Court of Appeals, Fifth Circuit, affirmed.

On further appeal to the U.S. Supreme Court, the Court held that the Eleventh Amendment did not entirely bar the lawsuit. The allegation of a continuing constitutional violation—an equal protection violation by virtue of the state's unequal distribution of the benefits of school lands— was the kind of ongoing violation for which a remedy could be fashioned. The Court remanded the case for a determination of whether the variations in benefits received by the different school districts were rationally related to a legitimate state interest and thus valid. *Papasan v. Allain,* 478 U.S. 265, 106 S.Ct. 2932, 92 L.Ed.2d 209 (1986).

The Supreme Court has extended the *Rodriguez* doctrine to all costs associated with education, including transportation.

North Dakota statutes authorize thinly populated school districts to reorganize into larger districts for efficiency. Reorganized districts must provide for student transportation to and from their homes. School districts choosing not to reorganize were authorized by statute to charge students a portion of their costs for transportation. Parents of a nine-year-old student refused to sign a transportation contract with the school district. The family was near or at the poverty level. Claiming inability to pay the fee, the family made private transportation arrangements which were more costly than the school's fee. The parents sued the school district in a North Dakota trial court for an order to prevent the school district from collecting the fee on grounds that it violated the state constitution and the Equal Protection Clause. After losing at the trial court level, the parents appealed to the North Dakota Supreme Court which upheld the lower court decision on state and federal constitutional grounds. The parents then appealed to the U.S. Supreme Court.

The U.S. Supreme Court upheld the statute's validity. The parents claimed that the user fee for bus service unconstitutionally deprived poor persons of minimum access to education and placed an unconstitutional obstacle to education for poor students. The Court noted that the student continued to attend school during the time she claimed she was denied access to the school bus. The Equal Protection Clause did not require free transportation. Education is not a fundamental right under the U.S. Constitution. The statute bore a reasonable relationship to the state's legitimate objective of encouraging local school districts to provide bus service. Payment of bus fees was not directly imposed by the statute. The statute did not discriminate against any class and did not interfere with any constitutional rights. *Kadrmas v. Dickinson Public Schools,* 487 U.S. 450, 108 S.Ct. 2481, 101 L.Ed.2d 399 (1988).

In 1989, the U.S. Supreme Court ruled that a choice of law in a university contractor's construction contract superseded arbitration rights found in the Federal Arbitration Act. This was because the parties had intended to incorporate state arbitration rules into the contract. As state law controlled, the Court refused to set aside the judgment of the California courts.

An electrical contractor contracted with a California university to install conduits. The contract contained a clause in which the parties agreed to arbitrate disputes relating to the contract. The contract also contained a choice-of-law clause which stated that it would be governed by the law of the place of the project's location. A dispute arose concerning overtime compensation and the contractor made a formal request for arbitration. The university sued the contractor in a California trial court for fraud and breach of contract. The contractor claimed that it was entitled to arbitration under the contract and the Federal Arbitration Act (FAA). The court granted the university's motion to stay arbitration under a California statute which permits a stay when arbitration is the subject of pending court action. The contractor appealed to the California Court of Appeal, which affirmed the trial court's decision. The court of appeal acknowledged that although the contract affected interstate commerce, the California statute applied because of the contractual choice-of-law clause. The California Supreme Court denied the contractor's petition for discretionary review, but the U.S. Supreme Court agreed to hear its appeal.

On appeal, the contractor reiterated its argument that the court of appeal's ruling on the choice-of-law clause deprived it of its federally guaranteed right to arbitration under the FAA. The Supreme Court ruled that the FAA did not confer a general right to compel arbitration. Rather, it guaranteed the right to arbitrate according to the manner provided for in the parties' contract. The court of appeal had correctly found that the contract incorporated California law. The FAA was not undermined by the state law which permitted a stay of arbitration. The Court affirmed the court of appeal's decision for the university. *Volt Information Sciences v. Board of Trustees of Leland Stanford Junior University*, 489 U.S. 468, 109 S.Ct. 1248, 103 L.Ed.2d 488 (1989).

The Supreme Court held that a New York statute creating a separate school district that followed a religious enclave's boundary lines violated the Establishment Clause of the First Amendment because it was not neutral toward religion. The state legisla-

ture had impermissibly delegated civic authority on the basis of religious belief.

A New York school district provided special education services at private, religious schools to students with disabilities who were members of the Satmar Hasidic group. The group's religious beliefs include segregation of school-aged boys and girls, and separation from mainstream society. A U.S. Supreme Court decision in 1985 prohibited the state from paying public school teachers for teaching on parochial school grounds. See *Aguilar v. Felton*, Chapter Two, above. Hasidic children were then sent to public schools while the group continued to challenge the matter. The state legislature passed a statute establishing a new, separate school district entirely within the Hasidic community. The school district provided only special education services, and Hasidic regular education students continued to attend private religious schools. New York taxpayers and an association of state school officials sought and obtained a state trial court declaration that the statute was unconstitutional. The New York Court of Appeals held that the statute conveyed a message of government endorsement of religion in violation of the Establishment Clause of the U.S. Constitution. The U.S. Supreme Court agreed to review the matter.

The Supreme Court held that a state may not delegate authority to a group chosen by religion. Although the statute did not expressly identify the Hasidim as recipients of governmental authority, it had clearly been passed to benefit them. The result was a purposeful and forbidden fusion of governmental and religious functions. The creation of a school district for the religious community violated the Establishment Clause. The legislation extended a special franchise to the Hasidim that violated the constitutional requirement of religious neutrality by the government. The statute crossed "the line from permissible accommodation to impermissible establishment," and the Supreme Court affirmed the judgment of the court of appeals. *Bd. of Educ. of Kiryas Joel Village School Dist. v. Grumet*, 512 U.S. 687, 114 S.Ct. 2481, 129 L.Ed.2d 546 (1994).

II. SCHOOL ELECTIONS

In a 1966 Michigan school board case, the Court held that there was no constitutional reason why nonlegislative state and local officials could not be chosen by the state governor, legislature, or by another appointive process.

Michigan law provided that local school boards be elected by the people and that county school boards be chosen not by the voters but by delegates from local school boards. Each local board sent a delegate to a biennial meeting and those delegates elected the county board from candidates nominated by school electors. This system was challenged by a group of qualified and registered voters in a federal district court. The group also challenged actions taken by the county school board, claiming that the procedures governing the board's appointment unconstitutionally violated the Due Process Clause of the Fourteenth Amendment. The voters also challenged the system as a violation of the principle of one-man, one-vote because only one vote was given to each local school board. The district court held that the procedure did not violate the Fourteenth Amendment. The U.S. Supreme Court agreed to hear the case.

The Court upheld the procedure's constitutionality. It held that there was no constitutional reason why state and local officials of a nonlegislative character could not be chosen by the governor, legislature, or by some other appointive means other than elections. It noted that county school boards perform essentially administrative functions, and therefore are not legislative bodies. Local governments need flexible, experimental policies in order to meet changing urban conditions. The Court held that the "one-man, one-vote" challenge was irrelevant because the school board appointment process did not involve an election. The district court's decision was affirmed. *Sailors v. Board of Education*, 387 U.S. 105, 87 S.Ct. 1549, 18 L.Ed.2d 650 (1966).

When a state limits participation rights in the election of school board officials, it must administer the vote fairly. The Court rejected a New York school district's argument that the state had a compelling interest in excluding persons such as bachelors without children from participating in school board elections.

New York law provided three methods of school board selection. First, the school board could be appointed by the mayor or city council. In smaller districts, the school board was elected in general or municipal elections in which all qualified city voters could vote. Finally, in rural and suburban districts the school board was elected at an annual meeting of qualified school district voters. State education law also provided that voters voting at the annual meetings meet one of three qualifications: be the owner or lessee of taxable real property within the district, be the spouse of one who owns or leases property or be the parent or guardian of a child enrolled for a specified time during the next year in the local district. A bachelor who neither owned nor leased taxable real property, nor had any children and who lived with his parents, challenged the statute in a federal district court. He claimed it violated the Equal Protection Clause of the Fourteenth Amendment. The district court dismissed the complaint. The U.S. Supreme Court agreed to hear the case.

The Court observed that local school districts retained a great deal of control over school district policy. For example, local school boards choose what materials to use and whether equipment should be purchased. In addition, voters at annual meetings approved the yearly budget as submitted by the school board. The Court noted that the bachelor was only challenging the constitutionality of the additional voting requirements under New York law, and not the usual requirements of citizenship, residency and age. In other words, the bachelor would have otherwise been eligible to vote if not for the additional requirements. Thus, he argued, he was being denied equal protection of the law.

The Court examined the facts and circumstances behind the law, the interests claimed to be protected by the state and the interests of those disadvantaged by the classification. Because the right to vote is so important, the state must advance a compelling interest for such denial. The Court rejected the school district's arguments that the state had a compelling interest in limiting elections to community members primarily interested in the elections. The state had not shown that it had used the least restrictive means to allow only those primarily interested to vote. The denial of voting rights to some people was not justified. The Court reversed the district court's decision and held the statute unconstitutional. *Kramer v. Union School District*, 395 U.S. 621, 89 S.Ct. 1886, 23 L.Ed.2d 583 (1968).

In *Wesberry v. Sanders*, 376 U.S. 1, 84 S.Ct. 526, 11 L.Ed.2d 481 (1964), the Supreme Court required that one person's vote in a congressional election must be worth as much as another's, as near as practicable. This is the "one man, one vote" doctrine, which was later extended to state elections for legislators and finally to local government elections. Taxpayers began using the one man, one vote principle to challenge the election of school board members and trustees. The Court applied the principle to these cases.

Under Missouri law, separate school districts could establish a consolidated junior college district by referendum. They could also elect six trustees to administer their districts. The law also provided that the trustees be appointed among the separate districts by "school enumeration." School enumeration was defined by state law as the number of persons between six and 20 who lived in each district. Residents and taxpayers of the Kansas City School District challenged this provision as violating the "one man, one vote" doctrine and the Fourteenth Amendment's Equal Protection Clause. The district was one of eight that had combined to form a junior college district. The apportionment plan resulted in the election of three trustees, or 50 percent of the board, from the Kansas City school district, even though the district contained 60 percent of the total school enumeration in the junior college district. The taxpayers argued that this scheme unconstitutionally diluted their vote.

A Missouri trial court dismissed the case and the Missouri Supreme Court affirmed its decision, stating that the one man, one vote principle was inapplicable. The U.S. Supreme Court agreed to hear the appeal. The Court reversed the Missouri Supreme Court's decision, finding that the one man, one vote principle applied to school elections. It held that the Fourteenth Amendment required trustee positions within the junior college district to be apportioned so that each vote was given as much weight as any other in the district. It agreed with the taxpayers' argument that because the board of trustees had the power to levy and collect taxes, issue bonds, hire and fire teachers, supervise and discipline students and administer the district, it should be subject to the same apportionment requirements as other elective bodies. The right to vote is protected against debasement by the Constitution.

The Court concluded that the purpose of a particular election is not the determining factor in whether voting rights should be equal. Whether voting in a congressional election, or for the county sheriff, each person must have an equal vote. The Court held that when Missouri established elections for boards of trustees, rather than using appointments, it was obligated to ensure voting equality. *Hadley v. Junior College District*, 397 U.S. 50, 90 S.Ct. 791, 25 L.Ed.2d 45 (1969).

In 1973, the Court concluded that an injunction granted by a federal district court against a mayor's future action in appointing a city school board was unjustified, since the charges had arisen from the former mayor's actions.

Philadelphia voters amended their city charter to allow the mayor to appoint nine members of the city school board. Each of the remaining nine positions were filled by the highest ranking officer of one of nine designated categories of citywide organizations. The mayor was assisted by an educational nominating panel, whose members the mayor also appointed. The panel's function was to seek out qualified candidates for service on the school board and to submit nominees to the mayor. Under the charter, the mayor was required to appoint four of the panel's members from the citizenry at large. The mayor was then required to make his selection from the nominees.

The Philadelphia Educational Equality League, the league president, Philadelphia citizens and city public school students challenged the mayor's 1971 panel appointments. The citizens and the league alleged that he had violated the Fourteenth Amendment's Equal Protection Clause by excluding blacks from appointment to the panel. They claimed that the mayor had discriminated against qualified black applicants for panel positions and requested an order directing the appointment of a panel which fairly represented the racial composition of the school community. A federal court dismissed their complaint, holding that they had failed to establish evidence of racial discrimination. The U.S. Court of Appeals, Third Circuit, reversed, ruling that the group had established an unrebutted *prima facie* case of unlawful discrimination. The court then issued injunctive relief against a newly-elected mayor who had succeeded the incumbent during the court proceedings. The U.S. Supreme Court granted review.

Before the Court, the new mayor contended that federal courts may not interfere with an elected executive officer's discretionary appointment powers. The Court held that it need not decide this issue, since racial discrimination had not been established. It concluded that the court of appeals' finding of racial discrimination was based on three fragments of evidence, only one of which was based on the district court's finding. First, the court of appeals should have excluded a statement by the mayor that he would limit the number of blacks on the school board as inadmissible hearsay. Second, the court of appeals relied on the district court's finding that the deputy mayor had made a statement that he had been unaware of many "black-oriented organizations" whose members could qualify for panel positions. The deputy mayor's ignorance was irrelevant, since it was the mayor's job to fill the positions. Third, the court of appeals went outside the district court's findings to conclude that the number of black panelists was small in proportion to the black population. The Court concluded that the injunction against the new mayor's future action was unjustified, since the charges arose only from the former mayor's actions. *Mayor v. Educational Equality League*, 415 U.S. 605, 94 S.Ct. 1323, 39 L.Ed.2d 630 (1973).

Federal district courts have the initial chance to reapportion school board voting districts when a state system is challenged. The Supreme Court has established the rule that federal courts are to prefer single-member districts to multi-member or *at-large districts*.

In 1968, a white Louisiana resident brought a suit in a federal district court to challenge voting wards in his county. He contended that population disparities among the wards denied him the constitutional right to cast an effective vote in elections for school board members and members of the police jury, which is the governing board of the parish. Accordingly, the district court adopted a reapportionment plan which called for at-large election of the board members. For the next two years, elections were held at-large. After the 1970 census, the district court instructed the two boards to submit revised reapportionment plans. They resubmitted the at-large plan.

A black voter was allowed to intervene in the action on behalf of himself and voters similarly situated. The district court approved the submitted at-large plan and the black voter appealed to the U.S. Court of Appeals, Fifth Circuit, arguing that at-large elections would dilute the black vote in violation of the Fourteenth and Fifteenth Amendments, and the Voting Rights Act of 1965. The court of appeals, hearing *en banc*, reversed, concluding that at-large elections would dilute the black vote in the parish. In the court of appeals' decision, it suggested that multimember districts, requiring at-large elections, were unconstitutional unless they afforded greater opportunity for political participation or unless the use of single voting districts would violate rights. The U.S. Supreme Court granted certiorari.

The Supreme Court affirmed the court of appeals' decision but divorced itself from the court's broad statements regarding the constitutionality of at-large voting. It held that the district court had abused its discretion in not initially ordering a single-member appointment plan. The Court held that it is well-established that when federal district courts are called upon to reapportion districts to avoid voting disparities, single-member districts are to be used first unless there are special circumstances. The court of appeals' decision was affirmed. *East Carroll Parish School Board v. Marshall*, 424 U.S. 640, 96 S.Ct. 1083, 47 L.Ed.2d 296 (1976).

In 1978, the Court suspended a Georgia county education board rule which would have required county employees to forego their

salaries when running for political office. The rule violated § 5 of the Voting Rights Act.

A black administrator of student personnel services for a county board of education announced his candidacy for the Georgia House of Representatives. Less than a month later, the board unexpectedly adopted a rule, without federal approval, requiring that any board employee running for office would have to take a leave of absence without pay. As a result, the administrator was forced to take three leaves of absence, losing approximately $11,000 in salary. The administrator sued in a federal district court, alleging that the rule was invalid because it was a standard in regard to voting and therefore required federal clearance under § 5 of the Voting Rights Act of 1965. The administrator also pointed out that he was the first black from the county to run for the Georgia legislature since the Reconstruction Era. The district court held that the rule should obtain federal approval before it was implemented. However, the court declined to decide whether the rule itself had a discriminatory purpose or effect, refusing to rule on its compliance with § 5 of the Voting Rights Act. The U.S. Supreme Court agreed to hear the case.

The Supreme Court agreed that the rule was a voting procedure, thus subject to compliance with § 5. The Court noted that previous decisions had given § 5 a broad interpretation, in order to encompass any state enactments altering its election law. The rule in question imposed substantial economic disincentives for public employees seeking office. The Court ruled that although the leave of absence rule was established by a school board which itself did not conduct elections, the rule became subject to Civil Rights Act requirements because it affected the electoral process. The Court affirmed the district court's decision and the rule was suspended, pending its clearance of § 5 of the Civil Rights Act. *Dougherty County Board of Education v. White*, 439 U.S. 32, 99 S.Ct. 368, 58 L.Ed.2d 269 (1978).

The Supreme Court held that a change in voting practices that violates § 2 of the Voting Rights Act does not constitute an independent reason for denying preclearance under § 5 of the act. However, evidence presented in support of a § 2 claim might be relevant in a § 5 proceeding.

The Voting Rights Act of 1965 was enacted to eradicate certain widespread discriminatory voting practices. Section Two of the act bars all states and their political subdivisions from maintaining discriminatory voting practices, standards or procedures. Violation of this section may be shown where the electoral system is not open to equal participation because of race. Section Five of the act is limited in scope to particular states and their political subdivisions that are identified as covered jurisdictions. It prohibits the formerly common practice of passing new discriminatory laws as soon as old ones were struck down by freezing election procedures in covered jurisdictions unless the changes are nondiscriminatory.

A Louisiana school board that was covered under § 5 addressed population disparities revealed in the 1990 census by adopting a plan similar to one adopted by the parish's governing body that preserved a white majority in each of its twelve single member districts. The board rejected a proposal by the local NAACP that would have created two districts with a majority of African-American voters. The board complied with § 5 procedures by applying for preclearance from the U.S. District Court for the District of Columbia.

A three judge panel granted the preclearance request, and the U.S. Attorney General's office appealed to the U.S. Supreme Court, where it joined with the NAACP in arguing that a change in voting practices that violates the § 2 prohibition on discriminatory voting practices also constitutes an independent reason to deny preclearance under § 5. The Court rejected this argument, citing 20 years of contrary legal precedent and stating that the board would be improperly burdened by this presumption. The sections addressed different voting policy concerns and nothing in the statute justified presuming that a violation of § 2 was sufficient for denying preclearance under § 5. However, some of the evidence presented in support of a § 2 claim might be relevant in a § 5 proceeding. Because the district court had failed to consider evidence of the dilutive impact of the board's redistricting plan, the Court vacated the judgment and remanded the case. *Reno v. Bossier Parish School Bd.*, 520 U.S. 471, 117 S.Ct. 1491, 137 L.Ed.2d 73 (1997).

In the following Voting Rights Act case, the Court recited the general rule, applicable in all cases, that a claim is not ripe for adjudication if it rests upon contingent future events that may not actually occur.

Section Five of the Voting Rights Act of 1965 requires covered jurisdictions to obtain preclearance from the U.S. District Court for the District of Columbia or the U.S. Attorney General prior to the implementation of any state change affecting voting. Texas is a covered jurisdiction under § 5. The Texas legislature enacted a comprehensive statutory scheme for holding local school boards accountable to the state for student achievement. The law contains ten possible sanctions which can be imposed on school districts for failing to meet legislative standards governing the assessment of academic skills, development of academic performance indicators, determination of accreditation status and the imposition of accreditation sanctions. The two most drastic sanctions, appointment of a master or of a management team to oversee school district operations, require the exhaustion of the lesser sanctions first. In compliance with § 5, Texas requested administrative preclearance for the amendments. The attorney general approved most of the sanctions as not affecting voting, but determined that the appointment of a master or management team could result in a § 5 violation.

Texas appealed to the U.S. District Court for the District of Columbia, which held that the claim was not ripe for adjudication. The U.S. Supreme Court agreed to review the case, and stated the general rule that a claim is not ripe for adjudication if it rests upon contingent future events that may not actually occur. Texas had not identified any school district in the state which might become subject to the appointment of a master or management team and was not required to implement the sanctions until one of the remedies already approved by the attorney general had been exhausted. Because the issue presented was speculative and unfit for judicial review, the Court affirmed the judgment. *Texas v. U.S.*, 523 U.S. 296, 118 S.Ct. 1257, 140 L.Ed.2d 406 (1998).

III. ACCESS TO SCHOOL BUILDINGS

The Supreme Court held that an organization in New York could not use public school buildings for its meetings because it had not shown that other similar organizations had been allowed to use the buildings while its requests had been denied.

The Yonkers, New York, board of education denied a request by the Yonkers Committee for Peace that it be allowed to use the Yonkers public school buildings for a forum on war and peace. The committee then filed suit in a New York trial court, alleging that as a result of the board's denial, its members' free speech, assembly, and equal protection rights had been violated. The trial court dismissed the complaint, and the New York Supreme Court, Appellate Division, affirmed. The New York Court of Appeals also affirmed, without giving a reason for its decision. The U.S. Supreme Court granted certiorari.

The Court affirmed the state courts' decisions, holding that the committee had failed to allege that other organizations of a similar character had been allowed to use the school buildings for the purpose of public assembly, thus failing to make out an equal protection claim. The Court stated that the claim was "too amorphous" to be decided on its constitutionality. The state court's decision was upheld. *Ellis v. Dixon*, 349 U.S. 458, 75 S.Ct. 859, 99 L.Ed. 1231 (1955).

The Supreme Court held that a school district could not prohibit a church from using its facilities for the purpose of airing secular views with a religious point of view because the subject matter was permissible by law.

A New York law authorized local school boards to pass regulations allowing school property to be used in certain specified ways. A local school board issued regulations allowing social, civic, or recreational uses or limited use by political organizations, but provided that the school not be used for religious purposes. An evangelical church sought permission to use the school facilities to show a six-part film series on family values. The district denied the church permission to use the school grounds because the film was church-related. The church filed suit in a federal court alleging that the district's denial violated its First and Fourteenth Amendment rights. The court held for the district, and the U.S. Court of Appeals, Ninth Circuit, affirmed, holding that the school was a "limited public forum" such that the district could exclude certain groups where the exclusion was "reasonable and viewpoint neutral." The church appealed to the U.S. Supreme Court.

The Court assumed that the school property was a limited public forum and that the school was not open for "indiscriminate public use for communicative purposes." However, even in a limited public forum, government exclusion of a category of speech must be "reasonable and viewpoint neutral." The Court noted that viewpoints about family issues were not proscribed by the district's regulations. Although the film addressed the subject from a religious perspective, the subject matter itself was permissible. Therefore, the regulation discriminated on the basis of viewpoint and the exclusion of this particular church from school property was not "viewpoint neutral" even though the district excluded all religious organizations. Next, the Court determined that since the film was not to be shown during school hours and was to be open to those outside the church, the public would not perceive the district to be endorsing religion. Accordingly, permission by the school district would not violate the Establishment Clause. The holding of the court of appeals was reversed. *Lamb's Chapel v. Center Moriches*

Union Free School District, 508 U.S. 384, 113 S.Ct. 2141, 124 L.Ed.2d 352 (1993).

IV. SCHOOL DISTRICT LIABILITY

The Supreme Court has ruled that the Constitution does not impose an affirmative duty on either the state or its employees (who act in their official capacities) to protect an individual's rights. The Constitution only prohibits the state from depriving an individual of his or her rights.

A Pennsylvania high school student had been sexually abused by her band director. The student sued the school district and several school officials alleging that the officials had either known or had recklessly failed to discover that the band director was preying on his female students. The school district asked a federal district court to dismiss the case but the court refused. The school district then appealed to the U.S. Court of Appeals, Third Circuit, which affirmed the district court's ruling. The court of appeals stated that every reasonable school official should know that it was a breach of duty to take no action to protect a student from sexual abuse. The court of appeals held that the constitution mandated some affirmative action to investigate and protect students from abuse.

The U.S. Supreme Court vacated the judgment and remanded the case to the court of appeals for further consideration in light of *Deshaney v. Winnebago County DSS,* 489 U.S. 189, 109 S.Ct. 998, 103 L.Ed.2d 249 (1989). In *Deshaney,* the Supreme Court held that the state's failure to protect an individual against private violence does not constitute a civil rights violation. The Court noted that the Constitution does not impose an affirmative duty on the state to protect an individual's rights, but only forbids the state itself from depriving the individual of these rights. In light of this holding, the Court vacated the judgment and remanded the case for further consideration. *Bradford Area Sch. Dist. v. Stoneking,* 489 U.S. 1062, 109 S.Ct. 1333, 103 L.Ed.2d 804 (1989).

Similarly, the Court vacated the Third Circuit's holding in *Sowers v. Bradford Area School Dist.* The Court noted that since the case was governed by the holding in *Stoneking* (above), the student's 42 U.S.C. § 1983 claim against the school officials was improperly considered. The Court vacated the judgment and remanded the case. *Smith v. Sowers,* 490 U.S. 1002, 109 S.Ct. 1634, 104 L.Ed.2d 150 (1989).

The Supreme Court held that even though a state university would be reimbursed by the federal government for any adverse judgments against it, the university was still able to assert the defense of Eleventh Amendment immunity. It is the entity's potential legal liability, rather than its ability to require reimbursement, that determines the immunity question.

A New York mathematical physicist sought employment at the Lawrence Livermore National Laboratory, which is operated by the University of California pursuant to a contract with the federal government. He sued university regents in a federal district court, claiming breach of contract because the university agreed to employ him but then wrongfully refused to hire him when he could not obtain the required security clearance from the U.S. Department of Energy (DOE). The court held that the Eleventh Amendment, which provides for state immunity from lawsuits, barred his breach of contract action. The U.S. Court of Appeals, Ninth Circuit, reversed the decision and the U.S. Supreme Court agreed to review the case.

On appeal, the physicist contended that the Eleventh Amendment was inapplicable in this case because any award of damages would be paid by the DOE and not the state of California. The Supreme Court rejected this argument, finding that an entity's potential legal liability, not its ability to discharge the liability or to require a third party to reimburse it, was the relevant inquiry when determining the immunity issue. The Eleventh Amendment protects a state from the risk of adverse judgments even though the state may be indemnified by a third party. The Court reversed the court of appeals' judgment. *Regents of Univ. of California v. Doe*, 519 U.S. 337, 117 S.Ct. 900, 137 L.Ed.2d 55 (1997).

Title IX of the Education Amendments of 1972 prohibits sex discrimination by education programs and activities receiving federal funding. It contains no express private right of action to recover monetary damages, but one was implied by the U.S. Supreme Court in *Cannon v. Univ. of Chicago*, Chapter Three, Section III, above. In 1998, the Court held that damages are inappropriate in a Title IX case unless an official with the authority to address the discrimination fails to act despite actual knowledge of it, in a manner amounting to deliberate indifference to discrimination.

The U.S. Court of Appeals, Fifth Circuit, affirmed a federal district court decision granting summary judgment to a Texas school district in a Title IX discrimination action filed by a student who had an ongoing sexual relationship with a teacher. The district discharged the teacher after it learned of the relationship and the Texas Education Agency revoked his teaching license. However, the Fifth Circuit held that imposing liability on the school district would amount to strict liability because there was insufficient evidence that a school official should have known about the relationship. The U.S. government was included as a party to the action and joined the student's appeal to the U.S. Supreme Court.

The Court rejected the liability standard advocated by the student and the U.S. government, which resembled *respondeat superior* liability under Title VII. Title IX contains an administrative enforcement mechanism that assumes actual notice has been provided to officials prior to the imposition of enforcement remedies. An award of damages would be inappropriate in a Title IX case unless an official with the authority to address the discrimination failed to act despite actual knowledge of it, in a manner amounting to deliberate indifference to discrimination. The failure of the school district to devise an appropriate grievance procedure for harassment claims in this case did not establish deliberate indifference on its behalf. The Court affirmed the judgment for the school district. *Gebser v. Lago Vista Indep. School Dist.*, 524 U.S. 274, 118 S.Ct. 1989, 141 L.Ed.2d 277 (1998).

In examining whether Title IX creates a cause of action for peer sexual harassment, the Supreme Court held that school districts may be liable for deliberate indifference to known acts of peer sexual harassment under Title IX in cases where the response of school administrators is clearly unreasonable under the circumstances.

A Georgia student complained to her teacher of sexual harassment by a male student. The teacher did not immediately notify the principal of the harassment. Although the harasser was eventually charged with sexual battery, school officials took no action against him. The student sued the school board in federal district court under Title IX of the Education Amendments of 1972, which prohibit sex discrimination by education programs receiving federal funding. The district court dismissed the case and the student appealed to the U.S. Court of Appeals, Eleventh Circuit. The circuit court reversed the judgment but granted the board's petition for rehearing. On rehearing, the circuit court observed that if it adopted the student's argument, a school board must immediately isolate an alleged harasser to avoid a Title IX lawsuit. Because Congress did not discuss student-on-student harassment during consideration of the Title IX amendments, there was no merit to this assertion. The circuit court affirmed the dismissal.

The Supreme Court reversed, holding that school districts may be liable for deliberate indifference to known acts of peer sexual harassment under Title IX in cases where the response of school administrators is clearly unreasonable under the circumstances. A recipient of federal funds may be liable for student-on-student sexual harassment where the funding recipient is deliberately indifferent to known student sexual harassment and the harasser is under the recipient's disciplinary authority. In order to create Title IX liability, the harassment must be so severe, pervasive, and objectively offensive that it deprives the victim of access to the funding recipient's educational opportunities or benefits. The Supreme Court stated that the harassment alleged by the student was sufficiently severe to avoid pretrial dismissal, thus reversing and remanding the case. *Davis v. Monroe County Bd. of Educ.,* 119 S.Ct. 1661, 143 L.Ed.2d 839 (1999).

CHAPTER SIX

Students with Disabilities

In the 1970's, Congress passed major legislation affecting special education and the rights of persons with disabilities. The most important special education legislation was the Education for All Handicapped Children Act of 1975 (EAHCA), 20 U.S.C. §§ 1410-1420, which amended the 1970 Education of the Handicapped Act, 20 U.S.C. 1400 *et seq* (EHA). Another important EHA amendment is the Handicapped Children's Protection Act of 1986, which requires losing parties in EHA litigation to pay the prevailing party's attorney's fees. In 1990, the EHA was once again amended, and the act was renamed the Individuals with Disabilities Education Act (IDEA). Finally, in 1997, the IDEA was again amended, allowing, among other things, the removal of disruptive disabled students from class for up to 55 days. Congress expanded the rights of persons with disabilities in § 504 of the Rehabilitation Act of 1973, 29 U.S.C. § 794, which states that "[n]o otherwise qualified individual with a disability in the United States... shall, solely by reason of her or his disability, be excluded from the participation in, be denied the benefits of, or be subjected to discrimination under any program or activity receiving Federal financial assistance," and in the Americans with Disabilities Act (ADA), which extends the protections of § 504 to the private sector. States have also enacted their own statutes protecting individuals with disabilities and statutes regarding special education. A distinct new body of law has developed around these enactments.

The U.S. Supreme Court's ruling in *Southeastern Community College v. Davis* set the standard for all institutions, including private schools, whose programs or activities receive federal financial assistance for evaluating claims of handicap discrimination.

A female nursing school applicant, who was severely hearing impaired, claimed that the decision denying her admission violated § 504 of the Rehabilitation Act. Section 504 states that an "otherwise qualified individual with a disability" may not be excluded from a federally funded program solely by reason of his or her disability. In refusing to admit the applicant, the nursing school explained that the hearing disability had made it unsafe for her to practice as a registered nurse. The school pointed out that even with a hearing aid the applicant had to rely on her lip reading skills. It argued that patient safety demanded that she be able to understand speech without reliance on lip reading. Agreeing with the school, the Supreme Court held that the term "otherwise qualified handicapped individual" [as the statute then read] meant an individual who is qualified in spite of his or her handicap.

The applicant's contention that her handicap should be disregarded for purposes of determining whether she was otherwise qualified was rejected, as was her contention that § 504 imposed an obligation on the school to undertake affirmative action to modify its curriculum to accommodate her disability. While a school may be required to make minor curricular modifications to accommodate a disability, here the applicant was physically able to take only academic courses. Clinical study would be foreclosed due to patient safety concerns. The Court held that § 504 did not require a major curricular modification such as allowing the applicant to bypass clinical study. The school's denial of admission was upheld. *Southeastern Community College v. Davis*, 442 U.S. 397, 99 S.Ct. 2361, 60 L.Ed.2d 980 (1979).

Section 504 of the Rehabilitation Act forbids federal funding recipients from discriminating against otherwise qualified persons with disabilities. In the case which follows, the Supreme Court determined that a lower court had failed to consider a public university's argument that it was not required to pay for a handicapped student's special educational requirements in a case filed under § 504.

A deaf graduate student at a Texas university requested a sign language interpreter. The university refused to pay for an interpreter because the student did not meet university financial assistance guidelines. The student then sued the university in a federal district court under § 504. He sought an order which would require the appointment of an interpreter at the university's expense for as long as he remained there. The court granted his request for a preliminary order requiring the university to pay for the interpreter. However, the court stayed further consideration of the case pending a final administrative ruling by a federal education agency.

The university appealed to thc U.S. Court of Appeals, Fifth Circuit, which affirmed the preliminary order, but vacated the stay pending administrative action. The university complied with the order by paying for the interpreter. The student completed his graduate program. The U.S. Supreme Court granted certiorari to address the university's argument that the lower courts should make a final ruling on who was to pay for the interpreter. The student argued that the case was now moot in view of his graduation. The Supreme Court vacated the appeals court's decision and remanded the case for a trial on the merits to allow the university a full opportunity to argue for recoupment of its payments for the interpreter. *University of Texas v. Camenisch*, 451 U.S. 390, 101 S.Ct. 1830, 68 L.Ed.2d 175 (1981).

The IDEA's effectiveness may be contrasted with the failure of another Federal act, the Developmentally Disabled Assistance and Bill of Rights Act, 42 U.S.C. §§ 6001-6081, to vindicate the rights of a class of mentally retarded Pennsylvania state school and hospital residents.

In 1974, a Pennsylvania state school and hospital resident brought a class action suit against the school and its officials, also naming as defendants various state and local mental health administrators. The resident claimed that conditions at the institution violated § 504 of the Rehabilitation Act, the Developmentally Disabled Assistance and Bill of Rights Act, 42 U.S.C. §§ 6001-6081 (DDABRA), Pennsylvania mental health legislation, and the Eighth and Fourteenth Amendments to the U.S. Constitution. A federal district court held that the state legislation provided a right to adequate habilitation, but did not determine whether the student and class had habilitation rights in the least restrictive environment. On appeal, the U.S. Court of Appeals, Third Circuit, affirmed the district court decision and ruled that the class had habilitation rights requiring the least restrictive environment, based on its interpretation of the DDABRA. The U.S. Supreme Court reversed, holding that the DDABRA created no substantive rights. It remanded the case to the court of appeals. *Pennhurst State School and Hospital v. Halderman*, 451 U.S. 1, 101 S.Ct. 1531, 67 L.Ed.2d 694 (1981). (*Pennhurst I.*)

On remand, the court of appeals affirmed its previous decision in full. The U.S. Supreme Court again granted certiorari, and again reversed and remanded the case. It held that the Eleventh Amendment to the U.S. Constitution prohibited federal courts from ordering state officials to conform their conduct to their own state laws. On remand, the court of appeals would be permitted to consider a judgment based on the federal legislation. *Pennhurst State School and Hospital v. Halderman*, 465 U.S. 89, 104 S.Ct. 900, 79 L.Ed.2d 67 (1984). (*Pennhurst II.*)

In 1982, the Supreme Court considered its first EHA case, *Board of Education v. Rowley*. The decision construed the act narrowly, holding that it provided only a basic floor of educational opportunity for students with disabilities.

Parents of a nearly totally deaf child in New York brought suit against school administrators for failing to provide their child with a qualified sign language interpreter for all of her academic classes. The school district had supplied the child with a hearing aid as well as additional instruction from a tutor. A U.S. district court, in a decision upheld by the U.S. Court of Appeals, Second Circuit, ruled that even though the child was performing better than average in her class and was advancing easily from grade to grade, she was not performing as well academically as she would have without her disability. Because of the disparity between her achievement and her potential, the court held that she was not receiving a free appropriate public education as provided by the Education for All Handicapped Children Act.

The lower courts' decisions were reversed by the U.S. Supreme Court, which held that the Act is satisfied when the state provides personalized instruction with sufficient support services to permit the disabled child to benefit educationally from that instruction. The Court held that the individualized educational program required by the Act should be reasonably calculated to enable the child to achieve passing marks and advance from grade to grade. The Act did not require the school to provide a sign-language interpreter as requested by the child's parents. The Act was not meant to guarantee a certain level of education, but merely to open the door of education to children with disabilities by means of special educational services. Additionally, the decision noted that a state is not required to maximize the potential of each disabled child commensurate with the opportunity provided nondisabled children. *Board of Education v. Rowley*, 458 U.S. 176, 102 S.Ct. 3034, 73 L.Ed.2d 690 (1982).

Generally, medical services are excluded from "related services" under the IDEA/EHA unless the services are for diagnostic or evaluative purposes. However, the U.S. Supreme Court held in *Irving Independent School District v. Tatro*, that clean intermittent catheterization is a related service.

In the *Tatro* case, the U.S. Supreme Court ruled that clean intermittent catheterization (CIC) is a related service not subject to the EHA's "medical service" exclusion. The parents of an eight-year-old girl born with spina bifida brought suit against a local Texas school district after the district refused to provide catheterization for the child while she attended school. The parents pursued administrative procedures to force the district to train staff to perform CIC. After a U.S. district court held against the parents, they appealed to the U.S. Court of Appeals, Fifth Circuit, which reversed the district court ruling. The school district then appealed to the U.S. Supreme Court.

The Supreme Court affirmed that portion of the court of appeals decision which held that CIC is a "supportive service," not a "medical service" excluded from the EAHCA. The court was not persuaded by the school district's argument that catheterization is a medical service because it is provided in accordance with a physician's prescription and under a physician's supervision, even though it may be administered by a nurse or trained layperson. The court listed four criteria to determine a school's obligation to provide services that relate to both the health and education of a child. First, to be entitled to related services, a child must be disabled so as to require special education. Second, the school need provide only those services necessary to aid a child with a disability to benefit from special education. Third, EHA regulations state that school nursing services must be performed by a nurse or other qualified person, not by a physician. Fourth, the child's parents in this case were seeking only the *services* of a qualified person at the school, they were not asking the school to provide *equipment*. The court reversed those portions of the court of appeals ruling which held the school district liable under the Rehabilitation Act and which held that the parents were entitled to attorney's fees. *Irving Independent School District v. Tatro*, 468 U.S. 883, 104 S.Ct. 3371, 82 L.Ed.2d 664 (1984).

In *Smith v. Robinson*, the U.S. Supreme Court ruled that by enacting the EHA, with its detailed procedural and substantive safeguards for students with disabilities, Congress intended to close off any other federal law as a basis for any special education lawsuit. The Supreme Court would have foreclosed the use of either the Rehabilitation Act or the Civil Rights Act by disabled students. However, Congress responded to this situation by enacting the Handicapped Children's Protection Act of 1986 (HCPA) (P.L. 99-372) which amended the EHA and authorized attorney fee awards to students with disabilities who prevail in special education lawsuits. Moreover, the HCPA provided that in addition to the EHA, the Rehabilitation Act and the Civil Rights Act may also be utilized by disabled students.

In *Smith* the U.S. Supreme Court ruled that attorney's fees were not available under the EHA, the Civil Rights Act, or the Rehabilitation Act. The case involved a child in Rhode Island who suffered from cerebral palsy and other physical and emotional handicaps. The child's parents had prevailed in their claim against their local school district, and the district was obligated to maintain the child in his then current residential school placement while a dispute involving who was to pay for the placement was resolved. After the parents collected their child's tuition costs from the school district, they sought attorney's fees. The federal district court granted the fees under the Civil Rights Act and the Rehabilitation Act, both of which contained provisions authorizing an award of attorney's fees to a successful plaintiff. The U.S. Court of Appeals, First Circuit, reversed and denied attorney's fees, and the U.S. Supreme Court upheld the reversal.

The Supreme Court undertook a three-step analysis. First, under the common law, attorney's fees are not available unless a specific statutory provision authorizes them. Second, the EHA contains no attorney's fees provision. Third, by enacting the EHA, Congress intended to make it the exclusive remedy for public school students with disabilities, thereby preventing them from relying on either the Civil Rights Act or the Rehabilitation Act. An exception was made, however, for cases in which a school district deprives a disabled student of his or her procedural rights under the EHA. If a student proves that a school district denied him or her the procedural rights to which every disabled child is entitled, then an attorney's fees award under the Civil Rights Act would be justified. This is because the EHA places great emphasis on following certain procedures. If the district denies a student due process of law, then a due process challenge under the Civil Rights Act is a legitimate remedy. In the present case, however, there was no evidence that the school district had violated the EHA's procedural safeguards, and attorney's fees were denied. *Smith v. Robinson*, 468 U.S. 992, 104 S.Ct. 3457, 82 L.Ed.2d 746 (1984).

In *Honig v. Students of California School For the Blind*, the U.S. Supreme Court refused to rule on whether the state of California could be held liable under the EHA and the Rehabilitation Act for failing to inspect a school site. It dismissed the case as moot.

Students at a school for the blind in California brought suit against state education officials under the EHA and the Rehabilitation Act, challenging a move of the school to a new site. Among the objections to the move were allegations that the new site was in an earthquake-prone, dangerous area. The school had been granted permission to open over the protest of the students because some parents objected to the possibility that, if the move was blocked, no special school for the blind would be available. The students sought a preliminary injunction to stop the move and made the seismic safety claims a major focus of their lawsuit. A U.S. district court ordered studies of the site and, finding California's pre-construction investigation inadequate, the court granted the students' request for a preliminary injunction.

The state appealed this ruling to the U.S. Court of Appeals, Ninth Circuit, which held that under the Rehabilitation Act, California was required to make its school for the blind as safe as schools for nondisabled students. To the state's argument that the general anti-discrimination provisions of the Rehabilitation Act cannot be used to make an "end run" around the more specific provisions of the EHA, the court said that while the EHA is more specific than the Rehabilitation Act as to educational programs, the Rehabilitation Act is more specific as to physical facilities. The court found no conflict between the two Acts.

Finally, because a strong argument could be made that a seismically unsafe school denied the students a "free appropriate education" under the EHA, the Court of Appeals held that the district court properly granted the students' request for a preliminary injunction. The district court ruling was affirmed and the superintendent of Public Instruction of California appealed to the U.S. Supreme Court, which held that the question of whether the district court erred in issuing the preliminary injunction was moot; because after the district court's order, and prior to the Supreme Court's ruling, the tests had been completed. *Honig v. Students of California School for the Blind*, 471 U.S. 148, 105 S.Ct. 1820, 85 L.Ed.2d 114 (1985).

In *Burlington School Committee v. Department of Education of Massachusetts*, the U.S. Supreme Court ruled that public school districts must pay private school tuition and related expenses only where the school district fails to offer an appropriate special education program to a student with a disability.

The father of a learning disabled third grade boy became dissatisfied with his son's lack of progress in a Massachusetts public school system. A new individualized education program (IEP) was developed for the child which called for placement in a different public school. The father, however, followed the advice of specialists at Massachusetts General Hospital and unilaterally withdrew his son from the school system, placing him instead at the Carroll School, a state-approved private facility in Lincoln, Massachusetts. He then sought reimbursement for tuition and transportation expenses from the school committee, contending that the IEP was inappropriate.

The state Board of Special Education Appeals (BSEA) ruled that the proposed IEP was inappropriate and that, therefore, the father had been justified in placing his son at the Carroll School. The BSEA ordered the school committee to reimburse the father for tuition and transportation expenses, and the committee appealed to the federal courts. A U.S. district court held that the parents had violated the EHA's status quo provision by enrolling their child in the private school without approval. Thus, they were not entitled to reimbursement. The U.S. Court of Appeals, First Circuit, reversed the district court's ruling, and the committee appealed to the U.S. Supreme Court.

In affirming the court of appeals' decision, the Supreme Court ruled that parents who place a child with a disability in a private educational facility are entitled to reimbursement for the child's tuition and living expenses, if a court later determines that the school district had proposed an inappropriate individualized education program. Reimbursement could not be ordered if the school district's proposed IEP was later found to be appropriate. The Supreme Court observed that to bar reimbursement claims under all circumstances would be contrary to the EHA, which favors proper interim placements for children with disabilities.

In addition, under the school committee's reading of the EHA status quo provision, parents would be forced to leave their child in what might later be determined to be an inappropriate educational placement, or would obtain the appropriate placement only by sacrificing any claim for reimbursement. This result, found the Court, was not intended by Congress. However, the Court noted that "[t]his is not to say that [this provision] has no effect on parents." Parents who unilaterally change their children's placement during the pendency of proceedings do so at their own financial risk. If the courts ultimately determine that a child's proposed IEP was appropriate, the parents are barred from obtaining reimbursement for an unauthorized private school placement. *Burlington School Committee v. Department of Education of Massachusetts*, 471 U.S. 359, 105 S.Ct. 1996, 85 L.Ed.2d 385 (1985).

The Rehabilitation Act of 1973 prohibits discrimination against individuals with disabilities in programs receiving federal financial assistance. Under the Act, no otherwise qualified individual with a disability is to be excluded from employment, programs, or services to which he or she is entitled. Additionally, claims for alleged discrimination are sometimes brought under the Equal Protection Clause of the U.S. Constitution, which prohibits discrimination by guaranteeing that laws will be applied equally to all citizens.

The U.S. Supreme Court ruled that mental retardation is not a "suspect classification" calling for heightened scrutiny under the U.S. Constitution. The case arose when the operator of a proposed group home for mentally disabled individuals was denied a building-use permit by the city council of Cleburne, Texas. The city council determined that the group home would be classified as a "hospital for the feebleminded" under the zoning laws and proceeded to deny a permit to the group home. The operator sued the city in federal court, claiming that the council's action unlawfully discriminated against mentally retarded citizens in violation of the Equal Protection Clause of the U.S. Constitution.

The Supreme Court, while ordering that the group home be granted a permit, held that government regulations regarding mentally retarded individuals are not to be subjected to rigorous judicial analysis as are classifications based on race, alienage or sex. The Equal Protection Clause does not afford the same protection to citizens with disabilities as it does to minorities. Although the group home won its building-use permit, the Supreme Court's holding limited the scope of the Equal Protection Clause to cases involving irrational, unfounded or arbitrary action against the handicapped. *City of Cleburne, Texas v. Cleburne Living Center*, 473 U.S. 432, 105 S.Ct. 3249, 87 L.Ed.2d 313 (1985).

Grants, loans and tax credits or deductions are the most common forms of state financial assistance to private school students. Such financial assistance programs are constitutionally permissible as long as the state purpose underlying the program is to benefit both secular and religious education.

The U.S. Supreme Court unanimously ruled that the First Amendment to the U.S. Constitution did not prevent the state of Washington from providing financial assistance directly to a disabled individual attending a Christian college. The plaintiff in this case, a blind person, sought vocational rehabilitative services from the Washington Commission for the Blind pursuant to state law [Wash.Rev.Code § 74.16.181(1981)]. The law provided that visually handicapped persons were eligible for educational assistance to enable them to "overcome vocational handicaps and to obtain the maximum degree of self-support and self-care." However, because the plaintiff was a student at a Christian college intending to pursue a career of service in the church, the Commission for the Blind denied him assistance.

The Washington Supreme Court upheld this decision on the ground that the First Amendment to the U.S. Constitution prohibited state funding of a student's education at a religious college. The U.S. Supreme Court took a less restrictive view of the First Amendment and reversed the Washington court. The operation of Washington's program was such that the Commission for the Blind paid money directly to students, who could then attend the schools of their choice. The fact that the student in this case chose to attend a religious college did not constitute state support of religion because "the decision to support religious education is made by the individual, not the state." The First Amendment was therefore not offended. *Witters v. Washington Depart-*

ment of Services for the Blind, 474 U.S. 481, 106 S.Ct. 748, 88 L.Ed.2d 846 (1986).

In *Honig v. Doe*, **the Supreme Court held that suspensions and expulsions of students with disabilities constitute changes in placement under the EHA. Indefinite suspensions violate the EHA's "stay put" provision. The 1997 Amendments to the IDEA now allow schools to remove disruptive students from class for up to 55 days so long as they place the students in an alternative educational setting.**

Honig v. Doe involved two emotionally disturbed children in California who were given five-day suspensions from school for misbehavior which included destroying school property and assaulting and making sexual comments to other students. Pursuant to state law, the suspensions were continued indefinitely during the pendency of expulsion proceedings. The students sued the school district in U.S. district court contesting the extended suspensions on the ground that they violated the EHA's "stay put" provision, which provides that a student must be kept in his or her "then current" educational placement during the pendency of proceedings which contemplate a change in placement. The district court issued an injunction preventing the expulsion of any disabled student for misbehavior which arises from the student's disability and the school district appealed.

The U.S. Court of Appeals, Ninth Circuit, determined that the indefinite suspensions constituted a prohibited "change in placement" under the EHA and that no "dangerousness" exception existed in the EHA's "stay put" provision. It ruled that indefinite suspensions or expulsions of disabled children for misconduct arising out of their disabilities violated the EHA. The court of appeals also ruled, however, that fixed suspensions of up to 30 school days did not constitute a "change in placement." It determined that a state must provide services directly to a disabled child when a local school district fails to do so. The California Superintendent of Public Instruction filed for a review by the U.S. Supreme Court on the issues of whether a dangerousness exception existed to the "stay put" provision and whether the state had to provide services directly when a local school district failed to do so.

The Supreme Court declared that the intended purpose of the "stay put" provision was to prevent schools from changing a child's educational placement over his or her parents' objection until all review proceedings were completed. While the EHA permitted interim placement where parents and school officials were able to agree, no emergency exception for dangerous students was included. The Court concluded that it was "not at liberty to engraft onto the EHA an exception Congress chose not to create." The Court went on to say that where disabled students pose an immediate threat to the safety of others, school officials may temporarily suspend them for up to ten school days. The court held that this authority insured: 1) that school officials can protect the safety of others by removing dangerous students, 2) that school officials can seek a review of the student's placement and try to persuade the student's parents to agree to an interim placement, and 3) that school officials can seek court rulings to exclude students whose parents "adamantly refuse to permit any change in placement."

School officials could seek such a court order without exhausting the EAHCA's administrative remedies "only by showing that maintaining the child in his or her current placement is substantially likely to result in injury either to himself or herself, or to others." The Court therefore affirmed the court of appeals' decision that indefinite suspensions violated the EHA's "stay put" provision. It modified that court's decision on fixed suspensions by holding that suspensions of up to ten rather than up to 30 days did not constitute a change in placement. The Court also upheld the court of appeals' decision that states could be required to provide services directly to disabled students where a local school district fails to do so. *Honig v. Doe*, 484 U.S. 305, 108 S.Ct. 592, 98 L.Ed.2d 686 (1988).

In *Traynor v. Turnage*, a case involving G.I. Bill educational assistance, the Supreme Court determined that a Veterans' Administration regulation defining alcoholism was not invalid under the Rehabilitation Act.

Two honorably discharged veterans who were recovering alcoholics sought an extension of the ten-year Veterans' Administration (VA) limitation for receipt of educational assistance under the G.I. Bill. The ten-year limitation on educational benefits can be extended by the VA if the veteran can show he was prevented from using his benefits earlier because of "physical or mental disability which was not the result of ... [his] own willful misconduct." VA regulations state that the deliberate drinking of alcohol is considered willful misconduct. Both veterans requested an extension of benefits after expiration of their respective ten-year limitation periods. These requests were based on grounds that they were disabled by alcoholism. The VA denied their requests, stating that their alcoholism had been willful misconduct. One veteran sued the VA in a New York district court. The other veteran sought review in the

District Court for the District of Columbia. The New York district court held for the VA, but its decision was reversed by the U.S. Court of Appeals, Second Circuit. The District of Columbia district court ruled that the VA regulation was contrary to the Rehabilitation Act, but the District of Columbia Court of Appeals reversed that decision.

Noting the disagreement between the two federal appeals courts, the U.S. Supreme Court granted review and heard the cases together. The Court held that the Rehabilitation Act does not preclude an action against the VA. The Court noted that Congress had changed the time limit for benefits several times, most recently in 1977. The Rehabilitation Act of 1978 did not repeal the "willful misconduct" provision of the 1977 regulations. According to the Court, Congress had the right to establish the allocation priorities for veterans' benefits. The District of Columbia Court of Appeals decision was affirmed and the Second Circuit Court of Appeals decision was reversed. The VA prevailed in both matters. *Traynor v. Turnage*, 485 U.S. 535, 108 S.Ct. 1372, 99 L.Ed.2d 618 (1988).

In 1989, the Supreme Court ruled that while local school districts could be sued under the EHA, states were immune from EHA liability under the Eleventh Amendment. Subsequently, Congress amended the EHA by passing the IDEA, which abrogated the states' Eleventh Amendment immunity.

A student with a language-based learning disability and emotional problems was enrolled in a Pennsylvania public school. His father requested an administrative hearing to challenge the student's individualized education program (IEP). Meanwhile, the father enrolled the student in a private school for learning disabled students. The hearing examiner then determined that the original IEP was inappropriate. The school district and father both appealed to the Pennsylvania Secretary of Education, who remanded the case to the hearing officer with instructions to revise the IEP. After the revisions were made, the hearing officer determined that the revised IEP was appropriate. The secretary affirmed this decision.

The father sued the school district and the secretary of education in a federal district court. He contended that the district's revised IEP was inappropriate and that the state's administrative proceedings violated the EHA because the secretary was not impartial and extensive delays had occurred because of the remand. The court ruled in the father's favor, stating that he was entitled to reimbursement for the student's private school tuition plus attorney's fees. The court determined that the

Commonwealth of Pennsylvania, as well as the school district, were
jointly and severally liable under the EHA. According to the court, the
EHA abrogated the state's Eleventh Amendment immunity from damage suits.

The secretary appealed to the U.S. Court of Appeals for the Third
Circuit. The court affirmed the district court's decision and the secretary appealed to the U.S. Supreme Court, which agreed to hear the case.
The Court noted that Congress does not abrogate sovereign immunity
unless it specifically states so within a legislative act. The EHA did not
specify an intent to abrogate state immunity from lawsuits. Although
the Handicapped Children's Protection Act, a 1986 amendment to the
act, specifically provided for reduction of attorney's fees if the state or
local educational agency unreasonably protracts the resolution of an
EHA action, the EHA did not state an intent to abrogate sovereign
immunity. The Court reversed and remanded the court of appeals'
decision. *Dellmuth v. Muth,* 491 U.S. 223, 109 S.Ct. 2397, 105 L.Ed.2d
181 (1989).

**The Supreme Court held that federal appellate courts should
review district court determinations of state law without according
considerable deference to those determinations. In the following
case, an issue arose as to whether an overweight student had
substantially performed on a contract in which she agreed to lose
weight (to remain in a college's nursing program).**

An overweight Rhode Island student joined a college's nursing
program in her sophomore year. During her junior year, the college
began pressuring her to lose weight. She received a failing grade in a
clinical nursing course, for reasons related to her weight rather than her
performance. By school rules, the failing grade should have resulted in
expulsion from the program. However, the school offered her a contract
which allowed her to stay in the program if she lost at least two pounds
per week. She failed to lose the weight, was asked to withdraw from the
program, and transferred to another nursing program. She sued the
college in a federal district court, alleging that it had violated the
Rehabilitation Act and that it had breached an implied contract to
educate her. She was awarded damages for breach of contract. The jury
determined that the student had substantially performed her obligations
under the contract so as to enable her to prevail on her claim against the
school.

The school appealed to the U.S. Court of Appeals, First Circuit,
which affirmed. The appellate court afforded considerable deference to

the district court's determination of how the state courts would have ruled on the issue. The school further appealed to the U.S. Supreme Court. The Supreme Court held that the court of appeals should have reviewed the case *de novo* (as if hearing it for the first time). The appellate court should not have deferred to the district court's determination of what state law would be. Instead, it should have examined the doctrine of substantial performance to ascertain whether it ought to be applied to a contract in an academic setting. The Court reversed and remanded the case. *Salve Regina College v. Russell,* 499 U.S. 225, 111 S.Ct. 1217, 113 L.Ed.2d 190 (1991).

The Supreme Court held that the parents of a special education student were entitled to tuition reimbursement after they unilaterally placed the student in an unapproved private school because the public school placement violated the IDEA and because the child received an otherwise proper education from the private school.

A South Carolina ninth-grader with a learning disability attended special education classes. Her parents disagreed with the individualized education program (IEP) established by their public school district. The IEP called for mainstreaming in regular education classes for most subjects, with individual instruction three periods per week and specific goals of increasing the student's reading and mathematics levels by four months for the entire school year. The student's parents requested a due process hearing under the IDEA, 20 U.S.C. § 1415(b)(2). Meanwhile, they unilaterally placed the student in a private school which specialized in teaching students with disabilities. The hearing officer held that the IEP was adequate.

After the student raised her reading comprehension three full grades in one year at the private school, the parents sued the school district for tuition reimbursement. The U.S. District Court for the District of South Carolina held that the educational program and achievement goals of the proposed IEP were "wholly inadequate" under the IDEA and that even though the private school did not comply with all IDEA requirements, it provided the student with an excellent education that complied with IDEA substantive requirements. It held that the parents were entitled to tuition reimbursement, a result that was upheld by the U.S. Court of Appeals, Fourth Circuit. The school district appealed to the U.S. Supreme Court.

The Supreme Court held that the failure of the school district to provide an appropriate placement entitled the parents to tuition reimbursement from the school district, even though the private school was not on any state list of approved schools. This was because the education provided to the student was determined by the district court to be appropriate. Moreover, South Carolina did not release a list of approved schools to the public. Under the IDEA, parents had a right to unilaterally place children in private schools. To recover private school tuition costs, parents must show that the placement proposed by the school district violates the IDEA, and that the private school placement is appropriate. The Supreme Court upheld the lower court decisions in favor of the parents. *Florence County School Dist. Four v. Carter*, 510 U.S. 7, 114 S.Ct. 361, 126 L.Ed.2d 284 (1993).

In 1999, the Supreme Court was faced with a case involving the scope of a district's obligation to provide related services. The parties disputed whether the requested services were related services which the district had to provide, or medical services, which the district would not have to provide under the IDEA's medical services exclusion. Adopting a bright-line, physician/non-physician rule, the court concluded that services which did not have to be performed by a physician were related services which districts must provide under the IDEA.

An Iowa student suffered a spinal cord injury which left him quadriplegic and ventilator dependent. For several years, his family provided him with personal attendant services at school. A family member or nurse performed catheterization, tracheostomy suctioning, repositioning and respiratory observation during the school day. When the student entered the fifth grade, his mother requested that the district provide him with continuous, one-on-one nursing services during the school day. The district refused, and the family filed a request for a due process hearing. An administrative law judge determined that the school district was obligated to reimburse the family for nursing costs incurred during the current school year and provide the disputed services in the future. The school district appealed to a federal district court, which granted summary judgment to the family. The district appealed to the U.S. Court of Appeals, Eighth Circuit, which concluded that the disputed services were related services the district was obligated to provide under the IDEA. Because the student required the services to benefit from his education, the district was required to provide them. The district appealed to the U.S. Supreme Court.

A majority of the Supreme Court affirmed the Eighth Circuit's opinion, argeeing that the requested services were not medical services. The court based its decision on the IDEA definition of related services, its previous holding in *Tatro,* above, and the purpose of the IDEA to make special education available to all disabled students. Adopting a bright-line, physician/non-physician standard, the court held that since the disputed services could be performed by someone other than a physician, the district was obligated to provide them. The Court rejected the district's assertion that a multi-factor standard, which included cost as a consideration, was appropriate. *Cedar Rapids Community School Dist. v. Garret F. by Charlene F.,* 119 S.Ct. 992, 143 L.Ed.2d 154 (1999).

UNITED STATES CONSTITUTION

Provisions of Interest to Educators

ARTICLE I

Section 1. All legislative Powers herein granted shall be vested in a Congress of the United States, which shall consist of a Senate and a House of Representatives.

* * *

Section 8. The Congress shall have Power To lay and collect Taxes, Duties, Imposts and Excises, to pay the Debts and provide for the common Defence and general Welfare of the United States; but all Duties, Imposts and Excises shall be uniform throughout the United States;

To borrow money on the credit of the United States;

To regulate Commerce with foreign Nations, and among the several States, and with the Indian Tribes;

To establish an uniform Rule of Naturalization, and uniform laws on the subject of Bankruptcies throughout the United States;

To promote the Progress of Science and useful Arts, by securing for limited Times to Authors and Inventors the exclusive Right to their respective Writings and Discoveries;

* * *

Section 9. * * * No Bill of Attainder or ex post facto law shall be passed.

* * *

Section 10. No State shall * * * pass any Bill of Attainder, ex post facto Law, or Law impairing the Obligation of Contracts, or grant any Title of Nobility.

* * *

ARTICLE II

Section 1. The executive Power shall be vested in a President of the United States of America.

* * *

ARTICLE III

Section 1. The judicial Power of the United States, shall be vested in one Supreme Court, and in such inferior Courts as the Congress may from time to time ordain and establish. The Judges, both of the supreme and inferior courts, shall hold their Offices during good Behaviour, and shall, at stated Times, receive for their Services a Compensation, which shall not be diminished during their Continuance in Office.

Section 2. The judicial Power shall extend to all Cases, in Law and Equity, arising under this Constitution, the Laws of the United States, and Treaties made, or which shall be made; under their Authority; to all Cases affecting Ambassadors, other public Ministers and Consuls; to all Cases of admiralty and maritime Jurisdiction, to Controversies to which the United States shall be a party to Controversies between two or more States; between a State and Citizens of another State; between Citizens of different States; between Citizens of the same State claiming Lands under the Grants of different States, and between a State, or the Citizens thereof, and foreign States, Citizens or Subjects.

* * *

ARTICLE IV

Section 1. Full Faith and Credit shall be given in each State to the public Acts, Records and judicial Proceedings of every other State.

Section 2. The Citizens of each State shall be entitled to all Privileges and Immunities of Citizens in the several States.

* * *

Section 4. The United States shall guarantee to every State in this Union a Republican Form of Government, and shall protect each of them against Invasion; and on Application of the Legislature, or of the Executive (when the Legislature cannot be convened) against domestic Violence.

ARTICLE V

The Congress, whenever two thirds of both Houses shall deem it necessary, shall propose Amendments to this Constitution, or, on the Application of the Legislatures of two thirds of the several States, shall call a Convention for proposing Amendments, which, in either Case, shall be valid to all Intents and Purposes, as part of this Constitution, when ratified by the Legislatures of three fourths of the several States, or by Conventions in three fourths thereof, as the one or the other Mode of Ratification may be proposed by the Congress; Provided that no Amendment which may be made prior to the Year One thousand eight hundred and eight shall in any Manner affect the first and fourth Clauses in the Ninth Section of the first Article; and that no State, without its Consent, shall be deprived of its equal Suffrage in the Senate.

ARTICLE VI

* * *

This Constitution, and the Laws of the United States which shall be made in Pursuance thereof; and all Treaties made, or which shall be made, under the Authority of the United States, shall be the Supreme Law of the Land; and the Judges in every State shall be bound thereby, any Thing in the Constitution or Laws of any State to the Contrary notwithstanding.

The Senators and Representatives before mentioned, and the Members of the several State Legislatures, and all executive and judicial Officers, both of the United States and of the several States, shall be bound by Oath or Affirmation, to support this Constitution; but no religious Test shall ever be required as a Qualification to any Office or public Trust under the United States.

* * *

AMENDMENT I

Congress shall make no law respecting an establishment of religion, or prohibiting the free exercise thereof; or abridging the freedom of speech, or of the press; or the right of the people peaceably to assemble, and to petition the Government for a redress of grievances.

* * *

AMENDMENT IV

The right of the people to be secure in their persons, houses, papers, and effects, against unreasonable searches and seizures, shall not be violated, and no Warrants shall issue, but upon probable cause, supported by Oath or affirmation, and particularly describing the place to be searched, and the persons or things to be seized.

AMENDMENT V

No person shall be held to answer for a capital, or otherwise infamous crime, unless on a presentment or indictment of a Grand Jury, except in cases arising in the land or naval forces, or in the Militia, when in actual service in time of War or public danger; nor shall any person be subject for the same offence to be twice put in jeopardy of life or limb; nor shall be compelled in any criminal case to be a witness against himself, nor be deprived of life, liberty, or property, without due process of law; nor shall private property be taken for public use, without just compensation.

AMENDMENT VI

In all criminal prosecutions, the accused shall enjoy the right to a speedy and public trial, by an impartial jury of the State and district wherein the crime shall have been committed, which district shall have been previously ascertained by law, and to be informed of the nature and cause of the accusation; to be confronted with the witnesses against him;

to have compulsory process for obtaining witnesses in his favor, and to have the Assistance of Counsel for his defense.

AMENDMENT VII

In Suits at common law, where the value in controversy shall exceed twenty dollars, the right of trial by jury shall be preserved, and no fact tried by jury, shall be otherwise re-examined in any Court of the United States, than according to the rules of the common law.

AMENDMENT VIII

Excessive bail shall not be required, nor excessive fines imposed, nor cruel and unusual punishments inflicted.

AMENDMENT IX

The enumeration in the Constitution, of certain rights, shall not be construed to deny or disparage others retained by the people.

AMENDMENT X

The powers not delegated to the United States by the Constitution, nor prohibited by it to the States, are reserved to the States respectively, or to the people.

AMENDMENT XI

The Judicial power of the United States shall not be construed to extend to any suit in law or equity, commenced or prosecuted against one of the United States by Citizens of another State, or by Citizens or Subjects of any Foreign State.

* * *

AMENDMENT XIII

Section 1. Neither slavery nor involuntary servitude, except as a punishment for crime whereof the party shall have been duly convicted, shall exist within the United States, or any place subject to their jurisdiction.

Section 2. Congress shall have power to enforce this article by appropriate legislation.

AMENDMENT XIV

Section 1. All persons born or naturalized in the United States, and subject to the jurisdiction thereof, are citizens of the United States and of the State wherein they reside. No State shall make or enforce any law which shall abridge the privileges or immunities of citizens of the United States; nor shall any State deprive any person of life, liberty, or property, without due process of law; nor deny to any person within its jurisdiction the equal protection of the laws.

* * *

Section 5. The Congress shall have power to enforce, by appropriate legislation, the provisions of this article.

APPENDIX B

GLOSSARY

Ad Valorem Tax—In general usage, a tax on property measured by the property's value.

Age Discrimination in Employment Act (ADEA)—The ADEA, 29 U.S.C. § 621 et seq., is part of the Fair Labor Standards Act. It prohibits discrimination against persons who are at least forty years old, and applies to employers which have twenty or more employees and which affect interstate commerce.

Americans with Disabilities Act (ADA)—The ADA, 42 U.S.C. § 12101 *et seq.*, went into effect on July 26, 1992. Among other things, it prohibits discrimination against a qualified individual with a disability because of that person's disability with respect to job application procedures, the hiring, advancement or discharge of employees, employee compensation, job training, and other terms, conditions and privileges of employment. The act also prohibits discrimination against otherwise qualified individuals with respect to the services, programs or activities of a public entity. Further, any entity which operates a place of public accommodation (including private schools) may not discriminate against individuals with disabilities.

Bill of Attainder—A bill of attainder is a law which inflicts punishment on a particular group of individuals without a trial. Such acts are prohibited by Article I, Section 9 of the Constitution.

Bona fide—Latin term meaning "good faith." Generally used to note a party's lack of bad intent or fraud.

Claim preclusion—(see Res judicata).

Class Action Suit—Federal Rule of Civil Procedure 23 allows members of a class to sue as representatives on behalf of the whole class provided that the class is so large that joinder of all parties is impractical, there are questions of law or fact common to the class, the claims or defenses of the representatives are typical of the claims or defenses of

273

the class, and the representative parties will adequately protect the interests of the class. In addition, there must be some danger of inconsistent verdicts or adjudications if the class action were prosecuted as separate actions. Most states also allow class actions under the same or similar circumstances.

Due Process Clause—The clauses of the Fifth and Fourteenth Amendments which guarantee the citizens of the United States "due process of law" (see below). The Fifth Amendment's Due Process Clause applies to the federal government and the Fourteenth Amendment's to the states.

Due Process of Law—The idea of "fair play" in the government's application of law to its citizens, guaranteed by the Fifth and Fourteenth Amendments. Due process is accorded when the government utilizes adequate procedural safeguards for the protection of an individual's liberty or property interests.

Education for All Handicapped Children Act (EAHCA)—1975 amendments to the Education of the Handicapped Act (see below). The EAHCA provides federal assistance to state and local agencies for the purpose of educating children with disabilities and also places a number of requirements on those agencies if they wish to receive this money. Local school districts and states may be sued by disabled children, parents or guardians if a free appropriate education is not provided.

Education of the Handicapped Act (EHA)—Now known as the Individuals with Disabilities Education Act (IDEA), it is the federal legislation which provides for the free, appropriate education of all children with disabilities.

Enjoin—(see Injunction).

Equal Pay Act—Federal law which requires that male and female employees be paid the same wages for the same work.

Equal Protection Clause—The clause of the Fourteenth Amendment which prohibits a state from denying any person within its jurisdiction equal protection of its laws. Its coverage is limited to intentional discrimination. Although the Constitution does not contain any explicit guarantee of equal protection on the part of the federal government, the

Supreme Court has interpreted the Due Process Clause of the Fifth Amendment to embody the concept of equal protection of the laws.

Establishment Clause—The clause of the First Amendment which prohibits Congress from making "any law respecting an establishment of religion." This clause has been interpreted as creating a "wall of separation" between church and state. The First Amendment, though by its terms limited to the federal government, was made applicable to the states, and its sub-entities, by the Due Process and the Immunities and Privileges Clauses of the Fourteenth Amendment (see, Incorporation Doctrine, below). In order to pass muster under the Establishment Clause, any government action must have a secular purpose, neither promote nor inhibit religion, nor excessively entangle church and state (see *Lemon v. Kurtzman*, infra).

Ex Post Facto Law—A law which punishes as criminal any action which, at the time it was performed, was not a crime. Prohibited by Article I, Section 9 of the U.S. Constitution.

Exclusionary Rule—Constitutional limitation on the introduction of evidence which states that evidence which is the result of any constitutional violation is excluded from trial.

Federal Tort Claims Act—Federal legislation which determines the circumstances under which the United States waives its sovereign immunity (see below) and agrees to be sued in court for money damages. The government retains its immunity in cases of intentional torts committed by its employees or agents, and where the tort is the result of a "discretionary function" of a federal employee or agency. Many states have similar acts.

42 U.S.C. §§ 1981, 1983—Section 1983 of the federal Civil Rights Act prohibits any person acting under color of state law from depriving any other person of rights protected by the U.S. Constitution or federal laws. Accordingly, a vast majority of lawsuits claiming constitutional violations are brought under § 1983. Section 1981 provides that all persons enjoy the same right to make and enforce contracts as "white citizens." Section 1981 applies to employment contracts. Unlike § 1983, § 1981 applies to even private actors, and is not limited to those acting under color of state law. These sections do not apply to the federal government, though the government may be sued directly under the Constitution for any violations.

Free Exercise Clause—The clause of the First Amendment which prohibits Congress from interfering with citizens' free exercise of their religion. This clause contributes to the "wall of separation" between church and state. The First Amendment, though by its terms limited to the federal government, was made applicable to the states, and its sub-entities, by the Due Process and the Immunities and Privileges Clauses of the Fourteenth Amendment (see Incorporation Doctrine, below).

Handicapped Children's Protection Act of 1986 (HCPA)—The HCPA, an amendment to the Education of the Handicapped Act (see above), encourages students with disabilities to bring lawsuits against school districts or states if a free appropriate education is not provided by requiring losing defendants to pay attorney's fees and money damages to the disabled children.

Incorporation Doctrine—By its own terms, the Bill of Rights applies only to the federal government. The Incorporation Doctrine states that the Fourteenth Amendment makes the Bill of Rights applicable to the states.

Individualized Education Program (IEP)—In order to ensure that children with disabilities are given an appropriate education, school officials must prepare an IEP, which is updated annually, with the participation of the child's parents or guardians. The Act also provides an administrative procedure for challenging determinations made in an IEP.

Individuals with Disabilities Education Act (IDEA)—An amendment to the EHA which renames the act and expands the group of children to whom special education services must be given.

Injunction—An equitable remedy (see Remedies) wherein a court orders a party to refrain from performing some specific action.

Issue preclusion—Also know as collateral estoppel. Legal doctrine in which issues that have been previously litigated cannot be relitigated.

Jurisdiction—The power of a court to determine cases and controversies. The Supreme Court's jurisdiction extends to cases arising under the Constitution and under federal law.

Mill—In property tax usage, one-tenth of a cent.

Nunc pro tunc—Latin phrase simply meaning "now for then." In judicial doctrine, giving retroactive effect to an action performed after the time it should have been completed.

Overbroad—A government action is overbroad if, in an attempt to alleviate a specific evil, it impermissibly prohibits or chills a protected action. For example, attempting to deal with street pollution by prohibiting the distribution of leaflets or handbills.

Per Curiam—Latin phrase meaning "by the court." Used in Supreme Court reports to note an opinion written by the Court rather than by a single justice.

Preemption Doctrine—Doctrine which states that when federal and state law attempt to regulate the same subject matter, federal law prevents the state law from operating. Based on the Supremacy Clause of Article VI, Clause 2 of the U.S. Constitution.

Prior Restraint—Restraining a publication before it is distributed. In general, constitutional law doctrine prohibits government from exercising prior restraint, but in the educational environment, school officials may exercise prior restraint over student publications based on curricular decisions, or on the grounds that the publication would disrupt the school environment.

Pro Se—A party appearing in court, without the benefit of an attorney, is said to be appearing pro se.

Remand—The act of an appellate court returning a case to the court from which it came for further action.

Remedies—There are two general categories of remedies, or relief: legal remedies, which consist of money damages, and equitable remedies, which consist of a court mandate that a specific action be prohibited or required. For example, a claim for compensatory and punitive damages seeks a legal remedy; a claim for an injunction seeks an equitable remedy. Equitable remedies are generally unavailable unless legal remedies are inadequate to address the harm.

Res judicata—The judicial notion that a claim or action may not be tried twice or re-litigated, or that all causes of action arising out of the same set of operative facts should be tried at one time. Also known as claim preclusion.

Section 504 of the Rehabilitation Act of 1973—Section 504 applies to public or private institutions receiving federal financial assistance. It requires that in the employment context an otherwise qualified individual cannot be denied employment based on a handicap. An otherwise qualified individual is one who can perform the "essential functions" of the job with "reasonable accommodation."

Section 1983—(see 42 U.S.C. 1983).

Sovereign Immunity—The idea that the government cannot be sued without its permission. The idea stems from the English notion that the "King could do no wrong." This immunity from suit has been abrogated in most states and by the federal government through legislative acts known as "tort claims acts." However, states retain their immunity to suit in federal court through the Eleventh Amendment.

Standing—The judicial doctrine which states that in order to maintain a lawsuit a party must have some real interest at stake in the outcome of the trial.

Statute of Limitations—A statute of limitation provides the time period in which a specific cause of action maybe brought.

Summary Judgment—Federal Rule of Civil Procedure 56 provides for the summary adjudication of a case if either party can show that there is no genuine issue as to any material fact and that, given those facts, they are entitled to judgment as a matter of law. In general, summary judgment is used to dispose of claims which do not support a legally recognized claim.

Supremacy Clause—Clause in Article VI of the Constitution which states that federal legislation is the supreme law of the land. This clause is used to support the Preemption Doctrine (see above).

Title VII of the Civil Rights Act of 1964 (Title VII)—Title VII prohibits discrimination in employment based upon race, color, sex, religion, or national origin. It applies to any employer having fifteen or more employees. Members of the Communist party are not protected by

Title VII, and discrimination based on age or disability is covered by other federal statutes.

U.S. Equal Employment Opportunity Commission (EEOC)—The EEOC is the government entity which is empowered to enforce Title VII, the Age Discrimination in Employment Act, the Americans with Disabilities Act and the Equal Pay Act (see above) through investigation and/or lawsuits. Private individuals alleging discrimination must generally pursue administrative remedies within the EEOC before they are allowed to file suit under these acts.

Vacate—The act of annulling the judgment of a court either by an appellate court or by the court itself. The Supreme Court will generally vacate a lower court's judgment without deciding the case itself, and remand the case to the lower court for further consideration in light of some recent controlling decision.

Void-for-Vagueness Doctrine—A judicial doctrine based on the Fourteenth Amendment's Due Process Clause. In order for a law which regulates speech, or any criminal statute, to pass muster under the doctrine, the law must make clear what actions are prohibited or made criminal. Under the principles of the due process clause, people of average intelligence should not have to guess at the meaning of a law.

Writ of Certiorari—The device used by the Supreme Court to transfer cases from the appellate court's docket to its own. Since the Supreme Court's appellate jurisdiction is discretionary, it need only issue such a writ when it desires to rule in the case.

Equal Employment Opportunity Commission (EEOC)

INDEX